SCHOOLING *in the* ANTEBELLUM SOUTH

THE RISE OF PUBLIC AND PRIVATE EDUCATION IN LOUISIANA, MISSISSIPPI, AND ALABAMA

SARAH L. HYDE

Louisiana State University Press
Baton Rouge

Published by Louisiana State University Press
Copyright © 2016 by Louisiana State University Press

Designer: Barbara Neely Bourgoyne
Typeface: Ingeborg
Printer and binder: McNaughton & Gunn, Inc.

Library of Congress Cataloging-in-Publication Data

Names: Hyde, Sarah L., 1981– author.
Title: Schooling in the antebellum South : the rise of public and private education in
  Louisiana, Mississippi, and Alabama / Sarah L. Hyde.
Description: Baton Rouge : Louisiana State University Press, [2017] |
  Includes bibliographical references and index.
Identifiers: LCCN 2016009624 | ISBN 978-0-8071-6420-4 (cloth : alk. paper) | ISBN
  978-0-8071-6421-1 (pdf) | ISBN 978-0-8071-6422-8 (epub) | ISBN 978-0-8071-6423-5 (mobi)
Subjects: LCSH: Education—Southern States—History—19th century. | Education—Gulf
  States—History—19th century.
Classification: LCC LA230.5.S6 H93 2017 | DDC 370.97509034—dc23
LC record available at https://lccn.loc.gov/2016009624

For my husband, Sam
and our children,
Clay, Andrew, Sammie, and Sophie

It's all for you

CONTENTS

Contents

TABLES

ACKNOWLEDGMENTS

This project began in a research seminar during my first year of graduate school at Louisiana State University. There are many people at LSU who helped me along the way. The environment within the LSU History Department during my tenure as a grad student was one that encouraged young scholars and supported new research, no matter how unlearned to start. I am grateful to have spent my graduate career studying under scholars such as Paul Hoffman, John Henderson, Victor Stater, Suzanne Marchand, Charles Royster, Benjamin Martin, Charles Shindo, Katie Benton-Cohen, Maribel Dietz, Christine Kooi, Meredith Veldman, David Culbert, and Karl Roider. Their many kindnesses helped a timid young student find her way in the historical profession. Thank you also to Mrs. Darlene Albritton for her love and support and to my friends and colleagues Heather Thornton-Young, Marc Patenaude, Christopher Childers, and Matthew Hernando. The T. Harry Williams Fellowship and the LSU Graduate School Dissertation Fellowship made it possible for me to work on this project full-time before entering "the real world."

There are several professors who deserve a special note of thanks. Dr. Paul Paskoff's enthusiastic response to my work was often a light on dark days. His kindness and warmth encouraged me to try harder and work longer in hopes that my work would find such a reception again. Dr. Gaines Foster shepherded me through my entire career at LSU, culminating with his tireless critique of my manuscript. My voice and my vision are much stronger because of him. I still worry that even in its final version, my book may fail to meet his high standards, but I hope he will be satisfied with the outcome. Dr. Alecia Long kindly reviewed an earlier version of this project and helped immensely with her careful critique and thoughtful suggestions. I am grateful to each of them.

I consider myself one of the lucky few to have worked under the mentorship of my major professor at LSU, Dr. William J. Cooper Jr. His boundless wisdom is matched by his gentlemanly kindness. The hours spent in his office reviewing chapters of my work page by page were some of the most intimidating meetings of my life, but needlessly so. His patience and guidance will always be remembered and appreciated. I am also grateful for his insistence that the work was worthy of publication. Without his encouragement, I may have never found the will to revise the manuscript and submit it for publication. I thank him for all he has done. I will always be proud to call myself a Cooper student.

I would also like to thank the folks at LSU Press who helped this study find the light of day. A special thank-you to Rand Dotson for guiding me through the entire publication process and to Gary Von Euer for his expert copyediting. I cringe at all the mistakes that might have been printed without Gary's careful attention. Thank-you also to Lee Sioles for acting as the production editor for this work and all her kind and careful attention to both myself and the manuscript.

In addition to the professional support received from those above, I must acknowledge the much more personal support from my family and friends. Researching, writing, editing, and rewriting is a solo endeavor, but I would not have been capable of getting anything done without my support system. I thank my parents, Linda and Dennis McIntyre. They created a home full of happiness and love. My mother always protected me from the worst of the world and convinced me that I could do anything. I try to instill that same confidence in my own children, and I am grateful that they get to have her for their Ginna. We are all stronger because of her. Thank-you to Dennis for his steadfast support and unwavering presence. A special thank-you to my father, Thomas Lipscomb, for his gentle guidance and reassuring confidence. Thanks also to my brother Matthew Lipscomb and my grandmother Shirley Ray Toups Lipscomb. I am lucky to have the most loving and supportive in-laws in the world. Thank you to my saint of a mother-in-law, Allie Hyde, and to my sister and brother-in-law, Margaret and Murray Quin. I am extremely grateful for decades of friendship with Wendi Luke, Marisha Carbo, Diane Rabalais, and Sydney Townsend. I owe a special note of thanks to Debbie

Edens, without whose love and care of my children I would be unable to leave the house. We are all grateful to have her in our lives.

A heartfelt thank-you to my husband, the indomitable Samuel C. Hyde Jr. He is truly one of a kind. I am happy to be on this journey with him. The man never tires, rarely rests, and refuses to slow down. Just being around him can be exhausting, but I cannot imagine life any other way. There is no one else I would want to be with during an August hurricane in south Louisiana, trapped with no electricity. He is the only reason to tolerate punk music and rugby. Although we share a profession, we are quite different creatures. Yet I have no doubt he is the only one for me. I thank him for his friendship and his love, and for giving me a family worth dying for.

Lastly, to my children. Nothing in this world matters without them. Despite the many roles I play, being their mom always comes first. Nothing is more rewarding, or more exhausting, than being their mother. Thank you to Clay, Andrew, Sammie, and Sophie for all the joy, laughter, love, and meaning you have brought into my life. Being a mom is hard, and trying to accomplish anything else in addition to parenting can seem impossible. And some days it is impossible. But there is always tomorrow. I marvel at my good fortune to have such amazing children. Clay and Andrew have grown into charming, intelligent, capable young men. I am proud to call them my own. While the first version of this study was complete before Sammie and Sophie came along, they have made its revision much more colorful. No doubt the final product was much delayed by pregnancy, birth, rocking, nursing, changing, cuddling, pregnancy (again!), birth, rocking, nursing, changing, cuddling—but what a worthy delay it was. As Sammie prepares for his first days of pre-K and Sophie readies for her first steps, I am so happy to get to share my days (and nights) with them. The fact that most of the revisions for this project were done after bedtime stories and goodnight kisses makes me proud. I'm a mommy first. Everything else comes second. And that is just as it should be.

Thank you, my little loves, for giving my life meaning. It's all for you.

Schooling in the Antebellum South

An Exploration of Learning in the Antebellum Gulf South

The importance of learning and intellectual development in southern society has long been overlooked by historians. Since the earliest travelers crossed the South, a myth emerged that portrayed inhabitants of that region as shiftless bumpkins content with illiteracy and ignorance. Numerous accounts have contributed to this perception. Frederick Law Olmsted's *A Journey in the Seaboard Slave States: With Remarks on their Economy,* published in 1856, offered one of the most caricatured accounts of slovenly, lazy, and inept southerners. Promising in his preface to analyze "the notoriously careless, makeshift, impersistent people of the South" and to highlight the "prejudice of the slaveholding community; and especially those features which are manifestly most to be regretted," he easily crafted his narrative to do just that. Before and after Olmsted's critique, historians have largely failed to acknowledge the role of learning in the lives of southerners. Even as recently as 2009, *The American South: A History* argues that "during the antebellum era no statewide public school system existed." The dearth of studies on southern education has led many to conclude that few schools existed and that learning played no central role in antebellum southern culture. This assumption, however, is based on the absence of studies examining precollegiate learning, not on the absence of learning itself. Education was deeply valued by southerners who inhabited the regions bordering the Gulf of Mexico prior to 1860.[1]

One of the main reasons for the paucity of studies on southern education is that the history of education concentrates on the establishment of public schools—first instituted in New England. This trend leads most historians to analyze southern education through a national, even northeastern, prism that compares all achievements there to the developments in the oldest states along the eastern seaboard. Such a comparison is unfair, however, because those long-established states did not suffer from the same unsettled conditions as those in the Gulf South. Examining the South apart from the context of New England and considering southern educational developments in light of the prevailing frontier-like conditions allows a more objective assessment of their progress, making the achievements of the southern states all the more significant.

This study examines lessons and learning in the Gulf South states of Louisiana, Mississippi, and Alabama. As the lands along the Gulf of Mexico became incorporated into the United States, state governments began to make provisions for public aid to education. In certain cases such funding went to private schools that already existed, while in other instances government appropriations helped create new schools. Few of these early institutions were public in the modern sense of the term; they relied on tuition income to supplement any aid received from state governments. In order to obtain public funding, legislative stipulations often required that a certain number of indigent children be admitted free of charge, but the stigma associated with receiving aid meant few families proved willing to accept such a label. As the antebellum period progressed, some southern states began to found public schools that all children attended gratis, leaving no distinction between those who paid and those who did not—one of the main arguments in favor of establishing such schools. This was the case in Louisiana, whose 1845 state constitution required each parish to offer free lessons to its citizens, along the lines of the model offered by the City of New Orleans since 1841.

In addition to public schooling, other forms of learning took place in the southernmost states. Louisiana, Mississippi, and Alabama each contained vibrant private schools, both secular and religiously oriented. As early as 1722 a Catholic priest established a boys' school in New Orleans, and five years later Ursuline nuns founded an academy that continues to this day. Even while battling nature to make homes in the wilderness, southerners exhibited an early interest in providing education for their children. Over time the number of schools increased along with the population, so that by 1860 at least a quarter million students attended schools in Louisiana, Mississippi, and Alabama.[2]

Despite the importance of formal institutions in educating children in the antebellum Gulf South, young boys and girls also enjoyed other opportunities for learning. The ubiquitous presence of tutors in the region attests to the importance of private lessons in educating younger members of the upper class. Also significant were less formal lessons offered inside the home by family members, be it an older sibling, aunt or uncle, or parents. Such lessons formed an educational foundation for generations of southerners whose agricultural society found great benefit in the informality of home schooling. The scattered settlement of rural society made it difficult because of transportation problems to situate a school where more than a handful of children could attend. Rather than leaving home to travel some distance to a formal school, children instructed in their own homes did not have to worry about travel or boarding. Additionally, parents often proved happy to have their young ones remain under the watchful eye of family members. Parents enjoyed the opportunity to supervise their children's instruction directly, relieving them of concern about the activities of their children or the quality of instruction being offered at faraway schools. The informality of home schooling also allowed total synchronization with the rhythms of family and agricultural life. Lessons could easily be put on hold when families needed young girls to help with a new baby or boys to tend the fields. Such accommodations perfectly suited the lifestyle of the agricultural South, yet previous historians have failed to recognize the importance of learning inside the home.

The ubiquity of private lessons, offered either by family members or by a hired tutor, has helped to discourage scholarly interest in learning in the antebellum Gulf South, yet southern education offers a rich field for investigation. While school segregation in the Jim Crow South has received intense scrutiny from scholars in recent decades, authors by and large have failed to examine the historical precedents laid down in the years preceding the Civil War, despite the substantial educational developments that took place during that period. The history of education more generally remains a vibrant field, with significant contributions from both historians and educators. The pivotal studies of Lawrence Cremin remain valuable, just as Bernard Bailyn's *Education in the Forming of American Society* (1960) and Michael B. Katz's *The Irony of Early School Reform: Educational Innovation in Mid-Nineteenth Century Massachusetts* (1968) continue to resonate with scholars and guide their thinking about education history.[3]

As for studies specifically analyzing schooling in the southernmost states, John Hardin Best explains quite succinctly that "the history of education in recent years has done its job remarkably well, with one striking exception: it does not explain the South." James Leloudis's impressive study of education in postbellum North Carolina remains a notable exception; he analyzes schooling and education reform, offering important insight into the role of learning in the American South. For the antebellum period, older studies continue to dominate the literature, such as Charles William Dabney's *Universal Education in the South* (1936) and Edgar W. Knight's *Public Education in the South* (1922). Educational conditions are also considered in a few broader historical works, such as J. Mills Thornton's *Politics and Power in a Slave Society: Alabama, 1800–1860* (1978), Steven M. Stowe's *Intimacy and Power in the Old South: Ritual in the Lives of the Planters* (1987), and Catherine Clinton's *The Plantation Mistress: Woman's World in the Old South* (1982). A few recent works of note explore women's education prior to the Civil War, including Christie Anne Farnham's *The Education of the Southern Belle: Higher Education and Student Socialization in the Antebellum South* (1994) and Mary Kelley's *Learning to Stand and Speak: Women, Education, and Public Life in America's Republic* (2006). Additionally, large numbers of theses and dissertations that remain unpublished offer valuable observations on southern schooling, such as Forrest David Mathews's 1965 PhD dissertation discussing Alabama and Georgia. Mathews denies the oft-repeated claim that southerners neglected education, arguing instead that "the history of schooling in the ante-bellum South is a story of progress despite difficulties rather than a record of delinquency despite reforms."[4]

The chronology of education developments in the Gulf South offers insight into that progress. Initial efforts by the state governments of Louisiana, Mississippi, and Alabama were not aimed at creating free public schools accessible to all. Instead, the governments focused on fostering education by extending access to private institutions—using public funds to support private schools and offset tuition so that families of more modest means would be able to afford the cost. Early efforts on behalf of education clearly reveal an acceptance by leaders that the state had a role to play in fostering learning. The original constitutions of Mississippi and Alabama specifically pledged the states to extend schooling, while Louisiana took measures to do so immediately upon entrance into the Union. From the beginning southerners accepted the premise that state governments should be involved in education endeavors, although it took decades before the idea took hold that states should not just support private schools but should establish and maintain their own institutions. In the 1820s and 1830s southern state governments used public funds to support private schools, with all three states setting up education funds to do so; however, the Panic of 1837 devastated these accounts. Both Mississippi and Alabama invested their entire school funds in their state banks, which failed during the Panic and wiped out the funds, while Louisiana's dire economic situation caused state leaders to slash education spending.

The economic downturn created a setback for education in the South, but one that would be overcome during the following decade. The economic recovery of the southernmost states coincided with the maturation of Jacksonian democracy there. The spread of this political philosophy, which assaulted vestiges of privilege within the political system and demanded greater democracy, began in the late 1820s and 1830s, but the positive effects of its reforms can be discerned in the Deep South more clearly in the 1840s. The establishment of statewide school systems there is one example of that change.

While the spread of Jacksonian democracy contributed to the demand for public education in the South, the desire for schooling can be attributed to two other sources. First, the political philosophy of republicanism rested on the premise that a representative democracy needed an educated populace to flourish. When southern states expanded voting rights, adherents of this philosophy argued that access to learning likewise needed to broaden so that more voters would possess the knowledge necessary to make good decisions. In addition, southerners embraced learning as a means of social mobility. Most parents exhibited an innate desire to have their children educated in hopes that it would contribute to their later success in life.

Influenced by these factors, residents in the southernmost states began to demand privileges formerly reserved for the elite. Along with the expansion of suffrage and the reduction of property qualifications to hold office, common southerners also insisted on greater access to learning. In the 1840s people in the South began to demand that their local governments do more to extend schooling for all white inhabitants. The larger towns and cities of the South were the first areas to attempt to support free public schools. The municipal governments of New Orleans and Natchez established public schools in 1841 and 1845 respectively, while Mobile did the same in 1853. The success of these urban schools motivated residents in rural areas to demand public schools in their neighborhoods. All three state governments responded, so that by 1860 Louisiana, Mississippi, and Alabama all housed statewide public school systems.

This study explores educational developments in the Gulf South as it progressed in fits and starts throughout the antebellum years. Although the southern states deserve credit previously denied them for developing school systems prior to 1860, this story is not one of continual progress over time. Setbacks and mistakes seriously marred the system, and some illiberal forces registered opposition to providing access to learning for families of lesser means. Additionally, fully one-half of the population of the southern states was denied access to schooling because slaves and free blacks were excluded from the system. Despite these failings, the history of education in the Gulf South prior to the Civil War shows that people there valued education and made considerable progress in developing school systems that most white children could access. The story of these developments offers important insight into the worldview of the people inhabiting the region and deserves inclusion in the larger narrative of southern history.

CHAPTER ONE

A Schoolroom at the Bottom of the Stairs

LEARNING INSIDE THE HOME

Céline Frémaux shivered in the cold and tried to hold her quill steady as she carefully conjugated her French verbs. She sat at a desk in a lower room of her family's home in Baton Rouge, Louisiana. Her mother used this room as a schoolroom, where she instructed her children daily. Céline tried to concentrate on verb forms rather than the aching chill in her hands. There was no fireplace to warm her, and it would be hours before the warmth of the sun finally offered her some relief. She glanced over at Leon—he had not yet written a single verb. She and her brother had to finish their French grammar before 7:30 or they would not be able to leave their desks for breakfast. Céline grabbed Leon's paper and jotted down a few verb tenses. She could not bear for Leon to be punished—he was her best playmate and the punishment might as well have been her own. It always made her nervous to help him with his work this way, but he was barely awake this morning. Too many mornings he failed to write a single word before the breakfast bell rang. So she risked her mother's wrath to try to help him. Their handwritings were similar enough that her mother likely would not notice, and at least they would be allowed a respite from their daily lessons for breakfast.[1]

So Céline recounted in her memoirs written years later. Antebellum southerners received their education in a variety of different settings— private academies and parochial schools as well as pauper and charity institutions and public schools. But many southern children learned outside a formal institution and in the familiar environs of their own homes. Wealthy planter families often hired private tutors to instruct their young, but not only the elite received lessons at home. Many parents arranged for relatives to take charge of the education of younger children, an unpaid

7

labor that has been almost entirely overlooked in the historical literature concerning education. Prevalent across early America, learning inside the home became an important form of education embraced by southerners. The frequency with which it occurred underscores that home instruction met a variety of needs peculiar to the South and served its cash-poor agricultural society particularly well. The ubiquity of lessons inside the home demands that such learning be included when discussing education in the antebellum South.[2]

The family member who took on the responsibility for educating younger members of southern households usually had themselves benefited from some sort of formal schooling, allowing them to spread their knowledge to young children in the family. The qualifications of a family instructor differed drastically from case to case, with some possessing little more than basic literacy themselves. Others, however, enjoyed advanced education, often attending a secondary school or college. Their own educational background affected the level of instruction they offered to younger family members, which meant that the quality of instruction and the courses offered could differ greatly from one family to the next. Some children simply learned the basics that might later be expanded upon through formal schooling and independent study, while others received an intense immersion into complex subject matter. One woman explained of her mother's tutoring, "When I was eight years old Ma began to start me on abstracts of ancient history. I would read a chapter and write it from memory on a slate. Ma corrected it. I had three lines for every mistake of any kind, and after lessons the slate work was copied in ink."[3]

Mothers provided the initial instruction for children in households across the Old South. In addition to cleaning, sewing, cooking, and caring for children more generally, many mothers in the Gulf South also considered it their obligation to educate their sons and daughters. In *The Plantation Mistress: Woman's World in the Old South,* when discussing the threefold responsibility of mothers in the antebellum South, Catherine Clinton first mentions the duty of educating children, along with inculcating morals and safeguarding their physical well-being. Clinton argues that most mothers in the South were ill-equipped to undertake this burden, calling them "undereducated as a group." Clinton's assessment may have been true for the early antebellum period, but as the years progressed schooling became more widespread and women as well as men benefited from greater access to education. Many mothers had been to school for a period of time and proved perfectly capable of instructing their children in the basics. Rather than the limits of her knowledge, the larger obstacle standing in the way of a mother's ability to impart a thorough education to her children was the demands on her time. The many chores that came with running a household often made it difficult to find the time to instruct children thoroughly. Yet many mothers were determined to do so and found the time and expended considerable effort instructing their young.[4]

The Frémaux family offers an example of this type of parent teaching. An immigrant French family who lived in south Louisiana, the Frémauxs offer insight into the everyday lives of a southern family, described by one historian as "non-plantation middling order," who "had manners and education but not much money." Husband León Joseph and wife Flore Caroline had five children, two daughters and three sons. León served as a civil engineer and never acquired much land or money. Flore Caroline hailed from a prominent French family displaced by the Revolution and had considerable trouble leaving the aristocratic Old World for a crude and tumultuous life in antebellum New Orleans. Flore and León's oldest child, Céline, wrote a memoir of her childhood from 1850 to 1871. Céline describes her father as a loving, affectionate man who doted on her as the eldest daughter, and her mother as a cold and often cruel woman who competed with her for her father's attention.[5]

In her memories of her childhood, Céline recounts how, much to the chagrin of the children, her mother provided the initial education for her siblings and herself before they entered formal schools at an older age. Frémaux believed that she and her siblings would have enjoyed a happy childhood if not for the incessant instruction from their mother. While one might assume that the lessons offered by a family member proved less rigorous or disciplined than those of a hired teacher, the instruction that the Frémaux children received from their mother proved both quite advanced academically and very strict. Reading Céline's account of the harsh discipline that accompanied her mother's lessons, one is left hoping other children fared better from their instructors. She explains of her brother's French lessons: "He had his ears pulled so often that he was hardly ever without little scabs at the back of them and his head would be bumped against the wall so often that he used to say, 'As soon as I am big enough, I will run away.'"[6]

Celine's mother regularly offered lessons. Céline explains that even while they lived on a boat for several days waiting to travel from New Orleans to Baton Rouge, her mother continually forced the children to sit through lessons. Once the family settled in Baton Rouge, their mother regimented their routine very carefully. The children worked on French grammar in the mornings. If they failed to finish before the breakfast bell rang at 7:30, they would be brought a piece of dry toast to eat while they finished. Even while Flore was away visiting family or sick in bed, she made sure the children had assignments to keep them busy the entire time. Indeed, for Mother Frémaux even playtime meant an opportunity for learning. As Céline explained some years later, "We never played out of her hearing, so if we played 'ladies' and pretended to go traveling, we *had* to go to some place that really existed in that special part of the globe. If we mentioned a name of a city or a lake she would call out, 'Where is that city? What river runs near it? What is manufactured there?' And we felt as if we had an extra lesson on hand." Although Céline's resentment at her mother's incessant teaching is discernible in her memoir written decades later, few modern readers can help but be impressed by the tenacity with which her mother instructed her children.[7]

In addition to mothers who took on the responsibility of educating their young, southern fathers also took an active part in their children's education. Letters abound from men offering advice and instruction to their children while away at school, but some fathers did more. Ulrich B. Phillips cites such a case in *Life and Labor in the Old South*. Phillips notes an incident when a visitor seeking out a planter found him "a distance from the house, in the garden, which he called his office. He was instructing his children. . . . he had been so troubled to get his children educated, that at last he had found more satisfaction in doing it himself than pursuing any other method." Other fathers in the rural South did likewise, taking on the responsibility of educating their youngsters themselves rather than relying on the available schools or tutors.[8]

Aside from parents who taught their children, older siblings who themselves had received some schooling often helped educate younger brothers and sisters. The Ellises, a prominent family from a plantation region in Louisiana, offer such an example. After attending Centenary College in Jackson, Louisiana, and before moving to New Orleans to study law, older brother Thomas returned to his parents' home in Clinton where he took on the role of tutor for his younger sisters and brothers, one of whom later became a US congressman. Interspersed among his notes about politics, hunting, and reading law, Thomas records in his diary for 1855 and 1856 "hearing the lessons of the 'young'uns,'" and that he "stayed at home, all day . . . acting the pettifogger and the pedagogue." Thomas proved not to be as incessant a tutor as Flore Caroline Frémaux. While he did teach his siblings regularly, he also took plenty of time off to hunt and visit friends in the neighborhood. Just as he recorded the lessons he offered in his diary, he also noted his hunting exploits and social engagements. According to his own tally, between January and June of 1856, Ellis taught his siblings an average of twelve days per month, with the maximum number of days he spent teaching per month at eighteen and the minimum at six. Such a schedule differed drastically from the one recounted by Céline. Although Thomas did not offer lessons daily, his instruction of his younger siblings no doubt afforded them a basic education that could be expanded and enhanced in later years.[9]

Like Thomas, many siblings found themselves pressed into the service of teaching their younger siblings. Planter Thomas Batchelor and his wife Martha of Point Coupee Parish put great stock in their children's education. Their two daughters and five sons attended school at early ages. Older brothers Charles and James Madison attended Oakland College in Mississippi before entering the Kentucky Military Institute. Younger brother Albert followed them there, where he remained at the outbreak of the Civil War. Younger siblings Iverson, Tommy, and Mollie continued to attend school back home in Louisiana even after the war began, but their mother worried about how long their lessons would continue. Martha strove to ensure that her children received a good education, but as war descended upon the South, her options and ability were severely constrained. She wrote to Albert in Lexington, urging him to make the most of his time at school. Unsure how much more schooling they could afford, she observed that "you may even have to help educate your younger brother and sister." While the Batchelor brothers all eventually left school to fight for the Confederacy, daughters Kate and Mollie stayed in school, transferring to the renowned Silliman Female Collegiate Institute in Clinton, Louisiana.[10]

Martha Batchelor turned to sibling tutoring in times of need, and many other families had children teach their brothers and sisters only temporarily. While Flore Caroline Frémaux tortured her older children with incessant instruction, she later relegated that task to her eldest daughter. The trend of older siblings instructing brothers and sisters appears throughout the South, forming an important component of the education structure there.[11]

The types of lessons offered by family members differed based on their own experience. Since Thomas Ellis graduated from Centenary College and went on to become a lawyer and judge, he was capable of offering his siblings an advanced course of study. Céline Frémaux recounts lessons in ancient history from her mother, in addition to an intense immersion in French vocabulary and grammar. No doubt many family members offered less advanced courses. One scholar explains that lessons offered by relatives inside the home generally proved "very elementary. Plantation women commonly limited themselves to teaching the alphabet and geography."[12]

If a family member took on the role of tutor for others in the household, it created some interesting dynamics. Céline harbored deep resentment toward her mother and continued to criticize her even late in life. It may be surprising that in her later years she was unable to acknowledge the solid intellectual foundation her mother had laid for her, but beneath her critical assessment lies a hint of pride in her advanced intellectual pursuits—"Don't stare, reader; yes, I was not yet five years old and I wrote French verbs." Bertram Wyatt Brown argues in the introduction to her memoir that Céline resented her mother for stifling her creativity and "sense of selfhood." Céline considered her education to be her only personal possession. Perhaps it was all her mother gave her, but the persistence of Flore Caroline's instruction proved impressive, even if motivated by self-interest. Her memoir's editor argues that "Caroline's determination to inculcate her aristocratic social and cultural ideals in her children were most evident in the educational program she undertook with them." Regardless of her motivation, Flore Caroline ensured that each of her children were educated to her own high standards by providing their initial instruction herself.[13]

As with the Frémauxs, family tutoring could cause conflict for members of the household. In the Mordecai family of North Carolina and Virginia, children received instruction from mothers, older sisters, and aunts, and the arrangement contributed to tension within the family. Older sister Ellen expressed resentment at her father and especially her stepmother for expecting her to live in their home to tutor her younger half-sister, Emma. While one sister complained of too much responsibility, another became agitated for not being given more duties. Ellen's sister Caroline tutored her brother's children and expressed frustration at having to share control of the nieces and nephews she so carefully instructed. The frustration expressed by the oldest Mordecai sister may prove most surprising. Rachel Mordecai Lazarus, after teaching in her father's private academy and reading and corresponding with educational theorist Maria Edgeworth, came to believe that the home was the ideal place for learning and teaching. This belief, according to her biographer, led to Rachel's decision to marry a man whose financial security would allow her to instruct at home her younger sister as well as her stepchildren and future biological children. Despite her considered pedagogical theories and the excitement with which she embarked on this endeavor, Rachel soon found herself frustrated, exhausted, and racked with fears of inadequacy. She came to reconsider her theories on home instruction and eventually enrolled all her children in formal schools. "She complained that her intellect was shriveling from exhaustion and neglect," and died at the age of fifty, "leaving young daughters still to be educated."[14]

Although family instruction may have contributed to conflict within households, many southern children took great pleasure in lessons offered by family members and often developed bonds with their family instructors. As Catherine Clinton explains, "Parents encouraged their own unmarried sisters to live with them to assist with the schooling, an arrangement which strengthened kinship ties; many children became especially attached to tutor-aunts." A pupil often repaid a tutor relative for his or her time spent teaching them to learn to read or write with feelings of loyalty and love that lasted throughout their lifetime. The bonds forged during these early lessons often remained some of the strongest ties in a young person's life.[15]

Lessons offered by family members usually came early in life to younger children who needed instruction in the basics of reading, writing, and arithmetic. As a student progressed, teaching was often shifted to a professional teacher, but that shift did not necessarily mean moving to a schoolroom outside of the home. The omnipresence of private tutors in the antebellum Gulf South reveals another important form of schooling available outside the conventional classroom. Southern families with the financial means to do so often hired private teachers who came into their homes to tutor their children. A particular room in the house or a building in the yard was usually set aside for use as a schoolroom.

Private teachers lived with the family who hired them, offering lessons regularly to all the children of the home of the appropriate age, boys as well as girls. Some families allowed neighbor children to attend lessons as well, and sometimes several local families combined to hire one teacher to instruct their children jointly. Some children received the entirety of their education from private tutors hired by their parents, while others utilized such lessons in preparation for more advanced study they would later undertake at a college or university.[16]

Most tutors in the South, like antebellum teachers more generally, tended to be male. Men who took on teaching jobs often saw them as only a temporary occupation. Many young men out of college would teach for a few years while saving up money for additional schooling or preparing to open their own business, until they found a lawyer or doctor to study under, or while they looked for work as a minister. Many of these entrepreneurial young men hailed from northern states and journeyed south in search of work and wages.[17]

Because many tutors considered teaching to be only a temporary profession—a means to an end—their devotion to their work differed drastically. Historian Joseph Tregle writes that private tutors "generally proved a disgrace to the profession, intellectual mountebanks with a reputation for drunkenness and dissoluteness exceeded by hardly any other group in the community." One scholar of antebellum Natchez describes the exploits of a confirmed drunkard who served as a tutor for three different Natchez families. In his diary, the tutor described drunken trysts with the dancing instructor and music teacher in their employer's drawing room. Such behavior probably led Methodist preacher Thomas Griffin to label the typical tutor "a hog stealer who was whipped out of North Carolina."[18]

While men on the make did not always devote themselves wholeheartedly to their teaching duties, plenty of tutors in the antebellum Gulf South proved exceptionally devoted to their work. Many tutors received their own education at leading colleges in the Northeast, such as one who advertised in the Baton Rouge *Weekly Advocate:* "The subscriber, recently graduated from Yale College, intending to remain in Baton Rouge or its vicinity, for some length of time, is desirous of obtaining a situation as instructor in some genteel family, either in the town or its neighborhood. All branches taught belonging to a finished English education—terms reasonable."[19]

Unfortunately for those devoted to educating young southerners as tutors in private homes, the pay often proved insufficient for an independent lifestyle. Existing evidence shows that tutors in the Deep South received an average income of about $400 a year, ranging between $200 and $600 annually.[20] Since most private teachers lived in the home of their employers, room and board must be added into their salary. In addition, the job often came with advantages other than the financial compensation that helped make certain teaching jobs quite attractive. Tutors in wealthy homes often enjoyed a lifestyle far above their means. In his newspaper advertisement for a private instructor, J. H. Taylor described his lavish summer and winter homes.[21] Although he paid only $400 a year, the lifestyle undoubtedly added to the appeal for many educators. Another important benefit for many tutors was the use of the family library. Tutoring in antebellum Natchez while preparing to be a lawyer, Seargent Smith Prentiss took great interest in his employer's extensive library filled with law books placed at his disposal. He wrote home to his mother that he considered his access to their books "as good as a hundred [dollars] a year at least."[22] One expert on education in antebellum Alabama explains it was generally acknowledged that tutors took great interest in the family's library and "in some instances the entire library would be moved to the tutor's quarter."[23]

Considering the wages received, it should not be surprising that many tutors moved around in search of better terms. One tutor in Mississippi left the home of the wealthy Natchez family that employed him to take a job in rural Hinds County, but after accumulating an income deficit of $150 in less than a year, he returned to work for the original family. Many tutors in the antebellum Gulf South followed a similar path, moving around regularly hoping to contract for more money. More accomplished tutors did not have to advertise their services in order to procure employment. Those who excelled at their craft quickly earned a reputation for themselves and became much sought after by families in the area. When a tutor's services were no longer needed by the current employer, several families might be waiting in the wings to try to entice the tutor to work next with their children.[24]

Abraham Hagaman offers an instructive example of a tutor working in the antebellum South. Hagaman was born in New Jersey and attended Princeton College. After graduating at the age of eighteen he took on tutoring jobs in Virginia and Mississippi before becoming a minister.

Once ordained, Hagaman continued to teach in addition to carrying out his regular religious duties. In 1836 he moved to Louisiana, where he opened a book and drug store, served as a deputy, and conducted the parish census, all the while continuing to teach and minister a church.[25]

Hagaman typifies most tutors in the Gulf South in many respects. Northern-born and college-educated, he started teaching in the South before deciding on a permanent profession. Also like Hagaman, many young men who became tutors hoped to enter the ministry some day. Like many of his colleagues, Hagaman moved around in search of better pay and situations. That he took on other jobs before starting a family also proved typical of such teachers. As other scholars have noted, earning the salary of a private tutor usually did not allow maintenance of one's own family or household.[26]

While most private tutors were male, some women did take on the role of teachers inside private homes. Like their male counterparts, Catherine Clinton explains, "these governesses were generally young, never married, and northern born and educated." Usually marriage meant a woman relinquished any teaching duties she formerly performed. In the household of Judge Clayton in southern Mississippi, for example, Miss Scales taught for two years before marrying. After her marriage, she was replaced by another unmarried young woman, Miss White from Lamar, Mississippi. As the antebellum period progressed, more women took on jobs teaching both in schools and in private homes. As the Gulf South states entered the Union, teaching remained the exclusive domain of men, but that fact changed as schooling became a more dominant part of southern society. As more schools appeared across the South and the literacy rate inched upward, there were more and more women teachers at the helm of classrooms, both inside the home and out. The feminization of the teaching workforce corresponded with the spread of learning across the South. This trend is discernible when one examines the various state and local education reports and census figures. It attests to the emergence of a woman's sphere outside the home, where only certain jobs were open to the fairer sex.[27]

Regardless of a teacher's gender, the relationship between tutors and the families they served often proved quite complicated. Some families developed affectionate ties with the teachers who joined their household. One scholar explains of tutors in Montgomery, Alabama prior to the Civil War that a tutor was "well received in a family, respected, and his welfare safe-guarded." John Davis, who taught in a private home, described his experiences teaching: "The affability and tenderness of this charming family in the bosom of the woods will ever be cherished in my breast. . . . My wants were always anticipated. The family Library was transported without entreaty into my chamber. . . . And once, having lamented that my stocks of segars [*sic*] was nearly exhausted, a negro was dispatched seventy miles to *Charleston* for supply of the best *Spanish*." Although some teachers found welcoming homes where they were respected and valued, in other instances families treated tutors merely as hired servants. Historian Joseph Tregle notes that the treatment of private teachers was an impediment to inducing qualified applicants to take such jobs. "Few able men found any attraction in the work," he argues, "for patrons frequently expected tutors to work out in the fields when the need arose or to fill in at any other chore, no matter how remote from the atmosphere of the classroom." Another scholar explains that teachers often were recently arrived in an area with few friends or relatives or any sort of support network. Such a situation often led them to rely on their host family for more than just wages, but also to help develop social connections and learn about their new area. In addition, tutors who stayed in the home of their pupils remained ever under the watchful eye of their employer, giving them little chance for unsupervised activity.[28]

An example from 1779 highlights some of the peculiarities that could arise in relationships between tutors and their employers. Pedro Flouard, a tutor in New Orleans, sued his previous employer, Francisco Ense, for the amount contracted to educate Ense's children. Ense refused to pay because the tutor failed to remain for the entire length of the contract, but Flouard informed the court that he could not stay in Ense's home because the family failed to feed him adequately. Whether the dispute arose from Flouard's unreasonable culinary demands, from the Ense family's inhospitality, or perhaps from financial limitations, this episode illustrates that the employment of tutors often did not go smoothly.[29]

Julius A. Reed, a Connecticut native who moved to Natchez, Mississippi, after graduating from Yale's theological school, encountered some problems while teaching in the South. Reed took a job tutoring the children of Judge John Perkins, a wealthy southern planter who owned land in Mississippi and Louisiana and maintained three separate residences. Certainly the lifestyle to which Reed was exposed proved far beyond his own means and would be considered quite a bonus to most educators, yet

Reed quickly came to resent his treatment by the Perkins family. Initially Reed appeared pleased with his host family, calling Judge Perkins "a man of his word of stern integrity & benevolent," and Mrs. Perkins "kind intelligent sensible & quite a favorite with me." He even had kind words for the Perkins children, calling them "pleasant scholars," although he noted that they "give me some trouble." Despite his initial favorable impression of the family, a hint of the divergent worldviews of the Yankee tutor and the southern planter family he served can be gleaned from Reed's comment that Judge Perkins "is very particular & expects me to dress genteelly."[30]

It was not long before Reed began to express his discontent with his treatment by the Perkins family. He wrote home: "There have been balls & *parties* without number but I have not been invited—and the family takes no pains to introduce me into company. From my conversation they must know I am not extravagantly fond of their routs but that does not account for their not sometimes taking me with them." Reed went on to comment, "I dont know whether they think my occupation degrading or myself not fashionable enough—although I care *very* little for the *parties* my pride is a little wounded—& it is somewhat problematical whether I shall continue a second year with this family." Clearly Reed hoped to be included in the family's social life, yet the Perkins viewed him as an employee rather than a social equal. He bemoaned how the Perkinses behaved toward him and noted that "the consequence of such treatment on the part of the family is that I am similarly treated by others & that I am scarcely invited anywhere."[31]

Reed recounted one incident in particular that upset him tremendously. A woman who lived nearby came to the Perkins's home and after meeting Reed invited him, in front of Judge and Mrs. Perkins, "to call often & without formality—to breakfast dinner or tea as might be convenient." Not long afterward the Perkins family accepted an invitation to the woman's home but intentionally concealed their destination from Reed, only informing him that they would be out for the evening. The next morning Mrs. Perkins told Reed that their hostess had "expressed some disappointment at your absence but I did not tell her *you* were not invited." This incident led Reed to the conclusion that the Perkins family "do not intend to treat me as an equal."[32]

Reed's experience in the home of Judge Perkins offers some insight into the precarious position of tutors in southern society. In no case was this more true than when it came to disciplining students. Parents and tutors often disagreed about the proper punishment for a particular offense. Most parents granted their employees little leeway when disciplining their children, and intuitive pupils often took advantage of the fact that their tutor's hands were tied. The expectations of parents often differed drastically in this regard, as illustrated by the case of Abraham Hagaman. Whereas his first employer insisted he was too gentle with his pupils and assured him the only remedy for their unruliness was free use of the rod, his next employment ended abruptly for, according to Hagaman, "I had given offense to Mr. Longhorn by exercising what he regarded as too strict discipline towards one of his children."[33]

The complicated dynamics involved in entrusting one's children to another's tutelage as well as inviting a stranger into one's home help explain why recommendations from family and friends played such a vital role in the process of hiring a tutor. As one scholar argues, "It was considered a most valuable service both to the friend and to the teacher, to give a recommendation, for in this manner the friend secured a proficient teacher, and the tutor secured a desirable position." It is not surprising that especially when it came to hiring northerners, parents in the Gulf South often took extreme care to secure trusted recommendations before bringing anyone into their home. A letter written by Charles Conrad to a friend in New Haven, Connecticut, in October of 1854 reveals his concern in hiring a teacher for his sons. Conrad was a prominent Louisiana politician who served as both a senator and US congressman in the 1840s before becoming secretary of war in the 1850s and later a delegate to the Confederate Congress. In the letter Conrad thanked his correspondent, William G. Walton, for his recommendation of Mr. Bacon and expressed his confidence in agreeing on the terms of his service, but also voiced concerns. He noted his awareness of a certain Mr. Bacon from New Haven who was "distinguished as a zealous & vibrant abolitionist," and inquired if that man was the father of his prospective employee. Conrad went on to comment that if so and if he shared "his father's principles and feelings in regard to slavery & slaves," that he "would not be a very pleasant inmate of my house," nor would a southern city be an appropriate place for him. Parents expressed a variety of concerns when procuring tutors for their children, ensuring that recommendations from trusted sources played an important role in the hiring process.[34]

The low status of teachers in southern society added to the need for recommendations. In 1857 the Louisiana state superintendent of education bemoaned, "The position of teacher, instead of being put, at all events, on a level with that of members of other professions, is sunk so low that as clerk, daily laborer, or almost any of the less responsible occupations." Another observer argued that teachers "are looked upon as an inferior sort of being of little sensibility, and not justly entitled to the regards of society." The poor reputation suffered by schoolteachers meant that the number and types of people willing to join the profession remained limited. Conversely, the fact that instructors themselves often considered teaching to be only a temporary occupation and that many performed their duties less than diligently helped ensure that the reputation of teachers in general remained low in the decades following the American Revolution. Yet as schools spread across the South and education became a more central theme in southern culture, the reputation of teachers and their status in southern society began to rise.[35]

Helping to bring about an increase in standing, many individual teachers were exceptionally well qualified and gifted in their craft and were valued by the families they served. According to one historian, "When the children in a family outgrew the services of an efficient tutor, other families eagerly awaited his release so that they could vie for his services." Despite the low status of teachers in general, individual tutors who attentively instructed their pupils made a name for themselves in the community and found their services much sought after by prominent citizens.[36]

Some parents went to great lengths to secure accomplished tutors for their children. In 1828 the Weston family of South Carolina paid for the Reverend Alexander Glennie to travel from England to tutor their children, while another family procured the services of a French teacher who agreed to move from Europe to the United States to tutor their children for $600 a year. Most families did not go so far as to bring instructors across an ocean from Europe to instruct their offspring, but many extensively researched a potential tutor's background and experience before bringing them into the home and exposing the children to them. Such a vetting process helped ensure that the tutor hired would prove satisfactory in regard to both their qualifications and their political proclivities, although not all parents vetted so carefully.[37]

Lessons inside the home offered numerous benefits for southern families that ensured many would continue to rely on tutors even as schools began to appear across the countryside. For those relying on relatives, one of the most obvious benefits was the pecuniary advantage gained from having a relative perform a job gratis that otherwise would require payment. Depending on the educational attainments of the family instructor, such teaching may have proved more rudimentary than that offered by a hired teacher, but some family members were well educated themselves and perhaps even more qualified than the teachers available for hire. Additionally, many families who could not afford to send their children to school or hire a private tutor were still able to provide their youngsters with a basic level of literacy through lessons from family members. Martha Batchelor wrote to her son while he was away at school that she may need him to help teach his younger brother and sister, "but I will never allow you to labour for them while I have a dollar." Clearly, family instruction only served as a last resort for the Batchelors, but many other parents eagerly utilized relatives as teachers for younger children in the home either out of necessity or desire.[38]

What may have been the main incentive to lessons inside the home also remained one of the major impediments to education in a formal school—the scattered settlement of southern society. One of the fundamental characteristics of antebellum southern society was its rural, agricultural basis. This feature directly impacted the educational system of the Old South. One study cites the settlement pattern in the South as the first factor affecting education there: "The population density in the southern states, even among the most populous, worked against a vigorous public school system." The authors go on to explain, "In view of the state of communications, roads, and modes of travel in the first half of the nineteenth century, an effort to bring children together regularly over considerable distances would have faced formidable difficulties." With families spread out on farms cultivating as much land as possible, it was very difficult to situate a schoolhouse where more than a handful of children could access it easily. Children walked to school, severely restricting the distance within their reach.[39]

Where schools did not exist within walking distance, another alternative was for children to board nearer the school—either with a family living nearby or at the school itself. But lodging was an expense many families could not afford, and the separation from family often proved trying not only for students but for their parents as well. Bringing a tutor into their home alleviated these concerns, eliminating the need for travel and the inconveniences associated with it during the antebellum period.

Time spent traveling to and from a schoolhouse or money spent boarding children near the school both were saved by having an instructor inside the home. The convenience this arrangement afforded is easily overlooked in the current age of cars and school buses, but remained foremost for rural southerners when making decisions about the education of their children.

While financial constraints and the inconvenience of antebellum travel led some families, who would have preferred to have their children enrolled in a formal school, instead have them receive lessons inside their home as a last resort, many parents actually preferred to have their young'uns laboring at their lessons at home. Private tutors offered parents the opportunity to supervise directly the instruction their children received as well as offering them a chance to keep their young ones under the watchful eyes of family members. Such oversight relieved parents of concern about the activities of their children or the quality of instruction being offered at faraway schools. One scholar of antebellum Natchez found several examples of children who withdrew from private schools in order to take lessons from a tutor at home instead. In 1842, for example, Margaret Dunbar withdrew from Elizabeth Female Academy when "she and her mother decided that employing a private tutor at their home would provide Margaret with a much better education as well as eliminate the separation from her family." Likewise, Clara Walworth did not like school despite the presence of her two sisters who also attended, so that the parents instead hired a private teacher to instruct their daughters inside their home. This decision may have helped Mary Shields, who had been attending a private academy, to decide to return home and take lessons from the Walworth tutor as well. Such examples reveal that even when private schooling facilities were available and financially feasible, many southern families preferred to have their children educated inside their own homes. Home schooling appealed to southerners for a variety of reasons and met a number of different needs.[40]

Another advantage gained from having lessons inside the home was the availability of children to help with the many tasks of running a household and farm. For small farmers, the more hands available to help, the better, including one's own children. The informality of home schooling allowed harmonization with the rhythms of family and agricultural life. Lessons could easily be put on hold when young girls were needed to help with a new baby or boys were needed in the fields. Such accommodations perfectly suited the lifestyle of the agricultural South. Even in well-to-do planter families where children would not be put to work in the fields with slaves, children were still needed to help with less laborious tasks, such as overseeing workers, helping in the kitchen, or entertaining. At one school in Louisiana that operated during the Civil War, the appearance of visitors caused the pupils' lessons to be put on hold so that the students could entertain and supervise the younger children who came to visit. The convenience of having youngsters learning at home where they could be taken from their lessons as needed appealed to many parents across the Old South.[41]

The prevalence of this type of learning illustrates that home schooling met a variety of needs peculiar to the rural South. Chronically cash-poor and isolated on farms and plantations with transportation slow and difficult, families who educated their children at home avoided many of the obstacles that would hamper efforts to introduce a systematic education structure to the South throughout the antebellum period. Parents who arranged for instruction at home found themselves able to exert full control over both their children's education and their discipline, something that many parents still find attractive today. The total synchronization with family life allowed by home schooling also proved especially important in the agricultural South and offered parents a convenience impossible in formal schools.

In addition to the many benefits of learning inside the home, such lessons often proved to be quite successful, as can be seen from the future accomplishments of students who learned in this manner. Thomas C. W. Ellis, who himself went on to become a district judge in New Orleans, could take pride in the accomplishments of the siblings he tutored. One brother, Stephen Dudley, followed in his tutor's footsteps and became a judge for the Louisiana State Court of Appeals. Younger brother Ezekiel John served in the state senate and the US Congress and as an officer in the Civil War. As for other children across the South, taking lessons at home from a family member in no way hampered their later success in life.[42]

The prevalence of learning inside the home and its suitability for rural southerners reveals the important role of such education in the antebellum Gulf South. Clearly, learning inside the home played an important role in educating young southerners, despite its oversight in historical literature. Among the few historians who have studied the history of education in the South, learning inside the home is almost completely neglected since works that do exist tend to focus on institutional education. Yet home instruction proved to be an important form of learning in the South just as it was in colonial and early America. While such lessons were less formal and regulated than those in the graded schools most of us are familiar with today, they should not be discounted as an unimportant form of education. Lessons inside the home from which generations of southerners benefited perfectly suited their agricultural society and occupied a central role in the education of the region.

## CHAPTER TWO

Learning beyond the Homestead

PRIVATE EDUCATION IN THE GULF SOUTH

Although learning inside the home was one of the earliest forms of instruction in the Gulf South, private schools provided one of the most consistent and dependable means of learning. Census records from 1840 reveal a total of 237 schools designated as "academies and grammar schools" in the three states of Louisiana, Mississippi, and Alabama. This number jumped to 480 schools in 1850 and 527 by 1860. Prior to the establishment of state systems of public education, private schools served as the primary agencies to which parents could turn to secure instruction for their children. Many of the schools established in the antebellum period continued to thrive for decades and earned reputations for their advanced courses and impressive teaching staff. Other private schools were more fleeting, operating only a few years while a teacher remained in town. Despite the varying degrees of permanence and quality, private schools abounded across the South and remained one of the most important avenues for learning in the antebellum period. Prior to the establishment of wholly public institutions, built and funded by state governments, southern legislatures looked to private schools to carry the burden for educating the majority of southern children. State legislatures aided and assisted these schools to a moderate extent, ensuring that private schools would remain a significant component of the southern education structure even after the establishment of statewide public school systems.[1]

There were many different types of private schools in the South. One institution that appeared very early on was known as an "old field school." Historian Frank Owsley explains: "These were elementary schools, in which reading and writing and arithmetic and sometimes higher subjects were taught." The name described the location, where it was "built by members of the community on one of the fallow 'old' fields that had lost its productivity through overuse." Parents whose children attended the school maintained control over it, hiring the teacher and setting up the terms of his employment. Such schools charged tuition, "about two and one half dollars for a five or six months' term and one dollar for a six-week summer session," according to Owsley, although some schools also instituted provisions to allow attendance by children whose families could not afford to pay tuition. The term "common school" is also often used for these types of schools, implying a system where all students, regardless of age or ability, were taught in one common classroom. In some cases the school originated when a group of neighboring planters hired a teacher to instruct their children jointly, whereas in other instances a teacher initiated the school and ran it independently. However such an institution came into being, references to both common and old field schools abound in the literature from the antebellum Gulf South.[2]

Such a school existed in Clinton, Louisiana in the late 1820s. There a group of seven families together contracted with a teacher to run a school for their children. The fathers worked out an agreement with Thomas T. Hale to teach classes in 1828 in a schoolhouse located on the land of Samuel M. Simpson. Hale began teaching on the first Monday in January and continued classes for one calendar year. He agreed to teach the students "spelling, reading, writing, arithmetick, and English grammar, with most of the branches of polite literature usually taught in Grammar schools." The parents contracting with Hale promised to pay him a certain amount before the end of the year, with pledged amounts ranging from $25 to $125. The contract went on to stipulate that "all subscribers shall have equal privileges in the school and be at liberty to send their own children and as many or as few as they may choose and they who subscribe more than they can make with their own to have the liberty of sending others to make it up." The contract allowed Hale to teach additional students at a set rate, with a commitment from the teacher to conduct classes from eight o'clock in the morning to five in the evening with an hour and a half break for recreation. The contract closed with a commitment from Hale "to be punctual in his attendance [to] the school, to govern with impartiality and strict justice, and to use his best exertions to promote the moral as well as literary interest of his pupils."[3]

The following year Hale made a similar agreement with a different set of parents with a few notable changes. The contract for 1829 committed

Hale to conduct classes in a different schoolhouse with eleven families subscribing, up from seven the previous year. Whereas the later contract again allowed Hale to accept additional students, this year he was limited to only ten such students. The parents in 1829 were likewise limited in the number of children they could send. The 1828 contract explicitly stated that the families could send as many children as they chose, their own charges or others. The following year the subscribing parents were limited to only sending children "under their legal guardianship." It appears that both Hale and the families who employed him wanted some sort of limit on the number of children who could be brought to the school for classes. We can only imagine these small, privately owned schoolhouses being overwhelmed with families anxious to take advantage of the opportunity to have their children educated locally when a teacher appeared.[4]

In addition to small schoolhouses built by planters on their land, the Gulf South also housed a large number of private schools known as academies and seminaries. Such schools usually offered what today would be considered a high school curriculum, although many also housed an elementary department that catered to younger scholars. In the judgment of one expert on southern education, "academy and seminary both seem to mean privately founded and supported schools." According to the 1860 census, Louisiana housed one hundred fifty-two private schools, Mississippi one hundred sixty-nine, and Alabama two hundred six, serving more than twenty-two thousand students. Some schools that would be considered high schools today were called colleges before the Civil War. A scholar writing about education in the antebellum South explains, "The terms 'secondary' and 'collegiate' were used interchangeably. At times, discerning secondary schools from true colleges proves difficult, if not impossible, for the historian. The word 'college' attached to the school did not necessarily mean an institution of higher learning." Regardless of the precise classification, such schools formed an important part of the educational opportunities available in the Gulf South.[5]

The story of Lucy Fisher offers insight into the lives of private schools and their proprietors operating in the antebellum period. Fisher, born and educated in Connecticut, moved to Louisiana in 1834 upon the advice of her brother, who explained that teachers were in great demand in the Deep South. Her brother insisted she decline her first job offer to teach at a private school in New Orleans for fear of yellow fever, so Fisher moved to Baton Rouge. After tutoring for a few years, Fisher married and opened a private school with her husband. She continued teaching while raising her family. When her husband died suddenly in 1843, Fisher intended to return to her family in Connecticut, but her patrons begged her to stay. She continued running the school, which flourished, on her own.[6]

While schoolteacher Thomas Hale taught in schoolhouses previously built by local farmers on their own land, Lucy Fisher and her husband controlled the property on which they began their school. To the surprise of the community, after her husband's death Fisher stayed in the South and continued their academy. Enrollments increased so that the school soon outgrew the property. In the first session after her husband's death the school catered to forty-four pupils and enrollment increased until every room was full. Fisher recounts in her memoir how a grandfather of one of her pupils continually offered his assistance to aid the school in any way, at one point purchasing a new brick structure (of Fisher's choosing) in which she could conduct classes as long as she chose to continue teaching.[7]

The buildings and equipment that private schools offered could be important in attracting potential students. The advertising done by the Silliman Female Collegiate Institute in Clinton, Louisiana for the 1854–1855 school year reported its accommodations as "one two-story brick house, 50 by 60 feet, with a one story room adjoining, 24 feet square; a study room, 24 by 40 feet, and a two story brick building, 24 by 50 feet, all well finished." That school also boasted a range of scientific instruments, including "an Electric Machine of great power, with suitable articles for experimenting, a superior Air Pump with necessary appendages, a large Electro Magnetic Machine, and the largest and best reflecting Telescope in the South," among other instruments. The school also owned a number of musical instruments including six piano fortes "made expressly for this institute," four harps, a percussion organ "with the power of a common ten stop church organ," four guitars, four accordions, and six violins.[8]

Many schools in the South conducted classes in impressive structures that compared favorably to the most lauded institutions in the Northeast. Barton Academy in Mobile was such a school, which continues to impress onlookers today. "A handsome structure of colonial architecture" completed in 1836, Barton Academy was constructed as a public enterprise by the City of Mobile and funded through a lottery, but initially the structure housed private and parochial schools. The school building was quite impressive, with three stories containing a total of eight separate classrooms that could accommodate up to six hundred students. The designers intended the classrooms to house boys and girls separately, and the rooms to be subdivided if necessary. Originally Barton Academy housed four separate departments: an infant school for children under eight, a primary and a secondary department for female students, as well as a classical department for young men. That the City of Mobile built such a structure for school purposes so early in the antebellum period is impressive, and speaks to that city's progressive stance on education and the government's role in providing it.[9]

Despite the presence of large and commodious school buildings, the proverbial one-room schoolhouse catered to students throughout the Gulf South. Most schoolteachers did not enjoy Lucy Fisher's luck of having a generous benefactor offering to pay for school improvements, and few local or state governments took the progressive stance of the City of Mobile in helping to provide for such structures. The first school established in Alabama was described as "a log cabin with a door at one end, a huge fire place at the other, a window on each side closed by board shutters. The furniture consisted of puncheon benches and a shelf around the wall between the windows and the door. This shelf served as a depository for books and dinner buckets, also for a writing desk. On a shelf just outside the door the water bucket was placed, and on a nail beside it hung a long-handled gourd, which served as a common drinking cup."[10]

Many private schools in the Gulf South operated as family businesses, with a husband and wife both teaching classes along with siblings, children, and other relatives. Nicholas M. Hentz and his wife Caroline ran a private school together in Florence, Alabama, in the 1830s. The Taylor family ran a school in southern Louisiana headed by patriarch Sereno Taylor, who served as the school's principal, with his wife and daughter both teaching classes and additional relatives sometimes joining them to teach. The business of educating was a family affair for the Taylors, which extended to the construction of a new schoolhouse on the Mississippi Gulf Coast that family members helped to build and furnish. When a young male cousin of the Taylors took charge of a school near Jackson, Mississippi, he brought his sister with him as an assistant. Lucy Fisher likewise surrounded herself with family as she made a career as an educator, teaching alongside first her brother and later her husband. After her husband's death she called on her sisters who came from Connecticut to help her manage her school in Baton Rouge. Many schools in the Gulf

South operated along similar lines, functioning as family enterprises in which all members had a role in the maintenance of the school.[11]

One job often allocated to family members involved housekeeping. Many schools boarded students due to the difficulty of travel and the distance between home and school. Often a wife, sister, or daughter would be placed in charge of upkeep of the boarding facilities, as Lucy Fisher put her sister Dorothy in charge of housekeeping for her school. While boarding students added immensely to the maintenance of a school, it often proved necessary in order to attract pupils. Outside of larger towns, few children lived close enough to a school to allow daily travel to and from home, so that provisions had to be made to board pupils nearby. Some schools allowed for such provisions at the school itself, where in other instances families living nearby would board pupils and see to their supervision for a specified fee. An example of this type of arrangement was an agreement between J. William Henderson and John T. Faulk in 1833. A contract signed by the two men states, "It is this day understood that J. Wm Henderson [does] agree to take four children in as boarders for J. T. Faulk and pay the teacher for their tuition." The document goes on to stipulate that "They are to go to school from Mr. Henderson's house to the public school house [Prairie] Maroughe. Mr. Henderson boards them, loading, washing, & provision." For his assistance, Faulk agreed to pay Henderson $26 a month for ten months "if the school continues in operation that long."[12]

Children often grew very attached to the families with whom they boarded. Young Mary Baker boarded with a couple while attending school in Lexington, Kentucky in the 1810s. She grew quite fond of her surrogate parents and often wrote to her family in Natchez about their kindness and how much she would miss them once she completed her schooling. Schoolchildren across the South reported sentimental attachment to the families with whom they resided while attending school. Mollie Batchelor related her love for her guardian, Mrs. Jackson, with whom she lived in the 1860s while attending school. One father in south Louisiana boarded his two sons with two different "French families of the first respectability" while they took lessons. He believed that the families treated his sons "with great tenderness & affection," but went on to voice his concern that "I am afraid they are rather too much petted as neither of the families have any children."[13]

Some schoolmasters considered it an advantage to have their scholars boarding with them. An advertisement placed in a Louisiana newspaper in 1847 for a boys' high school noted, "Arrangements have been made by which a number of boarders may be accommodated. They will reside in the same family with the Principal, and be under his immediate control and supervision." Likewise Elizabeth Norton wrote to her sister in 1822 "it is a great change to have other people's children committed to our care, but I prefer boarders that we have the entire management of them to day scholars because we can do much more good to the former than to the latter." Norton's sentiment reveals that some teachers preferred to have their pupils under their immediate supervision not only in the classroom but outside it as well. Parents depended on other adults to look after their children while they attended school away, be it the schoolteacher himself or another adult with whom the child boarded. These chaperones played an important role in the student's life, for better or for worse.[14]

Sometimes a chaperone took supervision of another's child to an extreme, resulting in conflict with the student's family. William T. Palfrey was a planter in Bayou Teche, Louisiana, who served as a judge, sheriff, and state senator. He sent his daughter Sidney to Catholic boarding school in Maryland, which led to repeated clashes with the headmistress. Sister Mary Bernard Graham displayed no timidity when offering advice, though unsolicited, to Judge Palfrey about how to raise his daughter. Sister Mary constantly criticized and counseled the judge in a series of letters throughout the 1850s. Her initial concerns were minor, such as how the girl was informed about a death in the family and whether or not the child should wear black mourning garb. Over time the nun became more outspoken. She objected to Sidney spending time away from school to visit family nearby who Sister Mary believed distracted the girl from her academic pursuits. Her concerns fell on deaf ears, however, because Judge Palfrey continued to allow her to go spend time with her aunt and uncle as well as receive them at school for visits.

In 1853 Sidney asked her father to allow her to leave school permanently and return home, and unsurprisingly this request brought a strong response from Sister Mary. If she could not return home permanently, the child requested a home visit of at least three months. The nun told Judge Palfrey that such an extended vacation from school would cause so much irreparable damage to the girl's studies that she need not bother to return at all after that absence. Sister Mary clearly had very strong feelings about what was in Sidney's best interest, at one point lecturing the judge, "You have been too indulgent to her, & I am afraid that you will become sensible of this when it is too late." She went on to say, "I hope that you will let Sidney know how very much displeased you have been with her. A good lesson at this time might be of service to her during the rest of her life. She is fully impressed with the idea that she can do just as she pleases, & it will be well for you to let her see that she cannot."[15]

Sister Mary was bold to be so assertive with Judge Palfrey regarding Sidney's upbringing, but her opinions no doubt flowed from genuine concern for the girl's well-being. Many guardians grew attached to the children under their care, yet boarding students also added considerably to the chores of average schoolteachers as noted by Caroline Lee Hentz. Hentz and her husband Nicholas were not average schoolteachers. Caroline went on to become an influential novelist and Nicholas taught at George Bancroft's school in Northampton, Massachusetts, as well as at the University of North Carolina. Both spouses displayed a dedication to educating young southerners, yet both also noted the incessant trouble that accompanied caring for young people. Caroline recounted the toil of caring for students who had fallen ill and required constant care and attention. After describing the efforts expended to care for two sick students, Caroline penned in her diary, "how severe are [their] requisitions—that we must bend ourselves to such inconveniences—it seems to me as if I [would] rather earn my living by the sweat of my brow, then by such bondage of the spirit."[16]

Teachers who worked in southern schools much resembled those who tutored in planter homes before the Civil War; they tended to be northern-born and educated. Like tutors, many took on jobs teaching in private schools temporarily before embarking on a more lucrative career. While teaching in a school rather than a private home often offered the opportunity of enrolling more pupils and thus the possibility of earning more money, many educators considered the pay too low to entice them to make a career of teaching. It often proved necessary to take a second job to supplement teaching income. In 1819 a group of men arranged for Mr. William Ashley to open a school in Montgomery, Alabama, for the benefit of local children. The school flourished, but Ashley found profits too small to continue. The community, however, wanted to maintain the school, so they offered Ashley the job of jailer to supplement his income. Ashley accepted, and because the schoolhouse was located directly across the road from the jail, they devised an arrangement that likely caused many a mother to cringe. "He sat in the doorway of home while conducting his classes, and kept an eye on the inmates of the jail at the same time." Animated by the same entrepreneurial spirit that so many men possessed in the antebellum South, many educators found ways to continue teaching while supplementing their income.[17]

Although overall the pay for most teachers remained low, some parents and school administrators proved willing to pay considerable amounts of money to obtain qualified teachers. Thomas Ellis, who tutored his younger siblings at his parents' home in Clinton, Louisiana, received a job offer in 1855 to teach at Pine Bluff Academy. The written offer stated that school administrators insisted on having "a competent teacher, let it cost what it may," and asked Ellis to name his price. At Lucy Fisher's girls' academy in Baton Rouge, Fisher insisted that she "had spared no money to get the best teachers and to have our seminary second to none in the State." Some dedicated school administrators, like many parents in the antebellum Gulf South, proved willing to pay top dollar to procure qualified and competent teachers for their school. Experience and reputation often allowed competent teachers to command higher wages from their employers, who were willing to incur the costs to retain accomplished instructors.[18]

Yet even the most qualified educators might experience trouble with their students or their students' parents. Schoolchildren in the antebellum period, just like those today, had mischievous tendencies and would find themselves in a bit of trouble now and then. An 1857 letter home from a schoolchild in south Louisiana reports that although he had been attending all his classes regularly, he had been given a reprieve on April Fool's Day, since the students tricked the teachers by cutting the rope to the school bell so that classes never commenced. Commentaries from teachers, students, and family members reveal the need for constant discipline for unruly students, ranging from minor infractions to more serious offenses. One schoolteacher wrote with seeming satisfaction of the expulsion of two of his former pupils from their new school, one for disobedience and the other for his "ungovernable temper," which led him to stab another student. The teacher reported, "I am not at all surprised for I know them to be obstinate, self-willed boys, unwilling to be restrained and governed even for their own advantage." Joseph Lightsey attended school in Mississippi in the 1850s and witnessed a knife fight between two classmates, leading to the expulsion of both.[19]

Schoolchildren might cause teachers grief, but trouble with parents who paid their salaries often proved more serious. The expulsion of a particular student meant loss of wages, but when a teaching relationship ended as a result of dissatisfaction with the teacher, his entire career was threatened. In a profession that relied so heavily on reputation and personal recommendations, it was dangerous to allow a disgruntled student to have the last word about the competency of the teacher. Such a case is illustrated by William Lacey, the principal of the Southern Institute in Jackson, Louisiana, who had two girls removed from his school based on a report from one of the girls that Lacey had called her and her mother "fools." Lacey went to great lengths to explain the origins of the conflict to the girls' uncle, Judge Thomas Butler, a man of considerable prominence in the local community. Lacey decried Judge Butler's rash action of taking the girls out of his school and warned that "if the principle here adopted [was] universally acted on, no school in existence can survive its operation a single year. Every literary institution must inevitably perish under the influence of a rule so partial and so destructive." Lacey was not alone in his troubles. The accomplished teaching duo Nicholas and Caroline Hentz were interrupted at supper one evening by a rider bringing an aggressive note from the uncle of one of their pupils based on the "false statements of his niece." Students and teachers often interpreted incidents differently, with the result that many conflicts occurred between teachers and guardians based on misinformation and emotional reactions.[20]

Lawrence Daily, a schoolteacher in Mississippi, got himself into a dispute with one family whose children enrolled at his school but never actually attended. Daily believed himself entitled to remuneration nonetheless, since the two girls were not prevented from attending due to illness or other unforeseen circumstances, but instead chose to patronize another school in the area. Daily insisted that the decision to enroll the girls elsewhere could not possibly be based on his skills as a teacher, asserting, "I can venture to affirm (without vanity or boasting) that I am an acknowledged scholar which is generally known by all persons who are judges of Education within the Circle of my Acquaintance—and as to my Sobriety, attention to my school and moral behavior these are points that I never have been questioned upon." The teacher insisted on being paid the total sum due for tuition of the two girls, a total of $8, promising the family to "rest assured I will have my pay and will not be fooled or trifled with."[21]

Many teachers dealt with parents who did not pay them in a timely manner for services rendered, and many were forced to beg, plead, and cajole for payment. James Lemon served as both a doctor and a teacher in Tickfaw Station, Louisiana, and found it necessary to request overdue payment for services rendered in both capacities. A letter to J. A. Williams written in 1861 begins, "Please be so kind as to let me know when you will have some money for me on my warrant so that I can make arrangements to get it. I am greatly in need of some (for provisions). I cannot collect any from my patients for professional services as doctor so I call upon you for some for services as School Teacher."[22]

Some lucky teachers managed to avoid financial difficulty, but almost all felt tried and tested at some point in their careers. Parents often harbored exceptionally high expectations for those appointed to instruct their young, not only wanting them to tutor in academic subjects, but to look after their children's moral development as well. When E. Mazureau sent his son out of state for schooling in 1824, he made sure to express to the teacher in no uncertain terms what was expected of him. The father sent a letter of introduction to the teacher for his son to present upon arrival. First mentioning two mutual friends that the father and teacher shared, the man then listed his son's previous schools and subjects of study, noting both his strengths and weaknesses. From there, the father went on to outline his hopes for his son's treatment: "Young as he is & with little or no experience of the world, he will stand in need of a Protector that will act towards him the part of a judicious and good father, attend to his literary improvements, and give him, with respect to his conduct & general demeanor, the necessary directions to make him a worthy member [of] society."[23]

Some teachers struggled to live up to such high expectations, but many private schoolteachers in the antebellum South excelled in their chosen careers. One young man wrote to a cousin about a schoolteacher in his area: "All of the little boys are going to school and learning very fast. They have one of the best teachers in the county and they all like him very much. He never whips any of them except when they do something that is very wrong and then it is only a slap or two and it is all over as good as friends as ever." Another schoolgirl from Mississippi reported on the diligence of one of her teachers, who continued teaching despite his ill health. She noted that the man's wife "thinks he will live only a short time. I never saw such an awful looking object in my life—he looks like a corpse—but he will not stop teaching not withstanding his bad health—sometimes he is so very weak he can scarcely speak, but still we are never excused from any of our lessons."[24]

Diligent teachers who took pride in their profession managed to forge bonds with students and their families. While some instructors encountered difficulties with their students or the families of their students, some developed meaningful friendships that lasted throughout their lives. Baton Rouge private school proprietor Lucy Fisher remembered in her memoir, "I had over twelve hundred pupils in Louisiana and some were in my family eight years. Dear, good girls they were and now, after forty years, I correspond with some who have long been grandmothers."[25]

Just as some tutors in private homes received kind treatment from their host families, some private schoolteachers likewise enjoyed a favorable position in the community they served. John and George Leidigh, brothers from Pennsylvania, traveled south in 1859 to become the principals of the Brooksville Institute in Mississippi. The brothers found the legend of southern hospitality to be quite accurate, bragging to a brother back home, "We eat at a very good table—a first class Rail Road hotel— drink coffee twice a day—butter milk, which is considered a delicacy here, for dinner—no light bread, but warm wheat biscuits and excellent corn bread—cold and warm fowl, roasted beef, fresh ham, eggs, tomatoes, peas, beans, cabbage, water melon, etc." The brothers went on to report, "We are in the family of Col. J. D. Brooks, planter and proprietors of the Hotel—have the liberty of his splendid mansion—his reading room—the use of a fine piano, and two servants—'Kitty' to keep our room neat and 'Dick' to black our boots, etc." The Brooksville Institute catered to thirty students, and the Leidigh brothers remained at the helm throughout the year. George reported that he made $16 a month teaching music, but assured his brother, "You need not trouble farther how much money we may have yet: we are fully able to pay all our debts and buy a few hundred acres of prairie land besides." The brothers proved quite pleased with both their treatment and their income teaching in rural Mississippi.[26]

Students at private schools across the South often took their studies very seriously. Many parents today would no doubt be surprised to have their child ask to stay at school through vacation in order to study, but some students asked their parents' permission to do just that. Edward

Palfrey wrote to his father in 1848 with such a request, telling him, "I wrote to you to ask you if you are willing to let me and Fed stay here next vacation and study if Mr. Kellogg will teach us, for I expect we will get ahead of our class in Latin which I am in hopes we will; Mr. Kellogg says he thinks we could if we were to study hard." Another young man expressed similar sentiments to his family, noting his plans for Christmas vacation: "I will spend my time studying which will do me more good than coming home."[27]

Students across the Gulf South expressed an appreciation for their time at school. Antebellum children often realized that despite the difficulties encountered at school, they were lucky to have the opportunity to receive an education. Southern children willingly endured long absences from family and friends in order to work on their studies, and often wrote home with gratitude for the educational opportunities provided by their parents and guardians. Clearly these pupils took their studies quite seriously. Letters to friends and family from schoolchildren are filled with information about the classes they took, the teachers they had, and the classmates they knew. Their lives revolved around school.

While many mature young pupils expressed their appreciation for their educational opportunities, that does not mean that the adjustment to life at school was always easy. One young woman voiced her concerns about her cousin's ability to adjust: "I am afraid she will not find studying as pleasant as parties. I never saw a girl that did."[28] A North Carolina teacher described the transition to school for young southerners in the following way:

> These young persons have never felt the pressure of want and the necessity of exertion. While at home they have been accustomed to pass their time in ease and amusement, and when they leave that home for school or college the change must be irksome. The confinement of a schoolroom, the demand of close application to uninteresting studies, the stern obligation of performing a regular task, and the privations of a boarding house must go hard with a boy after being accustomed to ramble about his father's plantation, the dogs at his heels and a gun or fishing rod on his shoulder until he is tired, and then to return to the house, open his mother's pantry, and there fish with more success among jars of sweetmeats and jellies. . . . Would he consider it a very serious misfortune if for inattention to his books or some youthful prank he should be sent home to the scene of his former amusements? . . . He may a little dread the first interview; but he knows that after a good scolding, his time will pass as pleasantly as before.[29]

The teacher's comments are clearly borne out by the evidence. While students took their studies seriously, that does not mean they kept their noses constantly in books. They also found plenty of amusements while at school and got into a good bit of trouble along the way. From sneaking off school grounds without permission to writing letters in study hall, students admitted a wide range of offenses, although some were more serious than others. One young man, Thomas Ellis,[30] was temporarily expelled from his school in New York for attempting to board a ship leaving port with a classmate. His teacher wrote the boy's uncle to request his removal from the school, though he noted his affection for the student and his disappointment that he had to do so. It seems, however, that young Master Ellis was able to convince the teacher to allow him to stay on at the school. A repentant Ellis wrote to his uncle of the teacher's mercy, and promised that he would make up for his past bad behavior. The remorseful student promised his uncle in St. Francisville, Louisiana, "I have entered Mr. Peugnet's institution anew, with the firm determination to repay him by my future conduct, for the kindness he has shown me during my stay with him." Ellis continued: "I am [sensible] of the duty that I owe both to you and Mr. Peugnet. I am aware, I cannot conduct myself with too much propriety during the remainder of my stay at this institution and I will endeavor all in my power to show that I am not entirely regardless of the kindness that has been done to me, and of the trouble that I have caused."[31]

For most students, an expulsion from school proved more permanent. S. S. Morris did not conceal his opinions of the school he had attended, commenting to a classmate, "you say you are still in the cussed old school. You are hardly more sorry for it than I am. I hope you will soon be out of it." Morris then reveals the source of his disdain for the institution, noting, "I am sorry that you did not know that I was expelled till next day as I would like to had [sic] you gone with me." Apparently his correspondent, Joseph Embree, was hoping to leave the school as well. Morris wrote to him, "You ask me to meet you on the wharfboat some Saturday or Sunday to go with you. I will do so." The offending student expected his mother to take the news of his dismissal better than she actually did. "My mother is dissatisfied with my being expelled. The reason is that old Mae wrote her a pack of lies and she believes them. She does not think I was right in doing what I did," Morris wrote to his confidant, "so I intend leaving home." Morris continued, "you may expect to see me in Baton Rouge in a short time and you must be ready to go with me. As for money I have a horse that I am going to sell that will bring enough money for us both. If we succeed in our plans we will go to South America if you agree. Then won't we have a glorious time hunting all sorts of game and also catching wild horses in the prairies of South America." Big plans for a young man recently expelled from school. Morris ended his correspondence with a postscript, "You say that old Mae says I was sorry at being expelled; it is all a lie."[32]

Some students in the South left school not because they were asked to leave but of their own volition. James Gayle attended a school run by T. W. Mieure in Louisiana and wrote to a friend in 1860, "Tell me whether you will enter College this year or not. I will enter by next October. If I don't I will quit this school." Gayle did indeed manage to start college and by November was attending Oakland College in Mississippi. His determination to leave his previous school was tempered, however, by what he found once at college. He confided to a friend, "Well this is the meanest school in the world. It is worse than Mieure's. If I was back in Jackson I would like it much better. I will try to get the old man to let me come up there next session. If I have to stay here I will quit school and go out in the world in pursuit of my living and you know that I am too lazy to work."[33]

Other students encountered trouble at school not because of their behavior but because of their academics. Edward Palfrey was one of the six children of William T. Palfrey and Sidney Ann Conrad Palfrey of Louisiana. The family owned a plantation on Bayou Teche in St. Mary Parish. Besides owning a successful plantation, Edward's father also served as parish judge, sheriff, and state senator. During the 1840s Edward attended school with his brother in Naugatuck, Connecticut, and exhibited a commitment to his education. He wrote home to his parents about his schooling, relating that he hoped to get ahead in his studies by taking extra lessons from the teacher. In 1852 Edward enrolled at West Point, however, and he faltered academically. He abashedly wrote home to his father, "When I saw the certainty you manifested in my ability to pass here, I feel ashamed to think that your confidence was misplaced, and pained to think that your hopes of my future prosperity is to meet with disappointment and all on *my account*." Edward had unpleasant news to relate, noting, "I can hardly make up my mind to write this letter, for it is of such a disagreeable nature," and began to explain to his father the academic problems he was having at West Point. He assured his father that he tried his best: "Although I study hard and occupy the short intervals we are released in trying to make up for what I am [deficient,] still every day I make point blank failures and have got the poorest mark in my section . . . and as I do so badly at first in the beginning and from all appearances I do not see any hope or chance of succeeding." The disappointed son lamented that they had gone over all the algebra he had learned his entire life in the first week of school. The teachers went over subject matters so quickly that Edward felt he could not possibly learn all the information he was confronted with. He felt as though the teachers expected the students to be familiar with the subject already, so they did not take the time to explain it. Edward related, "if you are not accustomed to it and studied the book before, you become confused and embarrassed and know nothing, and this is my case. Having passed from lesson to lesson without understanding it, that now when I sit down to study a lesson I do not know the first thing I am studying about." The schoolboy regretted that he was so busy that he was not able to get much help out of class, which he believed would help immensely. He sardonically wrote home to his father, "Everything seems to combine against me, it seems to be the general impression of my class that I will be found deficient, and although they appear to wish me well and some advise me, the very idea of this impression discourages me and I cannot dispel from my mind the disagreeable certainty."[34]

Aside from his disappointing performance in algebra and the embarrassment he clearly felt, Edward had to endure the humiliation of writing to his father to tell him about his failures. The young man feared before he enrolled that his tenure at school would end in disgrace, but had been too timid to relay his concerns to his father. He worried that his father would think he was lazy or just was nervous about leaving home. Edward admitted that though he may be lazy by nature, he strove to overcome that trait and worked incessantly to improve while at school. He noted of his poor performance, "Whether it be from stupidity or want of knowledge is not for me to say though it may be both, but I do say it is not from want of study, that I solemnly declare. . . . I eternally have a book before me, and as I said before I do not know half the time what I am studying about." The son felt certain he would not pass, but be asked to leave the institution, and requested his father's permission to resign. Edward's mortification at his performance at West Point is obvious; however, he did go on to graduate from the illustrious military academy. He served as a lieutenant colonel for the Confederacy during the Civil War, where he was killed in battle.[35]

Although modern students could relate to Palfrey's horror at algebra, they could likewise identify with another topic that caused many a young southerner sleepless nights—love. A mother from Pickens, Alabama wrote to one of her sons about his brother, who she feared was in love with a young girl from a neighborhood family. The mother believed that her son William was completely "consumed by her" and that he could not study because of it. The mother also worried that William planned to propose to the girl in the near future, and that "it will crush him for life when she declines." James Madison Batchelor of Louisiana wanted to leave school before he graduated, and his brother Charles related his thoughts on that position to their mother: "I presume that the cause of it is that some fair creature holds in sweet chains of affection his beating heart & the hold being so very firm, the greatest uneasiness will constantly harass him until he gains admittance in the company of his adored where a sure remedy will relieve him." James had earlier revealed his interest in women. He wrote his younger brother from school that "I was very home sick for a while after I got up here but I expect the cause of it is I went to so many parties and another reason I left the girls on the wharf-boat. Henry and I got up on the top of the boat and waved our handkerchiefs at them as far as we could see them." According to James, he was not the only Batchelor brother who harbored romantic feelings for a young woman for he wrote of another brother, "Henry is dreadfully in love with Miss Lea."[36]

While young love proved a distraction from academic pursuits, many young southerners managed to keep their amorous feelings in check. Laura May Gayden remembered an incident with a young man she met on her journey out of state for school. She confided in her cousin in Louisiana, "When I was coming over to school there was a young man fell in love with me or at least acted as if he did." The young man tried to convince Laura to stay in Greenville for several more weeks and showered her with gifts, including trying to give her his watch. But Laura resisted his amorous appeals, explaining, "I did not like him and didn't want his watch. But he is as ugly as myself and has got but little more sense than I have, but I had sense enough to find that he had none." She also had enough sense to avoid letting a romance interfere with her schoolwork, unlike the schoolboys who found themselves consumed with love rather than their studies.[37]

Romance could offer a pleasant diversion from schoolwork, but another distraction proved much less enjoyable—illness. Children in the antebellum period were prone to suffer a variety of sicknesses, many of which could quickly turn life-threatening. Students attending boarding schools out of town were often far from family members when illness struck and were forced to rely on the nursing of teachers and other students. When Thomas Ellis attended school in Jackson, Louisiana during the 1850s, he reported staying home from social functions in order to tend to a sick classmate. Similarly, William T. Palfrey Jr., attending school in Lexington, Kentucky, missed an opportunity to hear Henry Clay speak because it was his turn to nurse a sick classmate. Some students enjoyed the care of siblings while away at school. James Batchelor wrote home to a younger brother that both he and his brother Charley had been sick, but that both had recovered.[38]

While students at boarding schools had to rely on the care of classmates, teachers, and guardians when they fell ill, their parents often suffered in their own way. Many, like Martha Batchelor, suffered from fear and anxiety about their children's well-being. The Batchelor family of Pointe Coupee Parish, Louisiana, had six children, all of whom attended boarding school at some point in their lives. Although the family clearly valued education and was willing to endure separation in order to procure it, the mother constantly pined for her children and worried about their comfort and well-being. Martha wrote to her son Albert in 1860, "You my dearest little children can never know the anxiety that fills a devoted mother's breast for the comfort and happiness of dear little children who are so far from home and in a land of strangers." She went on to note that while the children might worry about family at home, "what can your anxiety be compared with ours for your welfare? If any of us are sick we are all here to relieve each other and see that nothing is left undone, but to think of our dear little helpless ones being so entirely dependent on strangers." The anxious mother was later greeted with news that typhoid fever had claimed several lives in the town where her daughter attended school, and her concern was noticeably heightened. Because of the distance, however, she had to resign herself to the belief that the woman running the boarding house where her daughter stayed would take care of her daughter as best she could.[39]

With illness such a prevalent part of antebellum life, teachers and administrators constantly attempted to take necessary precautions to keep their students healthy. Sister Columba Morancy of Louisiana taught at a Catholic girls' school in Kentucky in the 1840s and 1850s. When cholera broke out in the vicinity, the school shut down and the nuns took all the students to Louisville for two weeks until the danger passed. The unexpected holiday took the place of Christmas vacation, which Sister Columba believed worked out well. August vacation had been "so warm and disagreeable, that it proved but a slight relaxation," but their time in Louisville had given the students a much needed break from their classes. The girls returned to their studies renewed and healthy, with a new zeal for their classes. Sister Columba knew that some in the community thought that the nuns acted too hastily in taking the girls away, but the parents not only approved of their measures, but registered sincere gratitude for their proactive approach in protecting the children's health.[40]

Unfortunately, not all illnesses could be warded off through diligent precautions. Mary Lancaster attended the school in Kentucky in the 1840s where Sister Columba taught. From available records, Mary seems to have been a motivated and determined student. She studied Spanish, French, and Italian and also took an active interest in national politics. Mary wrote to her parents in November 1840 about her time at school and apparently went home for summer vacation at the end of the spring semester. Unfortunately, by August 1841 Mary's family was receiving letters of condolences regarding her death. One former schoolmate wrote to Mary's sister Eliza how devastated their parents must be after just getting Mary back after a long separation to have lost her forever. Sister Columba wrote to Eliza from Nazareth regarding her sister's death: "The news reached us just as school was commencing, and it cast a gloom on the whole family. About that time last year, you were both returning to school, so carefree, and eager to commence your studies."[41]

Even when children were fortunate enough to avoid getting sick themselves, they often had to deal with sickness among friends and family. Eliza A. Bonner of Pickens, Alabama wrote to her son John while he was away at school about how sick his father had become. She recounted how she thought every day would be his last, and that she feared he would not make it through the summer; although she hoped he would live to see John when he came home from school, she doubted that likelihood. Martha Batchelor also wrote very candidly to her children about their father's health, noting he "is as weak as a child." News also came to school-children of sick friends. One student expecting a friend to join him at boarding school in 1858 instead received word that his friend had fallen ill and would not be able to attend.[42]

From the accounts of students and teachers in the South before the Civil War, it appears that most students enjoyed and appreciated their time at school. Young people who had not yet had the opportunity to attend school often exhibited a desire to do so. Bettie Morancy wrote about her youngest daughter: "Agnes is sitting by me trying to work out a few sums in multiplication. She is more anxious . . . to go to school since some of her cousins have been to see her. They are much farther advanced than she is although two years younger and she seems to feel the importance of an education already."[43]

Once at school, though many youth encountered difficulty with their studies and most who attended school out of town experienced homesickness, young southerners enjoyed their time at school. One young woman wrote to her cousin, "I have got down here to school at last and I reckon before next July that I will acquire such a prodigious amount of knowledge that I will not know what to do with it." She went on to brag about the accomplishments of students at her school, and relayed a story about one of her recently graduated classmates who fell down the stairs and "came near killing herself. I believe that she attributes it to an overweight of knowledge. But I hope mine will not break my neck for if it does I shall have very little use for it afterwards."[44]

Families took an active interest in the education of their younger members. Letters to children attending school are filled with advice about making the most of their time at school, not only from parents but from siblings and friends as well. Richard Brumby wrote his daughter Ann Eliza in 1858 while she was attending school in Alabama about the importance of a young lady's education. In addition to family members, friends also wrote with advice about getting through school. Jessie Menzies wrote to a friend: "Your studies I need not mention to you for I know it is second nature to you to be studious. Don't mind being laughed at . . . fools only will scoff at virtues which you possess and which they one day would give all they are worth to have."[45]

It appears from the available evidence that southern parents placed a high value on their children's education. Many families sacrificed financially so that children could attend school. John Palfrey was born in Boston in 1768, moved to New Orleans in 1803, and remained in Louisiana until his death in 1843. He kept up continuous correspondence with his sister and brother-in-law with whom his sons stayed in order to attend school. Their communication reveals his desire to pay for his sons' schooling despite his own financial difficulties. In 1810 he wrote that he would find a way to pay for his oldest son to attend college, despite his economic troubles. Many parents felt the same way. In 1837 Mr. Phipps, who worked as an overseer for the Ellis and Butler families who owned plantations in Mississippi and Louisiana, requested a transfer to a different plantation to allow his children to attend school without having to board. Such a request demonstrates that parents solidly in the middle class, like overseers, made sacrifices for their children to attend school.[46]

Many parents eloquently expressed the importance they placed on their children's education. One mother, commenting about her youngest daughter's desire to go to school, wrote, "As she is anxious to go [to school] I will send her as soon as I get home this fall. . . . I do not like to think of sending her from home so early but I [do not] intend to let feeling interfere with my duty as far as the welfare of my children is concerned." Martha Batchelor wrote in a letter to her son in 1860, "As for my children . . . if I can command the money they shall have an education if they get nothing else. Without an education they can not command anything but with it they may command the highest position."[47]

The value that parents placed on their children's education helped ensure that private schools would constitute an integral component of antebellum southern society. Prior to the establishment of a state system of public schools, parents turned to private institutions to procure for their children the blessings of knowledge. Private schools of different sorts abounded in the Gulf South, and parents and children across the region took advantage of their offerings whenever possible. As the antebellum period progressed, legislators in southern states became aware of their constituents' commitment to their children's education and responded by enacting statutes to help support local schools. Even as public institutions began to appear, private schools continued to serve children across the South and remain an essential component of the southern education system, as they do even today.

## CHAPTER THREE

Education as a Responsibility of the State

EARLY EFFORTS TOWARD PUBLIC SCHOOLS

The governments of the Gulf South states of Louisiana, Mississippi, and Alabama each made provisions to support educational institutions in their states prior to the development of statewide public school systems. While private schools and tutors served a number of the region's inhabitants, costs limited the pool of families who could afford to take advantage of those opportunities. State politicians showed an early inclination to extend the benefits of learning to more of their constituents through government subsidies. During the early decades of the antebellum period it became clear that the limited assistance provided by the legislatures in each state left many children without the benefits of a formal education, and all three states took steps to institute statewide public school systems before the Civil War. To understand the development and implementation of those systems, it is essential to examine the prior assistance offered by the state governments in support of education.

The early antebellum period was a time of experimentation in the Lower South, when state governments took steps to encourage schools in their areas. Even before they entered the Union, the governments of Louisiana, Mississippi, and Alabama passed statutes concerning education and, throughout the 1820s and 1830s, continued to alter their school laws in an attempt to bring more schools into operation. These initial attempts to encourage such institutions reveal an interest in education by southern politicians and exhibit a clear belief that state governments bore some responsibility for helping to bring basic instruction to their younger constituents. Furthermore, the early school legislation in all three states laid the groundwork for the general public school systems that they later instituted.

In 1812 Louisiana became the first of the three Gulf South states to join the Union. Even before statehood, the American governor of the Louisiana Territory, William C. C. Claiborne, advocated legislative measures to support public schools accessible to all. Although Louisiana's first state constitution, adopted in 1812, did not mention education, Claiborne remained as governor and continued to ardently support public education. He advocated a state-sponsored system of schools to provide instruction to Louisiana's white youth, including those financially unable to pay tuition. The governor repeatedly pressured the legislature to make educational provisions for the state, asserting, "You cannot Gentlemen, but be sensible of the importance of this subject; it embraces the best interest of the community and mingles with the warmest affections of the heart."[1]

Claiborne began a pattern that continued for decades in the Gulf South in which governors lobbied the legislatures for support of existing educational institutions within their states. Indeed, during Alabama's first legislative session as a state in 1819, Governor William Wyatt Bibb spent considerable time lecturing legislators on the importance of education in a republic that relied on the wisdom of voters for its well-being, noting, "Ignorance and civil liberty are unnatural associates where the people are the fountain of authority." Likewise, when he addressed the state legislature in 1829, Mississippi governor Gerard Brandon reminded the state's politicians of the connection between ignorance and despotism, arguing that "the one is rarely found to exist without the other." Given that, Brandon contended that a representative government depended on a virtuous and intelligent population in order to survive. According to the governor, "an enlightened people, reared under the auspices of free institutions, can never be enslaved by fraud of stratagem." Therefore, Brandon implored the legislators to make the extension of schools and learning one of their primary concerns.[2]

The successors of the original governors made the same point in annual messages to the legislatures that advocated education initiatives. Their advocacy ranged from simply extolling the virtues of learning and its importance in a republic, to offering concrete suggestions for the expansion of schools across their state. For instance, in 1833 Mississippi governor Abram M. Scott spoke in flowery terms of the importance of intellectual development for republican citizens: "As therefore, the diffusion of intelligence among a people, is confessedly necessary to enable them not only to enjoy the blessings of a free government, but to protect and defend their liberties, it becomes the first great duty of a Republic to provide for all its members the means of instruction." Alabama governor Henry W. Collier went further in 1851, urging the legislature to create the position of a state head to run the school system, outlining what duties he should be charged with, suggesting methods for grading schools and certifying teachers, and adding a proposal to include military exercises in the university's curriculum.[3]

A clear trend emerges from the governors' messages to their legislatures up to 1860, with executives speaking of the importance of education and often urging lawmakers to take specific action. Using Alabama as an example, between 1818 and 1860 the state (which transitioned from annual to biennial legislative sessions in 1846) held thirty-six legislative sessions. Of those, governors explicitly spoke about education in their annual messages twenty-seven times, or 75 percent of the time. In seventeen of those instances governors urged the general assembly to take specific measures to extend and improve schools across the state.[4]

Their support of education reform, however, did not translate into concrete measures to expand learning. Because the governors enjoyed no legislative authority, it is difficult to determine the sincerity of their statements in favor of education initiatives. Did they truly wish to see state-supported educational institutions established, or were they only paying lip service to a cause they dared not oppose? Most governors appear to have had a genuine desire to expand access to learning in their state. It is easy to identify the executives who did not fit this pattern, for even while extolling the importance of education, they tempered their support in obvious ways. Governor Benjamin Fitzpatrick remarked to the Alabama legislature in 1841, "Ardently devoted as I am to a judicious system of State Internal Improvements, and to a general diffusion of knowledge by common schools, the financial difficulties which threaten the State will probably leave us no other duty connected with these subjects, than a faithful and economical application of the existing funds." Most executives did not moderate their suggestions in this manner, but instead consistently urged action by state lawmakers.[5]

Schooled in the political theory of republicanism, most governors couched their arguments in favor of education legislation by using language that corresponded to that philosophy. The institution of universal white manhood suffrage across the South meant that white men would be voting and making political decisions regardless of their intellectual attainments. Because of the right of such citizens to be involved in the political process, the entire country stood to benefit by having a more educated voting population. As Mississippi governor Joseph W. Matthews told legislators in 1850: "Intelligence and virtue form the foundation on which alone we can rely for the support and perpetuity of our free institutions. Our government, being the exercise of the popular will, to preserve it from anarchy and destruction, it must be guided and controlled by enlightened public opinion." Governor Matthews used this argument to lobby for "a general system of common school education by a tax upon the persons and property of all citizens of the State."[6]

Clearly, republican political ideology led many chief executives to argue in favor of legislative action to spread learning to the mass of inhabitants. There also was a certain level of noblesse oblige—a desire to provide avenues for intellectual development to those younger citizens whose families could not afford to pay tuition at private schools. Such sentiment explains why early education initiatives focused on tuition exemptions for students in need.

An early interest in education is evident in the original organic law of many southern states. Although the 1812 Louisiana constitution is silent on the topic of schools, both the Mississippi and Alabama constitutions specifically pledge the states to support education. Mississippi's 1817 constitution promised, "Religion, Morality and Knowledge being necessary to good Government, the preservation of Liberty, and the Happiness of Mankind, Schools and the means of Education shall forever be encouraged in this State." That sentiment was echoed in Alabama's 1819 document, which pledged, "schools and the means of education shall forever be encouraged." The language used in the state constitutions is not original, for it echoed the sentiment of the Northwest Ordinance. But it reveals an early commitment to use the power of the state to bring education within reach for the children of their states. The earliest American governments in the Gulf South acknowledged the responsibility of the state to foster schools for their inhabitants. Despite this early commitment, it would take decades before leaders there realized the extent of action necessary to accomplish that end. Initial efforts to encourage schools were limited in scope and action, and it would take decades before the vigorous government policy needed to actually ensure access to schools for all children would be contemplated.[7]

Southern leaders did not initially try to create a public system of education, but instead focused on assisting the schools already in place—looking to the private sphere to shoulder the burden of bringing learning to the masses. One of the earliest ways in which the Gulf South legislatures encouraged education also proved one of their most frequent: the incorporation of private academies and seminaries. As early as 1811 the Mississippi Territorial Legislature incorporated Washington Academy and one year later incorporated Greene Academy. The acts of incorporation in all three states had much in common—they authorized trustees to act on behalf of the school, they often expressly exempted the school and all school property from taxation, they sometimes authorized the trustees to raise money through a lottery, and some institutions were granted an appropriation from the legislature for a few hundred dollars to help get the school started. The Alabama legislature, for instance, passed "an act to establish an Academy in the town of Sparta, and for other purposes," in December 1821, which authorized the trustees "to raise by Lottery, upon such scheme or plan as they may consider most advisable, the sum of two thousand dollars, to be appropriated to the building of said academy, and to create a contingent fund for the exclusive benefit of the institution." When the Louisiana legislature incorporated the Montpelier Academy in 1833, it stipulated that "to enable the trustees of the Montpelier academy to get said academy into operation, the sum of two thousand five hundred dollars, shall, for the term of four years, be annually paid to the treasurer of said academy."[8]

Throughout the antebellum period, the legislatures of Louisiana, Mississippi, and Alabama incorporated many academies, seminaries, and colleges. In fact, incorporations of specific schools became so frequent in Alabama during the 1850s that Governor John A. Winston began refusing to sign such legislation. He warned legislators in his 1855 annual message of his opposition to legislation pertaining to particular schools when the general statutes proved sufficient for the purposes intended. He explained, "Much of the legislation heretofore enacted, upon examination, will be found to be of a special character—of no general interest to the State." The general code of laws and statutes proved sufficient to allow most of the purposes intended without special legislation, yet such individual incorporations unnecessarily "encumber the statute books." The governor criticized legislators for wasting so much time working on statutes that pertained only to specific institutions and not the state as a whole. Leaders protracted the legislative session and filled the statute books with unnecessary laws, while taxpayers footed the bill. Winston promised the assemblymen that "acting under a sense of duty to the people of the State, and having such opinions, I cannot be expected to become a party to legislation of a like character." He kept his word, returning several bills for incorporation to the legislature without his signature with explanations that particular legislation "appears, to my mind, to be an act already provided for by the general law." He reminded them throughout the session, "I look upon all such special legislation as not only unnecessary, but pernicious, to the public welfare. With a knowledge of my opinions on such legislation, I am not expected by my constituents to become a party to it. I, therefore, decline to approve the bill."[9]

Acts of incorporations for private schools and bills detailing financial assistance to help keep such institutions afloat reveal an early desire to foster education by merely assisting the private sector. State leaders acknowledged that government bore some responsibility for bringing schooling to its people, but the idea of creating wholly public institutions had not yet taken hold. Instead, during the decades following statehood, southern governments chose to rely on private schools to educate the state's youth, assisted to a limited extent by their legislatures. It would take decades before it became clear that in order to accomplish its mandate of providing access to education for all inhabitants, the state would have to take a much more active role in running and supporting schools.

Aside from incorporating schools and academies, another form of early legislation pertaining to education dealt with the disposition of federal lands given to the states in order to support schools. The US Congress granted the sixteenth section of each township for the use of schools (or other lands if the sixteenth section was no longer available) as well as a certain allotment to support a statewide seminary of learning. Through this grant, Congress hoped that each state would support at least one school in each township, as well as a college within the state. Each state government was thus charged with managing these lands and using the income they generated to support education. In its first session the legislature of Alabama passed "an act to provide for leasing for a limited time the Lands reserved by the Congress of the United States, for the support of Schools, within each township in this State; for a Seminary of Learning, and for other purposes." This statute provided for the election of three agents in each township who would serve for three years and be responsible for renting or leasing the sixteenth section lands, the revenue of which would go to support schools. These agents, however, were not just financial officers. The same act required them to hire one or more teachers and arrange for one or more schoolhouses in their township. According to the bill, "The agents aforesaid, are hereby made the trustees of such schools, and are vested with all necessary power for the general superintendence, due organization, and well being of every such school or schools, applying with impartiality, the proceeds of each section, to the purposes of education alone . . . that all the inhabitants therein may partake of the benefits thereof, according to the true intent of the reservation." Thus in its first year of statehood, the Alabama legislature arranged for the election of local officials who would serve as government officers overseeing schools in their towns. In 1823 the legislature amended the law to provide for school commissioners for each township and trustees for each school district, carefully prescribing the responsibilities of each officer to be "that the said trustees of each school district, shall have power to employ a teacher or teachers for the same, at an annual salary or at a state price for each scholar, or on such terms as they may deem expedient; to cause a school house to be built and kept in repair; to purchase books and stationery for the use of the school; and make regulations for the use and preservation of the same, and for the admission of pupils into the school—to designate the pupils who shall be admitted to the school without tuition fees."[10]

Like Alabama, Mississippi and Louisiana also passed legislation dealing with education early in the antebellum period. In Mississippi's first session after admission to the Union, its legislature granted authority to county courts to lease the sixteenth section lands and employ the proceeds to support education. In 1820 the county courts were ordered to appoint three to five landholders to put schools into operation in each township. As early as 1811 the Louisiana territorial legislature began aiding schools in the state, offering a one-time payment of $2,000 to each county to build or purchase schoolhouses as well as an annual stipend of $500, which was increased to $800 in 1821.[11] In 1819 the Louisiana legislature required the police juries, the governing body of each parish, to oversee any schools in the parish that received state aid, and in 1821 it required the juries to appoint trustees to oversee the schools. The legislature also ordered the trustees to visit the schools in their parish at least twice a year to ascertain their general situation, including qualifications of teachers and numbers of students, and then to disburse the money granted to each parish by the state among those schools as the trustees saw fit.[12]

Each of the three states clearly valued education enough to make provisions concerning schools even before they joined the Union. This interest continued following statehood, with each state passing laws that charged public officers to oversee schools in their area, revealing their belief that the state had some role to play in providing education for its inhabitants. But while the legislatures passed general provisions regarding schools, all three states vested control of education in the local communities. The legislatures would not designate a central official to oversee education in the entire state until later in the antebellum period. As far as southern legislators were concerned, education, if not strictly a family affair, certainly remained a local concern.

These early provisions offered a loose framework that politicians hoped would foster schools in towns across their states. In 1830, Governor Moore of Alabama reported, "To the benevolent and patriotic mind, it cannot be otherwise than exhilarating to see the rapid advancement of seminaries for sound and enlarged education, spreading over our country: excellent schools suited to every capacity and means increasing daily." Despite the governor's favorable review, it was clear that the laws passed immediately following statehood needed revision in order better to encourage and support schools. During the 1830s and 1840s all three Gulf South states altered their school laws in an attempt to increase the availability of education in their areas.[13]

By 1821 Louisiana had appropriated money to build schools across the state and ordered police juries to appoint trustees to oversee the schools in each parish. The state allocated funds to individual police juries who disbursed the funds based on their assessments, allowing local governments to decide whether to build new schools or to support private ventures already in operation. Many private schools therefore received state funding throughout the antebellum period. In 1835 the state allotted parish schools less than $50,000 while it granted private institutions over $125,000, revealing a propensity to fund private schools rather than construct public institutions. In parishes where more than one school qualified for state aid, those schools shared the parish's education appropriation, usually in proportion to the number of children enrolled.[14]

Even where parishes chose to build new schools, students paid tuition to attend. While the state felt a duty to support education, it did not yet feel a responsibility to provide schooling free of charge. Instead the legislature required any school receiving state funding to admit a number of indigent children, who received free tuition and supplies.[15] This stipulation allowed a clear distinction to emerge between paying students and "pauper" students who attended free of charge. Though legislators considered this requirement their most significant contribution to education—ensuring that poor children would enjoy the benefits of education—they greatly misjudged its impact on the population. In 1833 Governor Andre Roman repeatedly insisted that "the radical vice of our system consist[s] in the odious distinction which it establishes between the children of the rich and those of the poor." He explained to the legislature that "a great number of persons will forego for their children the advantages of privilege, which appears to them to induce them, if accepted, to the level of those who live on charity and alms." Most parents refused to accept the label of pauper by sending their children to school without paying tuition. As one official explained in 1841, "One of the principal causes of the want of success attendant on our system of primary instruction is, in my opinion, to be attributed to the great repugnance felt by many families to send their children at the public expense to school where there are other pupils whose parents pay for their education." The negative distinction applied to free instruction would continue to haunt Louisiana in its later efforts to organize a more effective school system.[16]

While Louisiana's education initiatives during the 1810s and 1820s fell far short of the free public schools that many historians consider the benchmark in educational legislation, the system employed there offered many advantages for the Pelican State. Leaving decisions up to local officials meant that people most familiar with the idiosyncrasies of each parish would be making decisions on how best to encourage education in their area. Allowing local officials to decide if their constituents would be better served by using state aid to support private schools rather than building new schools meant that many parishes were able to save money on the construction of schoolhouses. Likewise, the state did not require parishes to put schools into operation that would compete with existing educational institutions. Given the scarcity of teachers in many rural areas of the South as well as the irregular attendance of many students, many parishes would have been unable to support an additional school had they been forced to provide it. The legislative stipulation demanding the admittance of students free of charge, although it generated some problems, was a progressive measure aimed at assisting Louisiana's neediest children. Although the state could not afford to finance the education of all its children and completely rid families of tuition expenses, it did attempt to provide for those who most needed it. That parents refused to take advantage of the offer does not detract from the good intentions of its supporters. The state had met Governor Thomas B. Robertson's challenge that he issued to the Louisiana legislature in 1823: "Let us begin at the beginning, provide for the education of those who are too poor to purchase it themselves."[17]

Louisiana continued to aid schools until the 1840s based on the laws passed before 1821. Occasionally new stipulations altered the basis of state appropriations in support of schools or added specific provisions regarding school administration. In 1827 the legislature changed the education appropriation for each parish to two and five-eighths dollars for every voter based on the most recent census, not to exceed $1,350 or to amount to less than $800 per parish. In 1828 the legislature required the administrators and trustees of schools in each parish to report to the grand jury at each session of the district court to deliver "a detailed account of the amount of money drawn from the State treasury for the support of public education, the number and situation of the several schools in the parish, the number of paying scholars and the number of free scholars in each school, and the amount paid to each teacher employed in the several schools," which was then to be forwarded to the legislature each session.[18]

The most significant change to come prior to the 1840s occurred in 1833, when the Louisiana legislature designated a central education official to supervise schools throughout the entire state. In his annual message of that year, Governor Andre Roman reiterated an earlier suggestion that the secretary of state be assigned the additional duty of making annual reports to the legislature on the status of schools across the state. Later that session the legislature responded with "an Act supplementary to the several acts relative to public education, approved April 1, 1833," which ordered the secretary of state "to prepare and submit an annual report to the legislature, containing a statement of the condition of the parish schools, and the scholars in them; of all colleges or academies patronized by the State, and the number of students in them; estimates and accounts of the expenditures of the public money, appropriated for purposes of education; plans for the improvement and management of the fund appropriated for public education, and for the better organization of the parish schools; and, generally, all such matters relating to his office of superintendent, and to the system of public education, as he shall deem expedient to communicate."[19]

The naming of a central school official to coordinate education policy and report on the progress of schools across the entire state was a progressive measure that public officials hoped would allow legislative policy to more accurately meet the needs of Louisiana's younger citizens. Unfortunately, conferring the title of state superintendent of education upon the secretary of state rather than creating an entirely new post meant that that official devoted little time to education. He relied entirely on reports sent to him from local education officers who often failed to send in the required information, leaving him very little to relay to the legislature. The first year following the new provisions, twenty-one of thirty-two parishes reported to the secretary of state, but this number dropped to fourteen in 1835, and only eleven parish officials reported in 1836, which the secretary of state claimed "renders it impossible to present any thing like a general view of the condition of the schools throughout the State."[20]

Despite such complaints, it is possible to ascertain a broad outline of education conditions from reports of parish officials. In 1833, there were 1,175 students in Louisiana who received education free of cost through state aid in the twenty-one parishes that reported to the secretary of state. The number of students receiving a free education ranged from six in Carroll Parish to one hundred fifty-two in East Baton Rouge Parish. Compensating for the parishes that did not report, the secretary of state estimated that in 1833 fifteen hundred students received free instruction subsidized by the state government out of about twelve thousand boys of school age, for which the state allocated $30,449.77 for the year. Throughout the 1830s school attendance remained low for both paying and nonpaying scholars alike. In 1836 Claiborne Parish supported seven schools that enrolled one hundred thirty students, twenty-eight of whom paid no tuition, while an estimated two hundred fifty children of school age who resided in that parish did not attend any school throughout the course of the year.[21]

The reports that did make their way to the legislature from across the state often voiced objections to the state's school provisions. In 1842 one parish reported, "our public schools are in a very poor condition and need the interposition of the State." Many districts echoed this sentiment; one official informed the legislature that "there are bitter complaints against our own public schools; it seems that for several years they have been most wretchedly kept, and a notorious abuse." Another parish officer explained in 1842 that "since 1822, public schools have been established in this parish and we are unable to designate one who has been benefited by it."[22]

The various governors of Louisiana during the 1830s continually criticized the system of public education. Governor Jacques Dupré noted in 1831 that despite the $50,000 state appropriation, very little action had been taken to advance public education. Many parishes, he asserted, neglected to open schools even though they received state monies for that purpose. Dupré's successor, Andre Roman, echoed that criticism, recommending the abolition of the entire system. An 1836 legislative committee on education agreed with this opinion, concluding that the existing school provisions proved completely useless. Governor Roman lamented that the state appropriated $354,012 for education between 1818 and 1831, and that in 1834 this outlay yielded the pitiful enrollment of 1,500 students throughout the state. Roman's statistics refer to the number of children educated at state expense, a privilege that few parents were willing to take advantage of due to the stigma attached. He reported to the legislature that "the plan in which these schools are established ought to be changed; since, notwithstanding the liberal appropriations of the legislature, they are far from producing the advantageous results expected from them." In 1835 the secretary of state reported that "the object of the legislature, which is, the extension of the benefits of education to all classes, is not attained. . . . The best interests of the state require a change of the present system." In 1842 one official went so far as to suggest to the legislature that all appropriations to parish schools in the state could be withdrawn without harming education in Louisiana.[23]

Although Louisiana's education system faltered during the 1830s, legislative measures initiated in 1842 came close to destroying any educational progress made in the previous thirty years. Following the advice of state officials, the legislature that year required each parish to raise a certain amount of funding to receive state aid. Secretary of State George A. Eustis explained that "the material advantage of this plan is that it creates a direct interest in the judicious expenditure of the money, for more care will be taken in the disbursement of that which is raised directly from the people of each parish." In concurrence, the legislature in 1842 began granting state appropriations to parish schools based on the amount raised by local taxation; the state granted two dollars for every one dollar collected in the parish, not to exceed a state disbursal of $800 per parish. Though it was reasonable to expect local support and consistent with the provisions of other southern states, the unwillingness of Louisiana parishes to raise the necessary funds further hindered educational development in the state. The superintendent of education explained to the legislature that although supporting schools through parish taxes remained highly desirable, such a measure "would likely be to throw a greater burthen [*sic*] upon some of the parishes, which, strong in minor population, are weak in resources, and therefore least able to bear its pressure." He also feared that residents would object to such a scheme, noting "the unwillingness . . . of the people, in the unprovided state of the school fund, to be taxed for the maintenance of their schools." Despite such unflattering assessments of the likelihood of parish taxation, this requirement became state law in 1842.[24]

Besides placing a larger burden on the unprepared and seemingly unwilling parishes, the Louisiana legislature in 1842 also suspended appropriations to most of the private academies and colleges that it had previously supported. Though some schools received a three-year extension, most private schools were stripped of the state aid that had supplemented their income for years, forcing many to close. This alteration makes little sense to modern observers since Louisiana's system relied largely on awarding public funding to private schools. From the very beginning Louisiana allowed each parish the option of spending its education funding from the state to support private schools rather than insisting on the building of entirely new public institutions. Many parishes therefore had relied entirely on private schools to educate their children, using the public appropriation to offset tuition costs and ensure the admittance of indigent children as required by law. For the state to suddenly yank its support of private institutions, a major component of its system by its own doing, represented a failure of the state's education policy that would result in further deterioration of its school system.[25]

Both provisions instituted in 1842, requiring local funding for schools to receive state monies and cutting off appropriations to private schools, harmed education in the Bayou State, but both can be attributed to the financial situation resulting from the Panic of 1837. Across the country, the late 1830s and early 1840s was a time of retrenchment, and unfortunately schools suffered cutbacks which harmed the progress of education in the South. In 1842 one Louisiana official noted, "Under the present system of Public Education it is impossible to make good scholars, nor even to receive a common education." The secretary of state conceded in 1844 that "there seems to be many defects in the present system." Two years later, the harsh assessment of public schools by Secretary of State Charles Gayarré echoed throughout the state. He proclaimed, "The system of Public Education adopted in this state has proved a complete abortion from its birth day. The reports I allude to form a well concatenated chain of indictments against the present establishment of our Parish Schools." Gayarré concluded, "It must be inferred that, on the part of the Administration at least, a lamentable indifference exists with regard to public education."[26]

There Louisiana's state education system stood until a new constitution, approved in 1845, forced dramatic overhaul. The changed constitution would bring public schools to many areas of the state for the first time. The retrenchments of the early 1840s would be undone, allowing education in the state to progress considerably. As in Louisiana, other southern states followed a similar pattern in which initial provisions on behalf of schools were adjusted during the 1820s and 1830s. The Panic of 1837 caused retrenchment across the South that retarded efforts toward public education, but with recovery from financial woes, new initiatives brought better and more efficient provisions permitting schools to thrive in many areas, and brought education within the reach of children formerly bereft of an opportunity for learning.

Like Louisiana, Mississippi, with the governor's urging, first moved to provide education for children who could not afford to pay private school tuition. Rather than relying entirely on the income from the sixteenth section lands donated by the federal government for the support of education, in 1821 the Mississippi legislature created a Literary Fund to pay to enroll children and provide them with necessary supplies. The fund came from confiscations and fines not otherwise assigned, and after a certain amount of money was allocated to the counties for the education of their indigent children, the excess money remained as an endowment until it reached $50,000, when it would be distributed to the counties. A state board of directors, which included the governor, appointed county boards of school commissioners who administered the fund. The county boards were charged with identifying indigent children in their area whose tuition would be paid from the Literary Fund. The school commissioners decided whose schooling would be covered, how much would be paid for their tuition, and which schools those children would attend. In addition to administering the Literary Fund, the legislature also required a committee from the county boards to visit all the schools in each county and for teachers to demonstrate their proficiency to the school commissioners. However, this requirement amounted to little since the board did not have the authority to hire or dismiss teachers or in any way affect their employment.[27]

In 1824 Mississippi's legislature passed an education act that would govern most of the state's schools until a new system was instituted in 1846. It required the resident heads of household in each township to elect annually a board of trustees who were given complete control over the school lands, charged only with using the income from them in order to support education. The legislation gave the trustees authority to rent school lands, build schoolhouses, hire teachers, and make rules regarding the functioning of the schools. Like most of Mississippi's school legislation, however, the law was permissive, granting the trustees the authority to act on these fronts, but not requiring them to do so or penalizing them for failing to act. This characteristic, allowing action but not requiring it, hampered educational progress in the state throughout the antebellum years.[28]

The 1824 law offered a general outline for township control of schools, but Mississippi politicians continued to work toward providing more schools for their inhabitants throughout the antebellum period. In his annual message to the legislature in 1829, Governor Gerard Brandon reminded the assembled politicians of the importance of education to the state and urged them to do something for its support. In response, the legislature authorized a three-man committee "to devise a plan for a general system of education." Governor Brandon appointed Peter A. Vandorn, William Dowsing, and James Y. McNabb, who returned their findings to the house education committee at the next legislative session. That committee reviewed the suggestions made by these men and reported back that they "were pleased with some of the leading features of the system." The committee especially approved of their plan for establishing primary schools throughout the entire state; "on this branch of the subject, the views of the agents met the approbation and accorded fully with the sentiments of the committee." The committee affirmed the belief that government bore the responsibility to bring schooling to its citizens, noting that "the great object and policy of the government should be, to bring within reach of the most humble and indigent citizen, the means of obtaining the elementary principles of education—as lessening the wide gap between the educated and the ignorant, and as placing it in the power of all to become acquainted, and consequently to appreciate, the rights, privileges and blessings, of an American citizen."[29]

While the committee agreed with the suggestions on primary schools, it disagreed over secondary schools. The disagreement, however, came from the education committee's belief that more secondary schools were needed than the three-man panel suggested. According to the legislators, "With respect to schools of a higher grade, (viz.) Academies, to effectuate a general and complete system, your committee would observe, that the number recommended is too few to accomplish the objects contemplated. Those institutions should be as near the reach of pupils (who are qualified, and have evinced a capacity and qualifications for higher attainments from the primary schools), as possible."[30]

The major disagreement between the agents appointed by the governor and the legislature's education committee arose, unsurprisingly, over financing. Despite the legislators' insistence that they "look upon education as one of the primary objects of the government, and [one that] should never be lost sight of," they objected to the agents' suggestion that the entire state surplus be devoted to founding and supporting schools across the state. The committee went further in also opposing any new taxes to fund an expanded school system, arguing that no tax "can be imposed, that would meet with such decided approbation, as one imposed for literary purposes—particularly where it is general and uniform." Instead, the committee preferred to continue to rely on the Literary Fund.[31]

Despite the legislature's failure to act upon the recommendations for a general system of education that would extend schools across the state, according to the governor, schools across Mississippi were thriving in 1830. In his annual address to the legislature, Governor Brandon reported, "I congratulate the General Assembly, as well as my fellow-citizens, on the revival of the spirit of Education within our State. Schools and Academies are rising up in every country, under the influence of individual patronage, and are in a flourishing condition; which will doubtless be sustained by the fostering hand of the State."[32]

Throughout the 1830s, elected officials in Mississippi continued to express their support for state aid to education. After the approval of a new constitution in 1832, Governor Abram M. Scott reminded Mississippi's legislators of their requirement to encourage schools across the state, noting, "The propriety will readily suggest itself to you of immediately (by legislative enactment) laying the foundation of a general system of Schools and Academies, so organized that the means of instruction may be placed within the reach of the poorest of our citizens." In response to the constitutional requirements, the House Education Committee reported in late 1833, "The increasing resources of the country, the late acquisition of territory, and the consequent influx of population, seem to be sufficient guarantees to the state to justify her in adopting the free school system." The committee further went on to specify that they hoped the state would be financially able to support a free school in every township and an academy in every county, in addition to a college or seminary for the state as a whole.[33]

As in neighboring Louisiana, Mississippi legislators objected to a scheme in which the state paid only for indigent students, creating a distinction between students of means and those who relied on the state to cover their school costs. In 1836 Governor John Quitman urged the legislature to establish a system of free common schools that would be available to all white children in Mississippi. The House Education Committee reiterated its earlier suggestions for an academy in every county and a common school in every township. Following Governors Scott and Quitman, Governors Charles Lynch, Alexander McNutt, and Albert G. Brown all spoke out in their annual messages to the legislature in favor of a system of free public schools that would provide elementary schools in each township and a secondary school in each county. Despite the political rhetoric in support of such a system, a significant overhaul of the school system would not occur until later in the antebellum period.[34]

Architects of Mississippi's Literary Fund hoped that account would secure a permanent source of education support for the state's children. Unfortunately this was not the case. In 1826 the legislature authorized the governor to invest a portion of the Literary Fund in stock of the Bank of Mississippi. Two years later the entire fund was invested in stock, and in 1830 this stock was transferred to the Planters Bank. When the fund reached $50,000 in 1833 and according to law should have been distributed to the counties, rather than a cash payment each county received bank stock appropriated in proportion to its white population. Perhaps investing the education fund in the state bank could have yielded a significant return that would have brought more money to help educate children across Mississippi. Unfortunately, as a result of the Panic of 1837, the Planters Bank failed in 1840, taking out the Literary Fund with it. With that collapse, the state's means of supporting schools across the state vanished.[35]

The Panic of 1837 destroyed Mississippi's means of government support for education in the state. It is hard to exaggerate the impact of this financial crisis, as six years of depression enveloped the nation, causing banks and businesses to close and families across America to lose their homes, farms, and lands. The collapse of banks across the country destroyed the wealth not just of individuals and businesses, but of governments as well. The Mississippi Literary Fund was a casualty of the financial collapse of 1837, and its destruction left the state scrambling to attempt to revamp its funding scheme and again assist education within its borders.

While Mississippi struggled to overcome the setbacks wrought by the Panic of 1837, the challenge of doing so fundamentally altered the way the state supported schools. Alabama followed a similar course. The Cotton State amended its school laws throughout the 1820s and 1830s to little effect. Politicians in Alabama exhibited an interest in education, with governors continually urging the legislature to do more to encourage schools in the state. In his annual message to the legislature in 1827, Governor John Murphy commented, "The subject of Education commends itself to our most devoted attention, enjoined as it is by the commanding precepts of the Constitution, involved in the preservation of our happy form of government, and indispensable in every system for the promotion of social or moral happiness." He went on to assure them: "Every consideration urges the propriety of enlightening the minds, and improving the morals, of the whole body of the people. In the judicious prosecution of this work, no pains can be misapplied, no measure misspent, and no solitude pass unrewarded."[36]

Although legislators made early provisions to support education in the state and despite the clear interest in encouraging schools exhibited by many Alabama politicians, the status of education in 1830 revealed how little had actually been accomplished. According to one scholar, "Although public officials in the 1820s had planned for a state university and district schools and had made generous allowances for the development of academies, these programs were still embryonic in 1830. The University was not open; no more than 27 academies held charters; and the townships had only recently (1828) been allowed the sale value of their sixteenth sections—an authorization that probably was a prerequisite to actually constructing district schools." Education remained a recurring topic among governors and legislators throughout the 1830s as they attempted to adapt government policy to encourage more schools in the state. In 1830, Governor Gabriel Moore began his message to the legislature by noting, "In redeeming the pledge I have given by accepting the call of the people to fill the post of Chief Magistrate, and to watch over the public welfare, I feel myself irresistibly drawn to solicit the attention of the Representatives of the public interest, as far as their legitimate powers extend, to the great work of the *diffusion of knowledge among the people.*" He assured his audience that the "fabric of civil liberty" rested upon "*the intelligence and virtue found in the body of the people,*" and that it was therefore the responsibility of the government to ensure that the state's residents enjoyed access to education.[37]

Moore clearly outlined his belief that the state government bore the responsibility for providing education to the state's inhabitants, basing his argument on republicanism. His 1830 message to the legislature eloquently illustrates the argument made by many antebellum southern governors:

> Where all legitimate authority eminates [*sic*] from the citizens, as in our happy form of government, we should tremble at even the anticipation of the unnatural union of ignorance and civil liberty: and when, gentlemen, we add that it is the sentence of the people that is final, not only on our labors, but on all the civil regulations of the State, the importance of education and intelligence is completely and unequivocally developed. For the body of the citizens to exercise that happy control over the acts of their public servants, deemed one of the most important features in our political system, they must be capable of appreciating not only their privileges, but their rights and duties: otherwise anarchy on the one hand, and a fearful invasion and destruction of public liberty on the other, would inevitably ensue.

Following his argument for legislation to foster education, Moore congratulated the gathered legislators on the "flattering progress" of schools already in existence. He argued that the spread of schools across the state and their rapid advancement was "strongly evidencing that the fact is already impressed upon the mind that the *increase of knowledge is the best security for sound public morality.*"[38]

Moore's desire for an educated constituency was echoed by other Alabama leaders during the 1830s. Historian Forrest Mathews shows that Alabama legislators in the 1830s attempted to expand on earlier school provisions. Initially, these plans relied on assistance from the federal government, as when the state petitioned Congress to grant four quarter sections of unsold land to individual academies in the state, the income of which could be used to establish female departments for schools. But later in the decade, Alabama politicians began to make plans for a more comprehensive school system for the state's youth.[39]

In the legislative session that began in November 1835, Governor Clement Clay commented on the disposition of sixteenth section lands across Alabama. He argued that the federal government clearly intended its grant to give every township a means to support a school, yet some of the sections designated to benefit schools proved worthless, giving certain townships no resources from which to support their schools, while others enjoyed more income from the grant than they needed to run schools. Clay insisted that the federal government must have meant for there to be some equality between the various townships in regard to income from sixteenth sections. The governor laid the responsibility for fixing this inequity at the feet of the US Congress, noting that "I am aware this subject has been heretofore brought before Congress, yet it cannot be improper to remind them of a claim so manifestly founded in justice."[40]

Unlike Governor Clay, who looked to the federal government to rectify the inequity, state representative Pleasant May placed that burden squarely on the shoulders of the state. The problem created by the unequal value of sixteenth section lands across the state meant that "the counties with the richest land, hence the wealthiest counties, naturally had the more valuable sixteenth sections, and the poorest counties, the least valuable school property. As a result, the constitutional scheme for education was of least help to those communities that needed state aid the most." According to Mathews, May desired to change the appropriation so that schools would truly come within the reach of all citizens. Yet despite his concern over the inequity of the sixteenth sections, May did not offer an alternative funding scheme and assured the legislature that he had no intention of lobbying in favor of a school tax, although he expressed his own willingness to pay such a tax: "Next to the support of the Government, there is no object, for which I would pay taxes, with as much pleasure as to secure a system of general education."[41]

Though earlier governors spoke favorably of government support of schools, in 1838 Governor Arthur Bagby clearly outlined the state's failure to provide a general school system, telling the legislature, "Such has been the entire neglect of any attempt, at any thing like a general system of education in Alabama, that there is at this time, scarcely a school, or Academy in the State, in which, our young men can be fitted for College." It is interesting that Bagby would speak so harshly of the educational status of the state that previous governors had bragged about, revealing that many politicians merely paid lip service to the cause of education rather than actually attempting to expand and enhance the education system. Bagby could not tolerate such a situation, assuring the state's population, "This is an imputation under which, a people enjoying the manifold resources, and advantages that we do, ought not to consent, longer to labor."[42]

Initially the Panic of 1837 did not seem to hamper the state's commitment to fostering schools. Many proposals to reform Alabama's school laws were offered during the 1830s, though not until 1839 were any significant changes made. That year the legislature required the state bank to appropriate $150,000 annually to the school fund, which was increased to $200,000 in 1840. Each county would receive the income from its sixteenth section lands plus an amount from the bank appropriation necessary to bring its total school fund up to $200, increased to $400 in 1840. Governor Bagby, speaking to the legislature concerning public projects that would need to be postponed until an economic recovery, pleaded with the state's politicians that "education should be put in advance of every other interest. . . . I would rather be instrumental in imparting to the indigent and orphan children in the State of Alabama, the rudiments of a common English Education, than to enjoy the exclusive credit of constructing a railroad from Louisiana to the Lakes."[43]

The increased funding should have heralded a new era for education in the state. The requisitions from the state bank could have provided schooling for young Alabamians and support for struggling local schools. Unfortunately it was not to be. As in Mississippi, Alabama's politicians tied the state's school fund directly to the state bank, and as a result of the Panic, as in Mississippi, the bank failed. When it did so in 1843, the citizens of the state lost their public school fund. As with the Mississippi Literary Fund, Alabama's efforts fell disastrously short of their expected promise.

It is revealing of southern state politics that the same fate befell the school funds of both states. The desire to utilize education funds in order to finance state banks reveals politicians' commitment to state-run financial institutions. But what does it say about their interest in education? Even when legislators appeared to be making a move that would benefit learning institutions—investing the funds to draw interest and accumulate more money for the system—they did so in such a bungling manner that it proved harmful. Legislators were concerned about propping up the state bank more than they cared about protecting the education fund. So when the failure of the banks wiped out the education funds, the people mourned for the schools while lawmakers mourned for the bank, providing an example of how the sentiment of lawmakers and their constituents differed on the subject of education. Legislators were behind the curve in meeting the demands of the populace for education initiatives.[44]

An interesting phenomenon highlights the legislature's willingness to support education initiatives. In 1844, southern politicians were debating accepting a distribution of the federal surplus to the states, which was passed as part of the compromise ending the Nullification Crisis. Henry Clay had been promoting this distribution scheme to rid the federal government of the embarrassing wealth it had amassed as a result of the protective tariff. Democrats, especially southerners, who opposed the protective tariff balked at Clay's plan, wanting to use the embarrassment of riches in the treasury to lobby more effectively for repeal of the tariff. But the idea of a large distribution of federal money proved irresistibly attractive to the states.[45]

Interestingly, education became tied up in this debate. In order to receive their portion of the federal surplus, states had to petition the federal government to request distribution of the money. In Alabama, the legislature twice voted down Whig measures to request the funds from Congress. To make this distribution more palatable to the Democratic majority in the state legislature, Whig lawmakers proposed using the money to establish a common school fund. But Democrats would not be so easily lured. State senator Benjamin Hudson reported for the select committee tasked with considering the proposal, announcing to his colleagues that "the Legislature has twice refused to accept her share of the proceeds of the sales of public lands, upon the principle of distribution, because it is but another mode of sanctioning the protective tariff." He went on to explain, "The application of the fund to the support of common schools does not change the principle upon which it would have to be raised, if received at all. For these reasons in brief the committee concluded that it is inexpedient to pass the bill." The Whig effort did not succeed, and Alabama continued to refuse her portion of the federal surplus.[46]

The Democrats' opposition to the protective tariff is well documented, so their refusal to accept the federal distribution makes sense. In abstract terms, refusing the federal funds was justifiable. Emptying the federal treasury of the surplus would have stripped the Democrats of that tool for bludgeoning the opposition. Yet the Whig effort to use the disbursement to establish a common school fund cast the issue in different terms. Rather than an abstract lump sum, the money now was tied directly to the educational welfare of the state. The Whigs hoped that by doing so, they would make refusal to request the dispersal more politically dangerous for the Democrats. Rather than just a vote against the protective tariff, their denial to accept the funds was now a vote against a common school system. It was a clever maneuver by the Whigs, who were linked more directly with support for state education initiatives than were the Democrats. But the party of Jackson would not be so easily dissuaded.

Regardless of party affiliation, elected officials responded to their mandate to extend learning with only halfhearted measures meant to appease the populace, but lacking a sincere conviction to provide education accessible by all. Initially, state legislatures focused on supporting schools established by the private sector by offering a small appropriation designed to get a school off the ground or to save it in times of financial trouble. Using income from the sixteenth section of each township set aside by the federal government for the support of schools, the legislatures supported the learning institutions established throughout the states. These measures, while no doubt offering a valuable level of assistance to the receiving institutions, did not substantially improve access to learning in most areas of the South. It was not until the ideas of Jacksonian democracy percolated throughout the region bordering the Gulf of Mexico that residents began to demand that their legislators do more. Once the major urban centers in the South established public schools, the populace insisted that their state officials establish similar schools in rural areas. Before we consider the implementation of statewide public school systems in the 1840s and 1850s, we must examine how urban education progressed in the antebellum South.

## CHAPTER FOUR

The Genesis of Public Education in the South

URBAN PUBLIC SCHOOLS

Although statewide school systems would not come until later in Louisiana, Mississippi, and Alabama, successful public schools did exist in the early antebellum period. New Orleans, Natchez, and Mobile all established schools sustained by the city and state governments. The experience with these urban schools influenced the establishment of the statewide school systems instituted later, and in the case of New Orleans, stood as an example for the rest of the South of a successful free public school system. The establishment of public schools in all three cities reveals the value southerners attached to education and evidences that they were willing and able to support schools run by local governments rather than by private individuals.

Without question, New Orleans housed the preeminent public school system in the Gulf South and one of the most notable in the nation. Surrounding areas looked to its example when they began to implement their own systems, and many towns adopted methods identical to those exercised in the Crescent City when establishing their first public schools. In the discussion leading up to the establishment of a free public school in Natchez, for example, the New Orleans school system was continually referenced, and when the Natchez Institute was established in 1846, the board adopted "the rules, regulations, and organization, of the New Orleans schools, almost entirely." To understand how New Orleans came to house such a thriving free public school system, one must consider the city's history of supporting schools through government funding.[1]

Louisiana took steps toward creating schools in New Orleans as early as 1805, when the territorial legislature authorized the establishment of a private upper school called the College of Orleans, but stymied its establishment by not providing funding. Six years after the passage of the initial legislative act calling for its organization, the state allotted part of the surplus in the treasury to support education, granting $15,000 to establish the college with an annual appropriation of $3,000. Although the War of 1812 distracted attention from the college, annual appropriations from the state increased to $4,000 in 1819 and $5,000 in 1821. Despite the expanded funding, in 1817 a legislative committee appointed to inspect the College of Orleans reported very unfavorably on its conditions. Sebastian Hiriat, the committee chair, noted that "in a large commercial city like New Orleans, all the necessaries of life sell at a high price, the board of the pupils was of course fixed at such a high rate that none but the richest could afford to send their children as permanent students in the College." Not only could none but the wealthy manage to pay for the college, attendance among even the privileged also remained pitifully low. As Hiriat explained, "The original number of pupils diminished as soon as the first ardor for whatever is new had subsided." A legislative resolution prohibiting professors from simultaneously teaching at private schools had "a fated effect" according to the committee, since most teachers chose to work for private academies rather than teaching solely for the college. The resignation of the college's English teacher left the students without any instruction in the national language, and not long after, the College of Orleans "soon degenerated to a common school."[2]

Despite such unflattering observations, the legislature continued to support the college financially, in 1823 adding to its annual appropriation the revenue from the licensing of gambling houses. Although in 1823 another legislative committee reported much more favorably on the conditions of the college, the state withdrew appropriations in 1825 and abolished the College of Orleans the following year. The school's closure resulted from public controversy surrounding its president, Joseph Lakenal. Lakenal had been a well-respected educator in France, but his politics led him to leave the continent for Louisiana. He was a republican at odds with Napoleon, but his relationship with the Bourbons, resulting from his involvement with the convention that ordered the execution of Louis XVI, proved even more contentious. He moved to Louisiana after the fall of Napoleon, but his past regicidal behavior proved intolerable to many French people in New Orleans who remained loyal to the Bourbons. This scandal contributed to the closure of the College of Orleans. Still inclined to support some sort of public education in the city, the legislature replaced the college with three schools—primary schools in both the American and French sections of town, and one secondary school referred to as a central school. The central school simply continued the curriculum of the college without enjoying the title. State officials assumed that these schools would cater to less wealthy inhabitants; as the regents of the school later noted, "Sublime, indeed, were the views of the Legislature who first brought into existence those philanthropic, benevolent, and charitable foundations. They were pregnant with the destinies of that class of our community, the most interesting, as it is the most unfortunate." Regrettably the schools did not fulfill these high hopes, though education specialist Alma H. Peterson refers to their governing board of regents as the earliest school board in the nation.[3]

The three schools established from the College of Orleans received an annual appropriation of $10,000 added to $15,000 raised from a tax on the two theaters in New Orleans. Although the institutions constituted "public" schools, established and supported by the legislature, they charged tuition: in 1830, $2.00 a month per pupil for the primary schools and $4.00 a month per student for the secondary school. In 1833, the three public schools in New Orleans were attended by 236 boys, "most of them admitted gratis"; 108 pupils attended the lower primary school, while 82 attended the upper primary and 46 the central school. Despite the low enrollment, the board of regents assured the legislature that the schools were well organized and did tremendous good, especially for students who would otherwise be without education because of financial limitations. The school board assigned a committee to conduct surprise inspections of the schools once a month and also instituted public examinations for all students twice a year. Following their first inspection of the schools, the regents reported that "although our committee had presented themselves unexpectedly, they found boys from eleven to sixteen years of age translating with a facility and especially with an acuteness of expression really remarkable, the French, English and Spanish languages, some of them translated without previous preparation, several Latin books, among them Virgil's [*Aeneid*]. Questions were put to them on Mathematics: they answered satisfactorily, problems were propounded and solved on the spot."[4]

Enrollment in the schools continued to increase so that in 1836 the two primary schools boasted 440 pupils while the central school catered to over 100. Of this total, 190 registered as pauper students educated at the expense of the state; the rest paid tuition. Unfortunately the number of students enrolled rarely coincided with the number of students attending class regularly. Although the board of regents reported an enrollment of 440 in the primary schools, according to later assessments average attendance remained at about 75. That such a small number of families chose to patronize the school speaks to the institution's inadequacy. Although later reminiscences may have been overly critical of these first public schools, the schools seem to have displayed an ineptitude that became rather legendary. The successors of the schools repeatedly emphasized their inadequacy; one critic of the system reported that "in reviewing the history of the past, we behold only the wrecks of noble enterprises, freighted with the hopes and expectations of the community, yet destined to common ruin."[5]

In 1836 a change in the governance of New Orleans took place that had significant consequences for public schools there. A new charter divided the city into three distinct municipalities in order to ameliorate ethnic tensions and allow the French and the Americans to control their own parts of the city. The charter granted control of each municipality to a separate governing council under the general supervision of the mayor and a general council (composed of all three municipal councils). The general council had very limited powers and could only rule on matters that affected all the municipalities; it had no power over the purse. This division allowed each of the three municipalities within the city to function semi-autonomously, fostering differing public school developments. The First Municipality or "Old Square" housed the French section of the city and encompassed the Vieux Carré. Americans enjoyed control over most of the city's uptown, which made up the Second Municipality, covering the Faubourg St. Mary between Canal and Felicity Streets, while the Third Municipality housed a mix of French, mulattos, and Germans in the Faubourg Marigny. This division of the city allowed public education in each municipality to develop independently.[6]

Groundbreaking progress for the city's public schools came from the American quarter, the Second Municipality. In 1840 one of the section's residents, Samuel J. Peters, visited Horace Mann in Boston to learn his suggestions for establishing a public school system in the Crescent City. Mann, secretary of the Massachusetts Board of Education, was the preeminent education reformer of the day. Peters brought what he learned from Mann back home to New Orleans where Joshua Baldwin, a police court judge, drafted a bill for the state legislature authorizing the city to establish free public schools. In 1841 the legislature passed Baldwin's bill, allowing each of the municipalities in New Orleans to establish free schools for white children within their domains, marking the watershed for public education in the city. The law authorized each municipal council to levy taxes to support the schools and appropriated state aid of two and five-eighths dollars per taxable inhabitant, the current appropriation to each parish, not to exceed $10,000. In 1845 the legislature increased this amount to five and two-eighths dollars per inhabitant, not to exceed $15,000. The legislation simply permitted New Orleans to attempt to institute public schools; it in no way required action.[7]

After passage of the statute, the three municipalities immediately commenced preparations for their schools, but the general population received the law with hostility. Catholic educators feared that state intrusion into the field of education would erode their power in the community while private teachers did not want the state to deprive them of customers. Wealthy citizens who could afford to pay tuition did not want to be taxed for the education of other people's children, and general public opinion opposed free "pauper" schools serving the entire community. According to municipal officials, "The community regarded the enterprise with distrust, if not entirely opposed to it." Despite local resistance, within one year all three municipalities opened schools in their districts that soon elicited praise from across the nation. Historians Donald E. Devore and Joseph Logsdon note that "New England educators who normally scoffed at the educational backwardness of the South took notice of the New Orleans achievement."[8]

Left to their own devices to implement the Act of 1841, the three municipalities established schools in their districts individually, though the boards remained in contact and cooperation with each other. When a new charter combined the municipalities into a single entity in 1852, it did not alter the successful school system, leaving control to the three distinct school boards. The Second Municipality led the way by adopting the proven methods instituted in New England, such as organizing the schools into grades, and incorporating the phonetic reading system and New England primers. The other municipalities imitated the Second, though taking a bit longer to implement their systems.[9]

The Council of the Second Municipality first appointed a board of directors of twelve prominent citizens to add to the council's standing committee on education. It immediately abolished the existing public school developed from the College of Orleans, noting with contempt the inferiority of the previous system and refusing to "build upon this apology for a system of public education." Critically remembering previous public school efforts within the state, the board of directors enlisted the aid of experts from other areas. Through correspondence with city administrators, Horace Mann suggested his former assistant J. A. Shaw to direct the organization of the city's school system. The school board immediately contacted Shaw, who accepted the offer and arrived in New Orleans in 1841, opening a school by the end of the year under his direction; he and two female assistants instructed twenty-six students in a single room. The directors expended great efforts to publicize the new public school to all residents in the district, even going so far as to require board members to visit homes in the municipality to inform families about the institution. Despite such publicity efforts, the board noted with regret that only 319 pupils enrolled at the school, a very small proportion of the children residing in the municipality, estimated at about 2,300. But the municipal council praised the school board, claiming that "this general apathy, to take advantage of such high privileges, only stimulated them to persevere and make more vigorous and extended efforts in behalf of the cause."[10]

The low attendance at the school's first session should not be surprising. If the school board's appraisal of previous public schools in the city was accurate, it stands to reason that families would hesitate to patronize the new institution established by the municipal council. In addition, many parents generally do not rush to send their children to a new school until its reputation is better established. Most significantly, in all areas of the nation, it took time before the idea of free public schools was accepted by the local population. Parents hesitated to patronize an educational institution that did not charge tuition but instead was supported by the government.

Despite a meager beginning, municipal officers noted with pride that not a week passed without new enrollments. In 1842 the total number of pupils attending the public schools in the Second Municipality reached 840, with a total of 1,397 students "belonging to and having participated in their advantages." According to the estimates of the Second Municipality council president, 2,300 white children between the ages of five and fifteen resided within the district, of whom about 500 attended private schools in addition to the over 800 attending public school, leaving about 1,000 children in the district without instruction. School officials reported proudly that despite the initial opposition of the community, the success of the schools remained evident by their ever-increasing popularity, high attendance figures, and the good behavior of students.[11]

When the success of the Second Municipality schools became apparent, the other two sections of the city commenced their efforts to institute such a system. The Third Municipality immediately attempted to imitate the schools of the Second, opening a school within a year although its attendance levels never reached those of the Second District. The First Municipality, alternatively, did not immediately establish its schools in the same efficient manner. Rather than organizing entirely new schools in 1841, the municipality attempted to improve two existing schools established there in 1825 after the abolition of the College of Orleans. Unfortunately these schools continued to fall far below expectations, and in 1843 the school board finally declared them a complete failure. Despite the funding provided for their support, $13,942.93 from June 1841 to September 1843, only one school remained in operation in 1843, catering to 115 male students. The instruction provided proved unacceptable and the academic achievements of the students fell far below the school directors' expectations. Accordingly, the First Municipality abolished the schools and instituted a new free school system based on the system of the Second Municipality.[12]

Public schools throughout the city advanced rapidly. In the Second District the first classes were held in a single rented room of a house on Julia Street, but within a year, due to increasing enrollment and the need for more space to facilitate "physical development," it occupied "four large and commodious houses" as well as a fifth structure built by the municipality. The Third Municipality soon distributed children in seven classrooms in two different districts, and by 1845 the First Municipality administered six schools. The number of schools, students, and teachers continually increased, as did the accompanying programs, soon instituting a lyceum series and adding libraries and other useful resources. As was the case across the South, despite the presence of a large free black community in New Orleans, Louisiana public schools were open only to white children, regardless of status.[13]

An examination of the rapidly increasing enrollment in the New Orleans public schools reveals the immediate success of the system instituted in 1841. The following table provides an estimate of the increase in attendance at the public schools, which suggests their growing popularity. In 1843, after only two years of operation, enrollment in the public schools of the Second Municipality increased from the original number of twenty-six students taught by three teachers to 1,574 enrolled students taught by thirty-three teachers. Likewise, attendance in both the First and Third Municipalities increased rapidly. In 1845 the combined enrollment in the three municipalities reached 3,336 students taught by 80 teachers, and by 1850 the number of students had climbed to 6,285. Officers of the Second Municipality bragged that a number of families moved within its borders strictly to gain access to its schools. The directors of the schools proudly claimed that the "accession to the public, and diminution from the private schools, is believed the most conclusive evidence of the former's superiority, and moreover, further evidences with what facility prejudices, even the most deep rooted, are dissipated by the force of truth and wisdom."[14]

Table 4.1: Increasing Public School Attendance in the
Three Municipalities of New Orleans, 1842–1850

	FIRST MUNICIPALITY			SECOND MUNICIPALITY			THIRD MUNICIPALITY		
Year	# of Schools	# of Teachers	# of Pupils	# of Schools	# of Teachers	# of Pupils	# of Schools	# of Teachers	# of Pupils
1842	—	—	—	2	7	840	2	2	110
1843	—	—	—	3	20	1156	3	4	230
1844	3	11	615	5	33	1574	3	4	230
1845	6	36	1029	6	37	1859	5	7	448
1846	6	38	1351	7	40	2004	7	10	672
1847	7	40	1512	8	46	2303	9	13	867
1848	9	43	1725	10	54	2693	12	15	902
1849	11	45	1850	13	57	2851	14	17	989
1850	12	50	2010	15	63	3155	17	21	1120

Source: Fay, *The History of Education in Louisiana,* 71; Peterson, "A Historical Survey of the Administration of Education in New Orleans," 55.

The city's school board designated three levels in the schools: primary, intermediate, and secondary. All children entered the primary department regardless of age, "until they have some knowledge of reading, writing on slates, and mental arithmetic." Primary school students received lessons in spelling, grammar, composition, reading, writing, and oral instruction of numbers. The intermediate department added to this curriculum the Latin and French languages, geography, US history, and declamation. Those courses continued in the high schools, where the students also learned algebra, geometry, natural and moral philosophy, and French and English literature and history. As the years progressed, more advanced courses appeared in the high schools, so that in 1859 students could choose from such classes as analytical grammar, Roman history, rhetoric, chemistry, botany, physiology, astronomy, trigonometry, surveying, and American constitutional theory. Students in all grades received vocal music instruction, in which the schools took special pride, noting that music creates the "happiest effects, both as to the moral and intellect," and that the "influence of music on the nation is no less obvious than on individuals." Beginning in 1841 the teachers also read scripture to the students in the mornings, "without note or comment," followed by a prayer. Although the directors insisted that the moral instruction provided in the schools was still nonsectarian, Catholic objections to what they considered Protestant instruction led to the discontinuation of scripture readings in 1850. Nonetheless the school directors assured the community that "care is taken to instill in their young minds the precepts of a high morality and principles of lofty patriotism."[15]

Public education proponents in New Orleans refuted the charge that public schools endangered morals and manners. Sardonically questioning if nothing vicious or rude ever entered private schools, local administrators insisted that "the sad results of unwise domestic training are not confined to the children of the poor." Although some doubted whether schools without a denominational affiliation could adequately supervise their pupils' emotional development, school directors did everything in their power to ensure that the schools maintained a respectable environment and that students received not only academic instruction but social as well, taking particular care to inculcate both manners and morals.[16]

One of the complications for schools in New Orleans involved the challenge of catering to a bilingual population. The First Municipality bore most of the burden, for while it remained predominantly French, the large American minority insisted on having schools conducted in English as well. In 1852, there were 1,288 students in the First Municipality schools who spoke French as their first language while 968 spoke English. The bilingual divide led to the costly practice of providing duplicate texts and teachers for both languages. Language proved a contentious point because control of the First Municipality's school board vacillated between the French and American inhabitants throughout the antebellum period, leading to frequent alterations in school practices and contributing to the volatility of relations between English and French speakers. In spite of the numerous changes to school policies, duplicate courses for both languages remained until the Civil War.[17]

On average, New Orleans public schools operated five days a week, ten months a year, though some schools operated eleven months, closing only in August.[18] Originally the schools in the Second Municipality conducted class a half-day on Saturdays, but the board of directors discontinued this practice in 1851. In 1856 the school board noted that their schools convened at 9:00 a.m. and remained open until 2:30 p.m., with a half-hour recess at noon. The principal teacher could also grant the students a ten-minute recess at his or her discretion. Six to seven hours a day seems to have been the normal session, though in 1859 the First District of New Orleans reported their schools conducted class for only three and a half hours a day. Some primary schools initiated the practice of dismissing pupils under eight years of age earlier in the afternoons in order to allow teachers to work more closely with older students. Students underwent examinations twice a year, in December and June, with the school board often attending.[19]

The large amounts expended by the city to maintain its public schools allowed teachers' salaries in New Orleans to compare favorably with those received in other sections of the country. When the Second Municipality first hired Shaw to direct its schools in 1841, it offered him a salary of $3,500, a very generous sum even in the North. In 1856 principal teachers (head instructors) in New Orleans's boys grammar schools received $1,320, more than the same position received in Cincinnati or Philadelphia and only $180 less than it received in New York. School directors also boasted about the comparatively higher salaries enjoyed by female teachers in New Orleans. For instance, while Boston paid their male grammar school principal teachers $1,800, female principal teachers received only $450. In contrast, New Orleans paid female principal teachers $1,000, with men in the same position receiving $320 more.[20] These figures are included in Table 4.2.

Table 4.2: Annual Salaries of School Teachers in Various Cities, 1856

	Male Principal Teachers	Female Principal Teachers	Male Assistant Teachers	Female Assistant Teachers
Boston	$1,800	$450	$1,200	$450
New York	$1,500	$700	$1,000	$400
Philadelphia	$1,200	$600	—	$350
Cincinnati	$1,020	$504	—	$360
New Orleans	$1,320	$1,000	$1,000	$800

Source: *Annual Report of the Board of Directors of the Public Schools of the First District of New Orleans, for the Year ending June 30, 1856.*

Note: Philadelphia and Cincinnati did not employ male assistant teachers.

The high pay for New Orleans public school teachers is indeed impressive. Alma Peterson noted in her 1962 study that "to this day, the New Orleans public school system has never equaled the status it enjoyed relative to salaries of teachers that it held during the early years of its operation." Likewise, historian Thelma Welch concluded in her 1942 survey of teachers' salaries that this period was the only time in its history that New Orleans schools paid their teachers more than did other areas of the nation.[21]

A clear preference for female teachers emerges from the reports of the municipalities of New Orleans. In 1843 females accounted for sixteen of the Second Municipality's twenty teachers, and in 1854 it employed fifty-one female teachers and only fourteen males. The directors noted that they decided to hire mostly females "after mature deliberation," since women proved "better adapted to instruct young scholars, by their quicker perceptions; their instinctive fondness for, and tact in communicating knowledge; greater patience and more gentleness than the males." Despite such declarations, the pecuniary interest in employing women rather than men no doubt played a role in their decision, since female teachers received less compensation than males. Using 1856 as an example, male high school principal teachers received $1,800 compared to $1,200 paid to female principal teachers. These figures are included in Table 4.3 below.[22]

Teachers in New Orleans public schools consistently earned the praise of school administrators, whose assessments typically noted that "the teachers attached to the 3rd District Public Schools are ornaments, well

Table 4.3: Annual Salaries Paid to Public School Teachers in
the First District of New Orleans, 1856

	Male Teachers		Female Teachers	
High School	Principal Teacher	$1,800	Principal Teacher	$1,200
	Assistant Teacher	$1,500	Assistant Teacher	$1,050
	French Teacher	$700	French Teacher	$600
Grammar School	Principal Teacher	$1,320	Principal Teacher	$1,000
	Assistant Teacher	$1,000	Assistant Teacher	$800

Source: *Annual Report of the Board of Directors of the Public Schools of the First District of New Orleans, for the Year ending June 30, 1856.*

deserving the confidence which has been placed in them. Their general character is beyond reproach, their qualifications as teachers unsurpassed." All available appraisals regarding teachers in the city's public schools remain unflinchingly positive, repeatedly noting their diligence, attentiveness, and faithfulness. The school directors thoroughly examined all teaching applicants, claiming that "no teacher is employed in the schools, not in the Primary department even, who is not thoroughly versed in spelling, reading, grammar, geography, arithmetic and history of the United States; in order to ascertain this, every applicant for employment as teacher is required to undergo a rigid examination in all these branches." School directors in New Orleans not only expected their teachers to demonstrate academic achievement, but also to exemplify morality and virtue and employ only the best methods of instruction. "Teachers and scholars are thus rendered attentive to their duties," which thereby "ensures greatest good to greatest number, with the smallest means."[23]

The growing effectiveness and popularity of the new system was reflected in the number of teachers eager to work for the schools. After only one year the board of directors claimed that it received an abundance of teaching applications, commenting that "more numerous applications for situations have afforded more unlimited choice, and enabled the Council to appoint none but those experienced in teaching, and of a high standard in literary acquirements." Regardless of the number of applicants, school administrators wanted to train their own instructors. The legislature continually received requests insisting that the state should prepare its own inhabitants as instructors rather than importing teachers from other sections of the country. Accordingly, in 1858 the legislature authorized the establishment in New Orleans of a normal school to train teachers. The city added a normal department to its girls' high school, which accommodated thirty-seven students the first year and sixty-two in 1859. Proudly reporting that its graduates moved on to teach within New Orleans as well as across the state and beyond, the directors of the normal department claimed, "The growth and prosperity of the school during the past year, has been a source of gratification to those friends who hailed its first organization with pleasure, and who have faithfully continued to watch over its interests." In 1858, J. G. Parham Jr., superintendent of the Fourth District, reported that "nearly one-half of the teachers have been educated entirely and solely in the High Schools of the First and Fourth Districts of this city."[24]

Significantly, the public schools operating in New Orleans remained completely free to all students. Unlike in many other schools, where the term *public* simply connoted its support through some sort of state aid, schools administered by the Crescent City did not charge tuition. In contrast to the previous method of admitting poor children gratuitously, the public schools established in New Orleans after 1841 remained completely free to all children, the first example of free schools in the state. The board of directors praised the free system, pointing out that it produced impressive results and that rich and poor students sat side by side without any distinction among them, so that the school system "teaches the one as well as informs the other that adventitious wealth confers no superiority over the less fortunate competitor when engaged in the intellectual contest." The determination to establish an effective and productive system was also apparent in that not only were students exempted from tuition, but the schools also provided stationery and books for their students so that no one would be deprived of the benefits of education because of financial limitations. School administrators in New Orleans argued that although some citizens believed that the poor should stay ignorant, such opinions contradicted the egalitarian ideals upon which the nation was founded. They maintained that the responsibility to educate all citizens rested with the state and that it should do so free of charge since the nation's system of government demands that "the masses must be intelligent and virtuous; such only will make good members of society, and being able to comprehend their whole duty, will be able and willing to perform it."[25]

Although some feared that free schools would cater only to the less

fortunate segments of society, ensuring a situation where the rich continued to attend expensive private academies and only the destitute attended
public schools, this fear proved unfounded in New Orleans. The directors
of the Second Municipality schools boasted in their first report that "for
coming as many of the children do from opulent and influential citizens,
who before confided their education to the private schools, it affords the
most conclusive evidence, not only that the prejudices against public
schools in general, have yielded and been overcome, but that these public
schools, in their judgment, afford better opportunities for their children
acquiring a good practical education than the private ones." The schools
soon gained the support of the community so that by 1844 the directors
bragged that two-thirds of its population attended public schools and that
the condition and character of the schools therefore remained a "matter
of deep concernment to every good citizen." The directors proudly acknowledged the local support that the program garnered, claiming that
"the schools have greatly increased in usefulness, and have become so
firmly riveted in the affections and feelings of the people, that they are
no longer regarded as experimental, or their permanency considered as
questionable."[26]

The New Orleans community, although originally opposed to supporting a free school system, soon embraced the public schools of the city.
Referring to the public schools as "a system which finds an advocate in
every child, a protector in every parent, and a friend in every citizen," district directors repeatedly emphasized their value to the community. Intent
on extending the avenues of learning as far as possible, public school administrators instituted community programs that ingratiated larger and
larger segments of the city's population to the public school system. The
school system established a public library that housed over twelve thousand volumes by 1861 as well as a lyceum series offered to the New Orleans
community, which the directors hoped would "extend to the many the inap-
preciable advantages of knowledge—which, hitherto, have been confined
to the favored few." Such community programs helped rally more and
more supporters to the cause of public education in New Orleans.[27]

The transformation of public and professional impressions of the system proved dramatic. Not only did New Orleans officials provide schools,
libraries, and lecture series to the public, but they even made provisions
for young residents who lacked the freedom to attend school during the
day. Seeking to educate all the city's youth, by the 1850s all districts of

the city operated night schools. Although the Second District opened its evening school only to males, the other districts made their institutions available to young adults of both genders who worked during the day. Classes usually ran for three hours an evening, five days a week, for five to seven months a year rather than the standard ten-month term of day schools. In 1854 three night schools in the city enrolled 411 students, and by 1859 this number more than doubled in just one school, with attendance climbing to 849 students. While the operation of night schools may not seem like a significant contribution upon first consideration, such an undertaking reveals the determination of city officials. This provision suggests that those in charge of the New Orleans school system remained truly committed to educating the entire population, even those ordinarily beyond the reach of public schools.[28]

The extraordinary local supervision provided by the board of directors contributed significantly to the system's success. These men, appointed by the city council, took an active interest in the public schools that would remain unmatched elsewhere in Louisiana throughout the antebellum period. The board actively communicated with the teachers, closely examining all applicants for employment and meeting with all instructors semimonthly "for mutual conversation, discussion and improvement." The school board reported that these meetings proved very helpful to the teachers, who benefited by sharing experiences, and that the discussions contributed to uniformity throughout the various public schools. The directors suggested improvements to teachers and administrators and advocated on their behalf to the city council and the state legislature. The school board even provided subscriptions to an education journal for all its employees and planned to institute a teachers' association, which they explained would serve "as important means of exciting and maintaining the spirit of improvement in education."[29]

Dedicated local administrators gave the public schools an instant level of credibility and went far in contributing to their success and popularity. In addition to their advocacy for teachers, school directors made themselves a constant presence at the public schools of the city, requiring members to visit each school on a regular basis to observe its proceedings. School directors visited classrooms, evaluated teachers, attended annual exams of students, and suggested that parents and guardians do the same. Their constant presence as well as their palpable interest certainly made an impression upon both students and teachers, as well as the entire community, with one observer noting, "Few cities in the Union, if any, have more energetic, more vigilant, or more able Directors of Public Schools than New Orleans."[30]

Indeed, the system enjoyed the visible support of some of the city's social elite. Prominent figures in the New Orleans community became members of the city's school board. Samuel J. Peters, "a leading merchant and political figure," served the schools of the Second Municipality, and visited Horace Mann in Massachusetts for advice on how to set up the public school system initially. Many influential politicians sat on this section's school board, such as Joshua Baldwin, a former police court judge who was one of the original petitioners who asked the legislature to establish the public school system of the city, and who served as president of the Second Municipality's school board for eight years. In the Third Municipality, the council elected one citizen and one alderman from each ward to serve on its school board, while the mayor served on the board of the First Municipality. The service of established community leaders helped to bolster the reputation of the schools and reveals the importance that they attributed to public education.[31]

Prominent school administrators paid close attention to the progress of school students and found much to praise and applaud. In 1843 the school directors initiated the practice of awarding books and medals for excellent behavior and exceptional scholastic improvement but discontinued the practice of giving prizes the following year, insisting that pupils needed no rewards to induce excellence. They explained that the students' "natural desire not to be outdone, excites a sufficiently keen and wholesome emulation." In their judgment pupils did not need to be rewarded materially for their achievements, but sought to learn because of their "love of knowledge and pleasure and advantages consequent upon its acquisition."[32]

Aside from the exceptional local administration, one of the most important reasons for the success of the New Orleans public school system, especially when compared with public schools in the rest of Louisiana, remained the large amount of financing that came from the city itself. Although all public schools as well as a number of private schools that met state requirements received quarterly appropriations from the state, these funds remained far from adequate to support any standard school system; as a result New Orleans added significantly to this amount—contributing as much as ten times the amount appropriated from the state. At the time the 1841 act passed, the Second Municipality ordered the excess fees of the harbormaster to be applied to the public education fund, while the First Municipality established a 25¢ tax on each $1,000 of real property to benefit public schools. The Third Municipality levied a $10.00 tax per night on all social balls, the proceeds of which would be deposited into the public school fund. Such a creative tax on a socially active city like New Orleans ensured revenue, raising $2,500 in the first six months. According to the secretary of state, in 1843 the Second Municipality raised $11,000 to add to the state appropriation of only $2,300. School directors from New Orleans constantly lobbied for more money from the state, noting the drastic discrepancy between the cost to run the schools and the amount of state appropriations. In 1842 expenditures for public schools in the Second Municipality totaled $13,300, of which the state provided $2,300. Costs of maintaining and expanding the schools increased each year to $21,000 in 1843 and $26,000 in 1844, while the annual state appropriation remained fixed at $2,300. The large difference between these sums highlights the necessity of local taxation. New Orleans, through the perseverance of its school directors, procured the additional funds needed to run its schools. Wealthy benefactors bequeathed large sums to the city's public education fund at the same time the city council continued to increase the amount appropriated to support the schools. In 1861 the Second District reported that its annual appropriation from the city equaled $70,512, to which the city council added $10,000 that year to build a new schoolhouse. School administrators noted that financing public schools indeed drained much of the city's treasury, but that the cost was "promptly and cheerfully sustained by the people," who approved of incurring such expense in order to educate their children.[33]

In addition to local support provided by city government, New Orleans public schools benefited from a huge donation from a local millionaire. John McDonogh was a fascinating character in a city of interesting people. Born in Baltimore, McDonogh owned a large plantation in Algiers near New Orleans. Despite being a slave owner, he was a proponent of sending freed American slaves to Africa to live. He practiced a careful plan of emancipation, usually keeping slaves for fourteen years and then freeing them. He used slaves to do all his work, including managerial, refusing to hire white overseers or managers. He sent many of his freed slaves to the new Republic of Liberia to live. His liberal views on slavery and emancipation, along with his miserly ways, made him an outcast in

New Orleans. During his life, McDonogh amassed a fortune worth three million dollars (the equivalent of one hundred million dollars today). At his death, he left his estate to his hometown of Baltimore and the city of New Orleans, to be used to support free public schools. The bequest supported existing schools and led to the creation of new schools over the course of the next century, thirty-five of which bear his name.[34]

The resources of a thriving port city like New Orleans clearly gave it a financial advantage in gaining support for public education, but school administrators regularly reminded both the city council and the state legislature of the financial efficiency of New Orleans public schools compared to private schools in the area. In 1844 Second Municipality officials estimated that it cost the school system $1.47 for a student to attend public school for one month, including books and stationery. In contrast, the cost of private schools in the city averaged $5.00 per child each month, excluding supplies. In 1844, a total of 1,574 students attended public schools for the cost of $27,870. If the same number of children had attended private schools the cost would have reached $75,552, according to the calculations of school directors.[35]

While public schools certainly cost less to maintain than private schools, New Orleans public school directors frequently lobbied both the city and the state for more money. If the state allotted more money to support public schools, administrators argued, more students could be accommodated and attendance would increase. School directors suggested methods to increase the allotment from the state without raising the tax burden, such as changing the basis of the state appropriation from the number of taxable inhabitants to the number of pupils attending public schools, a move that would have ensured a larger appropriation for the city. Administrators in New Orleans constantly reminded the legislature how many more students they educated than other parishes, but how state appropriations failed to reflect this fact. In 1844, for example, East Baton Rouge Parish educated 118 children free of charge and received $800 from the state. The Second District of New Orleans alone educated 1,574 children that year and received only $2,300 from the state, providing $26,000 from its own treasury. While New Orleans did receive a larger appropriation than East Baton Rouge, about three times as much, it educated considerably more students, more than thirteen times as many. Administrators in New Orleans felt that their impressive enrollment figures should be rewarded through larger appropriations, but the state continued to allot funds based on the number of inhabitants rather than the number of students actually attending school. These numbers are included in Table 4.4 to highlight the case of New Orleans.[36]

Table 4.4: Number of Students Taught and State Appropriations
to Several Louisiana Parishes, 1844

Parish	Amount of State Appropriation	# of Students Educated	Amount Appropriated per Student
St. Bernard	$500	14	$35.71
Caldwell	$512	15	$34.13
St. James	$800	35	$22.86
Ascension	$600	49	$12.24
Pointe Coupee	$800	68	$11.76
Jefferson	$800	70	$11.43
West Baton Rouge	$520	46	$11.30
Natchitoches	$800	77	$10.39
East Baton Rouge	$800	118	$6.78
Rapides	$800	124	$6.45
Carroll	$800	127	$6.30
Lafayette	$800	164	$4.88
Ouachita	$800	175	$4.57
Average of above	$717.85	83	$13.75
Second Municipality of New Orleans	$2,300	1,574	$1.46

Source:[First] Annual Report of the Council of Municipality Number Two, of the City of New Orleans, on the Condition of its Public Schools (New Orleans: printed at the Office of the *Picayune*, 1845), 14.

In another attempt to procure more financing, school directors suggested taking money from other programs funded by the state, such as prisons. Emphasizing the benefits of public education, the school directors insisted that funding public schools proved a better use of revenue than spending money on "aged criminals, whose condition is the frequent accompaniment, if not almost the necessary consequence of ignorance."[37] While most of these proposals remained unimplemented, the creative suggestions and constant agitation by New Orleans school administrators highlighted the insufficiency of state funding. While the city's school board continually requested larger appropriations from the state, in the absence of such increases the city took it upon itself to provide the additional funding needed to support the free school system. Had New Orleans failed to provide additional revenue to support its public schools, the success of its schools surely would have been threatened.

The free public schools established by the City of New Orleans in 1841 thrived until the Civil War. Their success stood as an example to the rest of the state, and the legislature soon attempted to replicate the system across Louisiana. While arguably having the most successful public school system in the antebellum Gulf South, New Orleans was not the only urban area to establish public schools so early in the nineteenth century. Alabama's major urban center likewise established its school system prior to the rest of its state. Provisions allowing Mobile public schools to operate autonomously came in 1826 when the Alabama legislature passed "an act establishing schools in the county of Mobile," outlining the basic provisions of the city's school system. The law established a board of school commissioners who were given "full power and authority to establish and regulate schools, and to devise, put in force, and execute such plans and devices for the increase of knowledge, educating youth, and promoting the cause of learning in said county, as to them may appear expedient."[38]

Some of Mobile's leading men supported this drive for public education in the city, including Willoughby Barton, an early citizen and extensive landholder in the city who sponsored the bill in the state legislature, and prominent citizens Silas Dinsmore and Henry Hitchcock, who would both be instrumental in funding a new school building for the city. Hitchcock, the grandson of Ethan Allen of Vermont, was a successful attorney and real estate developer who went on to serve as judge, bank commissioner, and operator of the city's water works. Not only did Hitchcock serve on the school board and help finance the building of a substantial schoolhouse, he also donated land on which the Female Benevolent Society built houses for widows in the city. One contemporary called Hitchcock "one of the most enterprising, liberal, and public-spirited citizens Mobile ever had—whose name and works 'still live in the hearts of the people.'" As in New Orleans, the determination of a few prominent citizens was the key to establishing schools in Mobile.[39]

The 1826 law authorized Mobile to draw on new sources of revenue to support schools, including fines, penalties, and forfeitures, a $2.00 fee on suits in circuit and county courts, and 25 percent of the county tax, among other sources. Some merchants still managed to avoid paying their required share, however, leading the legislature in 1829 to require those liable to pay into the school fund to produce proof of payment to the city's school commissioners, who could then fine merchants who failed to pay. Some court clerks used legal loopholes to avoid paying their required share into the fund, while auctioneers offered such blatant resistance to the law that in 1836 legislators allowed Mobile school commissioners to require payment at the time of the auction and to "sell property themselves if the auctioneers balked at compliance."[40]

Despite these legislative stipulations meant to encourage public schools in Mobile, the city initially used its funds to support private schools already in operation rather than creating wholly public institutions. Yet as in New Orleans, some of Mobile's leading citizens continued to advocate public schools in the city, and in 1835 and 1836 built a beautiful building known as Barton Academy, named for the author of the 1826 school law. The state authorized a $50,000 lottery to raise revenue for its construction, in addition to a $15,000 loan from the city and private donations arranged by Henry Hitchcock and Silas Dinsmore. The three-story structure continues to stand in downtown Mobile as a testament to the work of these early public school enthusiasts. The first floor of the academy housed classes for the primary school in two classrooms, each of which could accommodate up to one hundred pupils. The second story was also divided into two classrooms of the same size where male and female high school classes were conducted. These rooms were further subdivided when needed so that no teacher instructed more than thirty students at a time. Unfortunately, despite the efforts made to finance its construction, the building left the school commissioners overdrawn in the amount of $12,000, leading them to charge tuition to retire this debt. The school charged $2.00 to $5.00 for enrollment in the primary and infant school, and $5.00 to $7.00 to attend the high school.[41]

In 1838 the Mobile school commissioners made arrangements for the admission of poor children who could not afford the school's tuition when they opened a boys' department that charged a reduced rate of $1.00 per month per child, where pupils studied spelling, reading, writing, geography, and arithmetic. In 1839 the school commissioners altered this provision to allow any young boy whose parents could not afford tuition to attend the high school free of charge. They also made provisions to instruct poor girls that year, authorizing the Free Female

Department in February 1839, with the board paying the teacher a salary of $2.50 a month per pupil. In 1839 one hundred fifty of Barton Academy's three hundred fifty students attended free of charge. An average of three hundred fifty students attended Barton Academy in 1839 and 1840, with a maximum enrollment of 470 students. That year the Classical Department enrolled eighty children, the Female Department catered to forty students, and eighty pupils attended the Juvenile Department, with the rest of the students attending the Free School.[42]

Mobile supported other schools in the area as well. In 1836 the city gave $600 for a school on Saw Mill Creek and also granted an appropriation for the building of a female academy at Spring Hill. City leaders devoted their main attention, however, to Barton Academy. Despite the school's contribution to education in the city, the school commissioners continued to struggle under the debt they incurred in its building. While the handsome structure stood as a testament to the city's support of education, the sale of the building was continually contemplated. Beginning in 1838, in an attempt to generate more income, school commissioners began renting rooms in the academy to local organizations, including the Franklin Society, the Philomathean Society, and the Mason's Lodge. In addition to the economic downturn associated with the Panic of 1837, a smallpox epidemic struck Mobile in 1839, further complicating school conditions. That year the commissioners closed the free departments for both genders and began charging rental fees to teachers who conducted classes in the school. These efforts failed to rescue the school board from its financial trouble, and in 1840 the building was auctioned by the sheriff to Colonel Thomas McGran, a cotton broker, who paid $5,000 for it. Samuel P. Bullard, a former school board member, sought reelection to help save the school, and along with other board members spent the next decade liquidating the board's debt. Bullard was a commission merchant in the city who served on both the city council and the chamber of commerce. In 1841 he became president of the school board and managed to get personal notes from six wealthy citizens and one business firm, which gave him enough capital to buy back the school.[43]

After the board discontinued the free departments of Barton Academy, it began channeling more of the city's education funding to private institutions. Unlike New Orleans, where the money designated to support education went solely to public institutions, Mobile continued to support private schools with public funds. In 1846 the state legislature passed "an act to aid free schools in the city of Mobile," which allowed taxpayers to put their school tax money into the city's general school fund or to apply it to a denominational school of their choice. Accordingly, the city government began aiding denominational free schools on a monthly basis, so that the Presbyterian, Catholic, Episcopal, and Methodist schools all received aid from the city in the 1850s. In order to add more money to their school appropriations, certain city officials once again began advocating for the sale of Barton Academy. The debate over its sale engendered a spirited discussion within the city over the future of schools in Mobile.[44]

In 1852, when the sale of the Barton building was suggested, the question centered around whether the city should continue to aid private schools that offered free classes, or again try to institute their own wholly public institutions. At the time the question was raised, private groups rented the Barton Academy, and the sale of the school building would add more money to the city's coffers that could be used to give more aid to private schools. According to one historian, "the proposal to sell the school property was seemingly routine. . . . Even so, the sale referendum proved to be a spark that set off a vigorous controversy in the city."[45]

Proponents of the sale of Barton Academy wanted to continue the system then in place in which the city distributed funds to private institutions that held free classes, using the income generated from the sale of the building to increase their appropriations to local schools. Many Mobilians, however, objected to what they saw as an abandonment of the public school system, and instead wanted Barton Academy to be used for what it was originally built for—to house *public* schools. According to one who took part in the debate, the proposed sale of Barton Academy "became a topic of supreme interest to the people of Mobile, and, in its discussion and consideration, stirred the popular mind as no other local subject had affected it for many years. Parties were formed, and the discussions were warm, earnest, and aggressive. The press took an active part, public meetings were held, and, as the election drew nigh, it became the absorbing topic everywhere in the city."[46]

General Walter Smith, deputy collector for the Port of Mobile, took the lead in favor of the sale, arguing that the city needed only to provide a common education for its children, not high schools, and that Barton Academy was not suited to that purpose. Instead, the Barton building should be sold and several plain buildings built throughout the city to house common schools. The *Mobile Advertiser,* run by Charles C. Langdon, vigorously opposed the sale and utilized its editorial pages to argue in favor of holding public classes in Barton Academy. Langdon had been a teacher before becoming a successful cotton merchant in Alabama. An active Whig, not only did he edit the paper, he also served as mayor for the City of Mobile from 1849 to 1856. In his absence Willis G. Clark wielded editorial control, and these two men enjoyed enormous influence, not only in the city but across the state. The pages of the *Advertiser* carried Smith's argument in favor of selling the building, which was refuted in the same paper by K. B. Sewall, an opponent of the sale. Sewall countered Smith's argument by noting that public schools in the city should include primary, grammar, and high schools, as in other states, and that Barton Academy was perfectly suited to house classes of different grades. The school had cost the city almost $100,000 and was at that moment free from debt. There was no way for the city to recoup that money by selling the building, which had a sale value of only $30,000. Langdon and Clark used their editorials to support Sewall's argument, and helped to turn public opinion against the proposal to sell a large, debt-free school building in order to build other schools, rather than utilizing Barton Academy for the purposes for which it had been built.[47]

According to a legislative provision passed in 1852, the city's school commissioners could sell the building if a majority of the county's voters approved the sale at an election in August of that year. The voices of Langdon, Clark, and Sewall, as carried by the *Advertiser,* clearly had an impact on the citizens of Mobile, for when it came time for the election, the voters overwhelmingly cast their ballots against the sale of the school: 224 voters favored the sale, with 2,225 voting against it, revealing considerable unanimity among the city's inhabitants in support of public schools. At the same election, the voters chose to serve as school commissioners men who had opposed the sale, including the *Advertiser*'s own Willis Clark, whom one scholar considers "the principal leader in the anti-sale movement."[48]

Given the results of the election, the school board immediately began reorganizing the city's public schools. A month after the election, the school board commenced its new plan for a public school in Barton Academy and began advertising for teachers. The school board divided itself into committees on teachers, schoolbooks, accounts, academy, and school laws. On the first Monday in November 1852, four hundred students attended class at the newly reorganized public school in Barton Academy. The following February, 109 students attended the high school, 209 the grammar school, and 536 the primary school, for a total of 854 students, more than twice the number of the previous year. As the number of students increased, the grades were changed to primary, intermediate, junior grammar, and high school. According to Clark, at the next school board election in 1853, public school opponents "made a zealous and persistent fight against re-election of the outgoing members, placing a ticket representing their views in the field," but they were soundly defeated by sitting board members.[49]

Because of the increasing enrollment in the city's public schools and the system's popularity, the school board made changes in 1854 to allow for better management and extension of the school system. Rather than relying entirely on the school board to oversee the schools, the board created the office of superintendent of schools, divided the city and county into school districts, and began establishing more schools to cater to more of the region's children. While the school board rejoiced in the schools' popularity, in Mobile public schools, like many across the South, some departments charged tuition. The primary and intermediate schools remained free, but the junior and senior high schools charged tuition. However, in Clark's words, "The rates charged, however, were so much lower than the charges for private schools that they did not seem at all onerous, and, as permits to attend the schools without charge were freely given to all pupils whose parents were unable to pay tuition for them, the means of acquiring a good education were brought, for the first time in Mobile, or Alabama, within the reach of all classes in the community." While the distinction between paying and poor students remained, Clark insists, "The schools attained so high a character, both with regard to discipline and thoroughness of instruction, that the rich soon sought them for their children in preference to sending them to the best private schools the city afforded."[50]

The schools in Mobile thrived; when the legislature instituted statewide public schools in 1854, it exempted Mobile County from the laws governing the state system, allowing schools there to continue to function independently. This action was similar to that taken by the Louisiana legislature, which took pains not to disrupt New Orleans's system when it instituted the provision of statewide education. Another indication of the progress of the city's schools came that year when the city suspended all education allocations to parochial schools, feeling confident that the public schools conducted in Barton Academy met the city's needs. In the 1850s the school's revenue increased throughout the decade, allowing the school board to lower tuition prices continually and expand the number of students attending free of charge. William F. Perry, the state's first superintendent of education, praised the city for its educational progress, noting that its system, which remained separate from the rest of the state, was in a "most flourishing condition." Perry complimented the city's school board, who "exhibited an energy and public spirit worthy of the highest commendation." He believed that the city's schools were "rapidly extending to every class of society."[51] The presence of able school administrators, like the ones in New Orleans, contributed to the success of the city's schools.

Mobile's school system progressed rapidly in the last decade before the Civil War. Although not as advanced as those in New Orleans, the schools there offered an affordable education to children who might not have otherwise attended school. As in the Crescent City, residents flocked to the public schools established in Mobile. The 1853 vote on selling Barton Academy reveals that city dwellers wanted a true public school in the city, and their patronage of that school showed their commitment to support such institutions.

Like both Alabama and Louisiana, Mississippi's urban areas were the first to establish public schools in that state. Prominently displayed on a historical marker in front of Franklin Academy in Columbus, Mississippi, are the words: "State's oldest free school. Has functioned since 1821. Worthy trustees, using 16th section income & employing able teachers, early made Columbus a cultural center in northeast Mississippi." The town of Columbus, located on the Tombigbee River, housed the third largest river port in Mississippi and served as the principal commercial center in the eastern part of the state. Incorporated in 1821, Franklin Academy was built upon the township's sixteenth section and supported by income from leases on town property. "Consequently, Columbus was distinguished from other southern towns by having a tuition-free public school for its white children, a school that lays claim to being the oldest of its kind in the Cotton Kingdom," notes one historian. In 1837 the school enrolled 100 girls and 150 boys, with separate newly built buildings for both.[52]

The town of Jackson, which would become the state's capital during the antebellum period, also established public schools prior to the Civil War, although unlike Columbus it could not boast of free schools. In his

1844 inaugural address, Jackson mayor John P. Oldham recommended the city establish a free school "for the education of poor, orphan children and others whose parents are unable to educate them." Four months later the city's aldermen passed a resolution that a common school be established within the city. Nineteen months later when still no such school existed, twenty-nine city residents, appointed by Governor Albert G. Brown, formed themselves into the Jackson School Association. This group petitioned the legislature for the donation of lots on which to build a school, which it did in 1846. That year the town built two brick buildings, each with a capacity to hold fifty students, which became the Jackson Male and Female Academies. These schools, like others across the South, charged tuition ($1.50–2.00 per month) unless students presented a certificate of need for free education from the county clerk.[53]

While public schools existed in both Columbus and Jackson, the main urban center in antebellum Mississippi remained the thriving river town of Natchez, which unsurprisingly boasted the largest public school system in antebellum Mississippi. Created in 1845, the Natchez Institute has been called by one scholar "the most ambitious undertaking of the city government and one of the most successful public schools in the Old South." In the months prior to its establishment, a spirited discussion on the value of public schools appeared in the city's newspapers. One citizen wrote to Natchez newspapers proposing an entire plan for public education in the city. In February 1845, another concerned citizen expressed his disappointment with the city's elected officials for failing to take any steps toward establishing a public school in the city, although they had pledged to do so during the campaign and had at that time been in office for over a month. The writer scoffed that the selectmen's promises regarding public education no doubt helped them win election. Public opinion was aroused, and Natchez residents demanded that their elected officials take steps to establish a public school in the town. Less than a week later, a plea to establish a public free school in Natchez ran in the *Mississippi Free Trader and Natchez Gazette*. The same paper excitedly reported on the "munificent donation" of Alvarez Fisk. Fisk, a leading merchant in the town, donated a lot in the city along with the buildings on it for the establishment of a public school. According to the newspaper, "It is the most suitable and convenient location for Public Schools that could be found in the whole city, and may be prepared, at a small expense, to accommodate a thousand pupils, with separate rooms for various classes, affording the people of Natchez an opportunity to establish a system of Free Schools under the most favorable auspices." In a letter to city officials conveying the property, Fisk stipulated that it "be used solely and entirely for the accommodation of Free Schools forever," and that all white children of Natchez, boys and girls, be allowed to attend free of charge.[54]

In the same article announcing Fisk's donation, the newspaper's editor carefully addressed opposition to public schools. According to the editor, "the only objection in the mind of any one as to the immediate adoption of the public school system" concerned increased taxation. Aside from the inherent value of education, which the editor believed more than justified increasing taxes, he also pointed out the comparatively low taxation rate of residents in Natchez and highlighted the many benefits public schools would bring to the city. Citing the case of New Orleans, the editor assured readers that a public free school would lead people to move into the city to gain access to its school, and that higher rents and increased property values would follow.[55]

Another concerned citizen wrote the newspaper echoing the editor's sentiments, insisting "it is now easily demonstrable, that 'public schools,' if established by taxation, not only will save money to the city, but will increase the business, and enhance the prosperity of the town." The writer listed a number of reasons why free public schools would benefit the city, including a belief that they would lead to increasing population, and in turn, a spike in rents; and would lead to higher profits for property owners. He also argued that schools would bring more laborers to the city as well as capitalists who would invest their money in city projects. According to the writer, "An increase of population would have the direct result of creating an increased demand for labor in its different branches; and the profits of labor would furnish the laborer with the means of contributing, by supplying his own wants, to the prosperity to men in every department of business and of trade." He closed with the plea to property-owners to support public schools as an important investment in the city's future prosperity.[56]

City officials could not ignore public demands for government-supported schools. The clamor by residents as evidenced in the town's newspapers revealed that the population insisted on public schools, forcing elected officials to act. In response to demands, the city's selectmen called a public meeting at city hall to discuss the issue of establishing a school and passing a tax for its support. At this meeting, a resolution passed allowing city officials to begin a school in the building donated by Fisk, levy a city tax to finance the school, and establish a board of visitors appointed by the city's selectmen that would oversee the functioning of the school.[57] As in New Orleans and Mobile, the actions of a well-respected and affluent citizen helped spur the establishment of a public school in Natchez. In New Orleans, Samuel J. Peters and Joshua Baldwin crafted the legislation to get the legal framework for such a school in place. In Mobile, Silas Dinsmore and Henry Hitchcock donated their own money as well as procuring donations from others to build Barton Academy. And in Natchez, the donations of Alvarez Fisk prompted the municipal government to establish a public school for the city's children. The actions of these few men sparked the establishment of schools in the urban areas of the South and initiated a commitment to providing schools for city children.

Opponents to the establishment of public free schools in Natchez seemed only to object to the increased taxation to support such an institution. Interestingly, Lucy Neal objected to the increased tax rate in general because she believed that "such a tax might be regarded as oppressive and unjust by two classes of our taxable people—white bachelors and persons of color." Neal went on to explain that she felt no sympathy for bachelors who could only blame themselves that they had no children to send to school. But since black children were prohibited from attending school, Neal felt that free black adults should be exempted from paying taxes to support the schools—an interesting point not often considered in discussions of public schools in the antebellum South.[58]

Despite concerns over taxation, by 1849 the school's board of supervisors bragged in its annual report about the success of the school. The school enjoyed a substantial enrollment of 555 students—300 boys and 255 girls. The ages of the pupils are shown in Table 4.5 below. Despite the large number of students enrolled, the board of supervisors complained about the average attendance of those students. Observing that in 1847 absences had been limited to one in fifteen students, they noted that in 1849 the number of absences had increased to one in five students. While a yellow fever epidemic struck the city soon after the start of the fall term, keeping students from going to school, the board did not pause before laying the blame with parents for allowing their children to miss so many days of school, asserting, "There can be no necessity for the absence of so great a number in Natchez. There is fault somewhere, and we do not hesitate to place it to the account of the parents." Parents' "injudicious indulgence" of their children clearly disappointed the board, but they also pointed out that despite the large number of absences, attendance at the Natchez Institute still outpaced that of Boston public schools.[59]

Table 4.5: Number of Students by Age Attending Natchez Institute, 1849

Age	# of Students	Age	# of Students	Age	# of Students
6	80	11	52	16	7
7	75	12	38	17	2
8	75	13	50	18	1
9	69	14	19	—	—
10	72	15	15	—	—
		TOTAL NUMBER OF STUDENTS			
Ages 6–10	371	Ages 11–15	174	Ages 16–18	10
	TOTAL STUDENTS ATTENDING, ALL AGES		555		

Source: *Fourth Annual Report of the Board of Visitors of the Natchez Institute: Also, the Report of the Board of Examiners. July 4th, 1849* (Natchez, MS: Printed at the Courier Book and Job Office, 1849), 4–5.

The board of supervisors believed that the Natchez Institute compared favorably with Boston public schools, not only in regard to attendance, but also when it came to expenses. The supervisors reported in 1849 that it cost about $7,000 per year to run the school. Looking at figures for the number of children of school age in Boston versus the amount of money spent on public schools there may make it appear that Boston conducted its schools more efficiently, but the board pointed out that those numbers were misleading. One must consider the number of children attending school and the amount of money spent to support those schools to get an accurate idea of the cost per child. According to the board, when comparing the number of students in public schools with the amount of money expended to run those schools, Natchez spent twenty cents less per pupil than Boston.[60] Clearly the board of supervisors included such a comparison in order to dispute the contention that the school could be conducted more efficiently.

Rather than focusing on cutting costs, the board pleaded for an addition to the public school system in Natchez—a normal school to train teachers. Insisting that such a school proved necessary to train competent instructors and pointing out that the state suffered from a dearth of teachers, the board insisted that the addition of such a school was vital to the continued success of the Natchez Institute and other public schools across the state. Not only did the board lobby for a normal school in the state, but it wanted that school located in Natchez, explaining "that the most eligible situation for a State Normal school, is Natchez, must be obvious to the slightest reflection." The presence of the largest public school in the state, a large number of students and teachers, the availability of schoolrooms and instruments, a large library, many private schools and seminaries, as well as the health of the city were all mentioned as reasons a normal school should be located in Natchez.[61]

The report closed by emphasizing the importance of public schools in general and praising the progress of the Natchez Institute in particular. Interestingly, included with the 1849 report of the board of supervisors is a report of the board of examiners that differs considerably in tone. While the board of supervisors praised the progress of the school, the examiners focused on suggestions for improvement, making the report more critical in nature. Their main complaint centered on the fact that not all students were tested in each subject, but only certain students examined in particular subjects. The examiners also pointed out the problem of having only one teacher in charge of sixty-six young boys "just from the nursery" (ages six and up).[62]

The examiners also found fault with the textbooks used. Rather than engage in a lengthy explanation of the problem, they merely included an excerpt from *The Grammatic Reader,* № 1 and № 2, used to teach children six to ten years old:

Example 1: "A predication is an association of words, forming a complete proposition. The predications are divided into intransitive—intransitive post adjective—intransitive post substantive—transitive and passive."

Example 2: "The prepositional gerundive phrases are divided into intransitive—intransitive post adjective—intransitive post substantive—transitive and passive."

Example 3: "This youth was delighted with the prospect of becoming a farmer." This is defined to be "an intransitive post-substantive prepositional gerundive phrase."

This may be "easy Grammar," but it would seem enough to make a child of eight years old cry out "Help me, Cassius, or I sink!"

Such advanced lessons for elementary grammar no doubt stumped many children, but they also reveal the high expectations held by teachers in the Natchez Institute. Assuming that comparable standards applied to all grade levels, the children who mastered their coursework at the institute no doubt exited with a thorough and complete education.

Despite offering constructive criticism, the examiners closed with praise for the school and especially the teachers it employed. The progress of the school continued so that in 1856 the school enrolled 856 students. The supervisors marveled at the success of the school, which then encompassed fourteen schoolrooms, a library, and a large exhibition hall, noting that "if the progress in all things had been as great as in this, during the last twelve years, Natchez would have been the first city on the Mississippi River." The board of examiners concurred in their annual report of the same year, noting "that, which was once regarded as a hazardous tax upon the people, and which cautious men feared might prove a failure, is now part of the settled policy of the city, bearing equally upon all, and distributing its benefits alike to all. How wisely it was planned, and how judiciously it has been conducted, it is easy to perceive; for it has met its largest promise; retained the confidence of its patrons, and given such an impulse to public education, as to place us far in advance of other portions of the State." The problem earlier cited of only examining certain children in certain subjects had been abandoned, with all children in each class taking exams in each subject. The examiners reported favorably on every class conducted by the school.[63]

The board of supervisors continued to lament the casual attendance of many students, but also insisted that such was the case in public schools across the country and that the situation in Natchez proved in no way unique. Another complaint voiced was that parents took boys out of school altogether at too early an age in order for them to begin working. Such a problem did not arise with female students, who were left to complete their studies, with the result that "the females of our country generally are better educated than the men." The supervisors insisted, "It is an evil of serious import. We do not complain of women knowing too much, but the men of too little. . . . Every facility is rendered to the boys, necessary to make them fine scholars. If any persevere in their determination to be stupid, they will have their way. We will endeavor to teach the ladies how to take care of them."[84]

As in the other major urban centers in the Gulf South, the establishment of public schools came from the demands of the population. The heated debate over the best method to institute schools and the criticism leveled at the town's elected officials forced action on the subject. The schools established there quickly enrolled large numbers and attracted praise from residents, revealing that public schools were created through community insistence and sustained through local support.

The school systems in New Orleans, Mobile, and Natchez shared similar characteristics that contributed to their success. Most obviously, the concentrated population offered by urban areas meant that the schools did not have to overcome the hurdle of sparse settlement, which plagued the establishment of schools in the rural South. More pupils and teachers concentrated in urban areas, and they enjoyed a much larger tax base upon which the city governments could draw to support the institutions financially. The benefits offered by the concentrated populations of these urban areas cannot be overemphasized in explaining the success of public schools in New Orleans, Mobile, and Natchez.

In addition to the advantages inherent in an urban setting, in each of the three cities prominent citizens took the lead in organizing the schools. This fact means that while some residents might question the value of public schools, the school systems had powerful and influential proponents to speak out in their favor. In New Orleans, Mobile, and Natchez, leading merchants and politicians not only lobbied for the creation of public schools, but took an active role in their supervision by serving on school boards or in other advisory roles.

Additionally, the city governments stepped in to fill the void left by the legislatures. In all three states, while the legislatures admitted that the state governments bore responsibility for helping to educate their youngest citizens, they all vested authority over school matters in the local governments. The states did very little to ensure the success of public schools—they appropriated an insufficient amount of money, and they offered little or no guidance or regulations on how to conduct the schools. But in New Orleans, Mobile, and Natchez, the city governments stepped in to take the reins. They appropriated additional money and created committees to supervise the schools and report on their progress. These committees interviewed teaching applicants, made decisions on books and other teaching tools, and attended the annual examinations of students. Without such consistent supervision, it is unlikely that the schools would have progressed in the same manner.

City governments would not have acted, however, without the insistence of residents. It was the local populations who demanded action, and officials responded to their pleas. The implementation of proposals for urban schools came as a result of pressure from citizens, and they thrived because local residents supported them. Patronized by local families and supervised by leading citizens, the schools in New Orleans, Mobile, and Natchez attracted attention from the rest of the South and were important in leading residents in rural areas to demand public schools of their own.

The school systems established in the urban centers of the Gulf South progressed up until the time of the Civil War. According to one beaming state official in New Orleans, "She wields the two mighty levers that move the world—commerce and education—and by her enlightened liberality in the cause of universal education, no less than by her energy and success in commercial pursuits, she deservedly takes the first rank among all the cities of the South." Throughout the state as well as throughout the nation, many took notice of the city's flourishing free schools. Not only instituting successful grade schools but also night schools, a normal department, an extensive public library as well as public lyceum and lecture series, the New Orleans school system rapidly became one of the major accomplishments of the city.[65]

The New Orleans school system offered a powerful and promising example to the rest of the Gulf South. The Natchez Institute, for instance, initially replicated the system established in New Orleans. According to school officials, "The first Board of Visitors were glad to adopt the rules, regulations, and organization, of the New Orleans schools, almost entirely." After getting the school off the ground, however, officials altered their school organization to better suit their particular needs. In 1856, they noted: "Now, and for years past, we have an organization peculiarly our own. Adapted to our own wants, as fitly, as those of any other city." In 1858 the Natchez Institute again reorganized, dividing the school into primary, grammar, and high school divisions.[66]

Like Natchez, New Orleans and Mobile continually altered and improved their school systems so that on the eve of the Civil War, schools in all three cities were thriving, witnessing increased enrollments, receiving large numbers of teaching applicants, and offering more advanced courses. While these cities enjoyed many advantages over the predominantly rural areas that made up the rest of the Gulf South, residents outside of the urban centers began to demand public schools in their areas during the 1840s and 1850s. The example of urban schools, along with the spread of Jacksonian democracy and the economic recovery following the Panic of 1837, would combine to lead residents to insist that their elected officials make good on their promise to promote education. All three states would do so before the eve of the Civil War.

CHAPTER FIVE

The Culmination of
Antebellum Education Initiatives

THE ESTABLISHMENT OF STATEWIDE PUBLIC
SCHOOL SYSTEMS IN THE GULF SOUTH

Each with an example of successful public schools in their major urban centers, the Gulf South states of Louisiana, Mississippi, and Alabama took steps to advance educational opportunities for all white children. Previous attempts to aid schools led residents in all three states to the realization that practical improvements in education demanded more comprehensive legislation. Once the Gulf South recovered from the Panic of 1837, the states of Louisiana, Mississippi, and Alabama passed laws to establish comprehensive public school systems.

Each of the states began making provisions to encourage education immediately upon organizing governments. Even before becoming a state, Louisiana's territorial government enacted education statutes and both Mississippi and Alabama pledged to support schools in their original state constitutions. The 1820s and 1830s were decades of experimentation in education policy, with each state passing laws to encourage and support education, but not yet instituting statewide school systems. Efforts on behalf of education faltered when the Panic of 1837 descended upon the South with a vengeance. The rise of cotton prices after the mid-1840s presaged an economic recovery in the Gulf South. As economic fortunes advanced, constituents in all three states began to demand action from their legislators on public education. The groundswell of popular demand for public schools would force all three governments to act in the 1840s and 1850s, bringing statewide school systems into existence for the first time.

Three fundamental adjustments emerged to create a climate for legislative action. Steady economic recovery in the aftermath of the Panic of 1837 offered potential access to funding not previously available. Additionally, the presence of thriving public systems in the major urban areas of all three states provided both an impetus and a roadmap for establishing public schools. In addition, the spread of Jacksonian democracy led middling southerners to demand inclusion in areas of privilege not previously offered to the less wealthy—including schooling. In earlier decades many viewed learning as something to be purchased and therefore a privilege of the elite who could afford it; in the 1840s southerners began to see access to education as a right of citizenship, and they demanded that their state governments provide it. Just as the push for white manhood suffrage sought to grant a larger segment of the population access to voting rights, southerners agitated for greater access to schooling, arguing that the state governments should step in to provide more schools at lower costs than what was currently available. This impulse is evident in Mississippi, where the Adams County Education Association met in 1838 to discuss "what are the difficulties that exist in the way of the establishment of permanent Literary Institutions in the South-west, how they may best be obviated."[1]

In the 1840s, a lively debate unfolded in the pages of the *Mississippi Free Trader and Natchez Gazette* over how best to establish a statewide public school system.[2] Natchez itself established a public school in 1845, so it is not surprising that that development would spark interest in expanding public education. But rather than the establishment of a public school there eliciting interest in education, the interest in education revealed by letters to the editor of that paper preceded the establishment of the public school known as the Natchez Institute. It was the agitation of the citizenry for a public school that led to the establishment of such a school. A correspondent labeling himself "P." wrote to the paper in February of 1845 about his disgust that the board of selectmen for the city of Natchez, elected on a platform promising to establish a public school there, had not yet acted to do so even though they had been in office for over a month. It is only after P.'s lively debate unfolded in the newspaper with another correspondent known as "Q." on the best system of schools, that city officials acted to establish a public school. Throughout the South, public officials acted to organize schools only when the citizens demanded it.[3]

In Louisiana, thriving free public schools in New Orleans stood both as evidence that such institutions could prosper and as a challenge to the rest of the state to attempt to provide such schools for rural children. Watching the schools in the Crescent City increase in enrollment and achievement each year, inhabitants in the rest of the state began to agitate for schools within reach of their own children. Although the state government passed legislation in 1841 authorizing the Crescent City to establish free schools, it did little else to support or maintain the schools. New Orleans schools thrived as a result of the support they received from the city's leading citizens and the municipal government, not as a result of legislation. Although Louisiana had instituted measures to support education across the state as early as 1821, the provisions had not yet yielded free public schools. As the 1840s progressed, popular agitation would finally force reforms that ultimately brought a statewide system of public schools into existence.

In combination with the impetus provided by the successful example of New Orleans schools, a more democratic mood swept through Louisiana, with citizens across the state demanding more from their government. Louisianians began agitating for democratic reforms to the state's organic law—changes that would have dramatic consequences for public education. The spread of Jacksonian politics led many citizens to question the political status quo, as did the movement of settlers into the state from regions with more democratic traditions. Although in the late 1830s the state senate twice managed to block efforts of the lower house to call a constitutional convention, by the mid-1840s the measure could no longer be thwarted. The 1844 popular vote on the calling of a constitutional convention revealed widespread support for a new constitution, with nearly 80 percent of voters favoring a convention. Democrats led the drive for a new constitution; the Whigs, though clearly less enthusiastic about the prospect, found it hard to oppose a measure that such a large portion of the population embraced. At the convention the two parties agreed on certain basic measures—universal white manhood suffrage, reapportionment, and an increase in the number of elective offices. Beyond these main points, however, the two parties split, with Democrats pushing for more reform and Whigs resisting their efforts. When the document finally reached Louisiana's voters, it was heartily endorsed by a large margin who favored adopting the new constitution.[4]

The resulting 1845 constitution democratized Louisiana's political system, curbing the power of wealthy legislators, taking steps to prevent common abuses of office, protecting civil liberties, and granting a much larger segment of the state's population the right to vote and seek office by abrogating property qualifications. As one historian explains, "the new constitution fulfilled the democratic aspirations of the vast majority of Louisianians" and gained the overwhelming support of the majority of Louisiana's voters. In addition to reforms of state law, the new constitution also mandated free public education for the entire state, a step that conscientious officials and ordinary citizens had been urging for decades. Many reveled in the promises offered by the new constitutional requirements. Isaac Johnson, elected governor in 1846, characterized such optimism when he proclaimed "that provision of the new Constitution, which adopts the Free Public School System, is destined, under judicious legislation to become a principle of light to the people, which, like the burning bush on Horeb, will burn and consume not: It is the dawning of a new and happy era in the history of Louisiana—there must be Free Public Schools—sayeth the Constitution."[5]

When delegates to the constitutional convention debated adding an educational provision to the state's organic law, they revealed their proclivities and assumptions about the role of the government in providing education to its citizens. The education committee passionately argued for free schools across the state, and many delegates spoke up to demand that the constitution ensure such schools. Preston Kenner, a Whig from rural Ascension Parish, argued that requiring the legislature to "encourage" schools was not enough; he wanted the language to read that the legislature would "establish throughout the State a system of free schools, for the education of all the children of the people of the State," and "raise the means for [their] maintenance and support." The debate that followed Kenner's suggestions led delegates from the state's urban center to take divergent positions based on party affiliation. Isaac T. Preston, a Democrat from Jefferson Parish near New Orleans, spoke against Kenner's plan to require the legislature to establish free schools. Preston argued that although he was "as great a friend to public education as any one," he believed that the legislature should be left to act on public schools as it saw fit, since "they had always shown great solicitude upon the subject." Modern scholars wonder if the legislative chamber guffawed at the blatant hypocrisy of Mr. Preston's statement. His contention provoked a sharp rebuke from Christian Roselius, a Whig delegate from Orleans Parish. Roselius railed against the previous action of the legislature, which in 1843 diverted the funds from the federal government's appropriation for a seminary of learning, instead using the income to pay off the state debt. He decried that the legislature "laid their sacriligeous [sic] hands upon this donation," and bemoaned that "the act consummating this outrage will remain a perpetual blot upon our statute books! I cannot find words to express my utter abhorrence and detestation of that act." Roselius went on to insist, "We should take warning for the future and place it beyond the power of the legislature to abstract the means exclusively belonging to education to any other purpose."[6]

The exchange reveals that rather than a divide between country and city, the debate over education in the 1845 constitutional convention pitted Whigs against Democrats. This split was in line with national trends, where the Whig Party endorsed government involvement in internal improvements and other such programs, and the Democrats wanted to keep government limited in power and involvement in people's lives. Yet it is interesting to note that while the Democrats opposed including a mandate for public schools, the constitution that instituted such a requirement is generally remembered as a Democratic document, with the 1852 constitution credited to the Whigs. Indeed, the provisions for public education in the 1852 constitution are often heralded as proof of its Whig authorship, but it merely repeated the clause of the 1845 document. Such a shorthand method of labeling the constitutions as "Whig" or "Democrat" obscures the important role of both parties in creating the documents.[7]

The finished product included Kenner's demand that the constitution require the legislature not merely to encourage schools, but to establish them. In order to fulfill its constitutional obligation, the Louisiana legislature passed a free school act on May 3, 1847, "to establish Free Public Schools in the State of Louisiana." The law established an entirely new administration to manage the public schools, headed by a state superintendent appointed by the governor. The statute also mandated a superintendent for each parish to be elected by the voters. Funding for the new system was derived from a mill and poll tax as well as proceeds from the sale of sixteenth section lands, which the US Congress allocated for the support of schools. The law explicitly intended for all white inhabitants between the ages of six and sixteen to attend school free of charge, while those older than sixteen but under the age of twenty-one could attend for at least two years. Police juries, the governing council of each parish, were directed to divide their parishes into school districts, and each parish received an appropriation from the state based on the number of school-age children residing therein.[8]

This act finally instituted wholly public free schools in Louisiana. Since no students were meant to pay tuition, no child in the state would be denied the benefit of schooling due to their inability to pay, and no distinction between pupils based on wealth would occur. State officers rejoiced in this provision, feeling certain that the democratic equality newly pronounced in the constitution would soon be exhibited in public schools across the state. Most officials believed that the problems inherent in the old system had been abolished, noting that "there can no longer a pretext exist for that vague, vacillating and improvident Legislation, which has, heretofore, disgraced our Statute Books on the subject." The legislature believed the new system of public education, fostered and maintained by the state, would work toward the benefit of all of Louisiana's inhabitants. As the state superintendent remarked in his first annual report to the legislature, "There is, in the great mass of our rural population, a yearning after the day, when they will have an opportunity of redeeming their children from the blighting touch of ignorance, which has been heretofore laid upon them and which even now threatens the expectancy of the State."[9]

The office of state superintendent served as a much needed addition to the school system. Unlike the previous post, which simply added a few requirements to the secretary of state's responsibilities, the new officer dedicated the entire year to the management of the school system. The law required the state superintendent to apportion school funds to each parish, receive reports from local officials, visit schools during the course of the year, and report annually to the legislature on school conditions. Governors enjoyed the prerogative of appointing the state superintendent, and most executives selected experienced education professionals. Alexander Dimitry, a longtime member of the school board of the Third Municipality of New Orleans, was the first to hold the post. Since New Orleans public schools were prospering, Dimitry's acquaintance with its system would prove beneficial to the new state program. The appointment of a New Orleans school official to this significant post heralded hope for the state, for if the successful methods instituted in the Crescent City could be extended to the rest of Louisiana, the state would be able to boast one of the most efficient public school systems in the nation. Unfortunately, such hopes would remain unrealized in many parts of Louisiana throughout the antebellum period.[10]

The axis through which the school system functioned centered on the working relationship between Dimitry and the corresponding parish superintendents. As specified in the 1847 statute, each parish elected a superintendent to oversee their local schools and handle all administrative tasks. The parish superintendent maintained public education funds and dispensed them throughout the parish to the various school districts. All correspondence—legal, financial, and otherwise—between the state office and the locale went through the parish superintendent. In addition, the law expected this officer to examine and certify teachers to be employed by the public schools.[11]

Under this legislation, which lasted until 1852, public schools began to operate throughout the state. Conditions differed from parish to parish, with some areas instituting successful schools that served large numbers of children while other locales had trouble procuring accommodations, finding teachers, and attracting students. But despite the obstacles faced in many parishes, no one could deny that the new system of education represented a dramatic improvement from the previous state-funded system. Even where officials encountered opposition and pessimism among residents, all remained hopeful that the new system would soon win converts to its cause and that education in the rest of the state would progress in the same successful manner initiated in New Orleans. As Superintendent Dimitry described his visits to the various parishes throughout the state, "In many an humble cabin, whilst suggesting bright hopes for the future, he has been made the depository of many a bitter regret for the past. In the course of his inspection he has encountered many a doubt to satisfy, many an opposition to subdue, and many a prejudice to overcome; but he has also been cheered by the manifestations of zeal and indications of support."[12]

Under the new guidelines public education progressed slowly; in 1848, one year after the passage of the free public school act, police juries in only nineteen parishes had organized school districts. Out of 49,048 children in the state between six and sixteen years of age, 2,160, or 4.4 percent, attended seventy-eight public schools established throughout the state. By 1849, however, 704 public schools operated for an average of six months a year, though in different parishes the length of school terms ranged from four to eleven months. In 1849 enrollment in reporting parishes climbed to 16,217 students, amounting to 56 percent of the school-age population in those areas. Clearly, public schools were finally beginning to make progress in the rural parishes of the state. As the Assumption Parish superintendent explained in 1851, "the general condition of the schools is good and improving. Many who were indifferent on the subject of public education are becoming more zealous, and the desire to have their children educated is becoming general. Much good has been effected during my administration, and the schools being well organized, their progress must be onward."[13]

The increased number of schools and students following the passage of the 1847 school law revealed the success of Louisiana's statewide school system. The following table includes attendance figures for the parishes that submitted information to the state superintendent of education, excluding the urban areas of Orleans and Jefferson Parishes. Such numbers prove that Louisiana's inhabitants embraced the new public schools. Noting the inefficiency of the previous school system, one parish superintendent reported, "Before, the parish had no more than three or four stinted schools, which hardly could stand the ground." He went on to explain that the new school system produced "a very satisfactory result, very. It must rejoice the friends of Free Public Schools; it is a triumph for those who have faith in the doctrine of progress; it will cheer up the hearts of those who have little faith in it, and are despondent."[14]

Table 5.1: Number of Children Attending Public Schools in Louisiana

Year	# of Parishes Reporting	# of Schools	# of Reported Children Attending School	# of Reported Children Not Attending School	% of Reported Children Attending School
1848	19	78	2,160	46,888	4.4%
1849	37	704	16,217	12,724	56%
1851	45	683	22,100	18,295	55%

Source: "Report of the State Superintendent of Education," *Louisiana Legislative Documents,* 1848, 5; ibid., 1849, 2; ibid., 1851, 6–48. Data for the year 1850 are not available.

As in Louisiana, the same time period in Mississippi witnessed new agitation on behalf of public education. Throughout the 1840s, Mississippi governors lobbied the legislature to take action to spread free schools across the state. Unlike in Louisiana, Mississippi did not need the impetus from a new constitution to spark the state government's actions on public schools; Mississippi's original constitution mandated state support of education. In 1840 Governor Alexander G. McNutt reminded the state's legislators of that provision, imploring them, "I again call your attention to that clause of the Constitution which enjoins upon us the encouragement of schools, and requires us to provide the means of education." McNutt served as an important lobbyist in favor of school reform. He carefully studied the condition of schools in the state and sent out circulars to the presidents of all the schools engaging them on the current education situation as well as their suggestions for reform. From their responses, which he passed on to the legislature, he concluded, "The correspondence satisfactorily establishes the fact, that education can be afforded as cheap in this State as elsewhere." The governor then called the legislators' attention to the revised statutes prepared by General P. Rutilius R. Pray. There Pray offered a plan for a "complete system of public instruction in free schools, academies, colleges and in a State University," based on the experience of other states. Most importantly, according to McNutt, Pray pointed out the necessity for an annual tax to support the schools. While opposition to increased taxation was expected, the governor insisted that the value of an educated populace would benefit the entire state, even those with no children or who preferred to patronize private schools.[15]

McNutt's pleas nonetheless went unheeded. In 1844 his successor, Tilghman Tucker, prodded the legislature to take action to establish free schools across the state. Tucker chided the legislators for failing to do more for education earlier, despite the arrangements put in place by the federal government to use sixteenth section lands to support schools. He argued that "the legislature has heretofore entrusted this important subject to the management and to the voluntary contributions of the citizens of the state." Tucker called on politicians to end their neglect of education and to lend it their pecuniary support in order to establish a system of schools across the state. The governor suggested the organization of a free primary school in every township with a new tax to support the schools for a minimum of six months each year. It is interesting that Tucker chose to use his last address to the legislature as governor to lobby so passionately for schools: "Although the suggestion may be considered rash, even indiscreet, by some, yet as this message will in all probability, be the last official act which I shall have the honor to perform in the legislative councils of the state, I feel under the most sacred obligations to present the subject [of public education], so as not to be misunderstood, and to urge its consummation." Clearly he hoped his efforts on behalf of education would be part of the legacy he left to the state. Yet like the pleas of his predecessor, Tucker's admonitions would go unheeded, and his successor would also feel compelled to lobby in support of schools.[16]

This trend of governors lobbying state politicians to do more to facilitate schools, and the failure of legislators to act, held true across the Gulf South. Several key factors contributed to legislative inaction. In the early 1840s, southern states were still recovering from the economic collapse of 1837, allowing politicians to bemoan a lack of funds to support schools. Additionally, the concept of education as the responsibility of the state had yet to take hold in the South. While certain public-spirited men did want the government to ensure access to education for all children, many did not. Historian Edward Knight wrote a very early history of education in the South, published in 1922, which despite its age still provides useful insight into the establishment of school systems there. Knight argues that two important principles had to take hold before free schools could be established on a large scale. First, residents had to accept "the democratic principle that education is the function of the State rather than a family or a parental obligation and that the responsibility of providing the means of education rests primarily with the State." Although Mississippi's and Alabama's constitutions pledged them to support schools, and in spite of the grant of the federal government of the sixteenth section lands to be used for that purpose, many still balked at state control of education. Next, Knight cites the belief that "the State has the right and the power to raise by taxation on the property of its members sufficient funds for adequate school support." He credits the establishment of permanent public school endowments as helping public opinion to shift in favor of schools as a public concern.[17]

In Mississippi, public sentiment began to shift in the mid-1840s. According to historian Edward Mayes, "about the year 1844, stirred by the tide of immigration and the growing illiteracy in the State, and perhaps by the agitation of the sixteenth section question, the general subject of common school education began to attract far more attention than ever before." Mayes credits Albert G. Brown for his efforts on behalf of public education, arguing that "too much praise can hardly be accorded to this gentleman for his unflagging interest in the subject of education." As a candidate for governor in 1843, Brown spoke in favor of free schools for all white children and he continued to lobby for education once in office. Historian Dunbar Rowland cites Brown as "perhaps the most popular man in the State—and the acknowledged leader of the Democracy." In his second inaugural address as governor given in 1846, Brown offered a plan for public schools across the state. He did so only after mature deliberation and careful investigation of the current state of schools in Mississippi, contacting town trustees and local politicians, as well as examining the methods implemented in other states by corresponding with school and political officials across the country.[18]

In his 1846 inaugural, Brown laid out a very detailed plan for free common schools in Mississippi. He suggested that a school fund of $250,000 be set aside, $200,000 of which would be a permanent fund. The governor calculated the interest he believed that fund would earn, and suggested a particular sum be designated to support a state college with the remainder going to lower schools. Brown urged the establishment of ten high schools, which would annually receive $800 from the state. He stressed the importance of secondary schools in preparing students to enter college and insisted that it was futile for the legislature to support a college without also supporting high schools.[19]

After elucidating his plan for upper schools, Brown moved on to his plan for common schools. He criticized the previous treatment of sixteenth section lands, which he believed Congress had wisely set apart for common schools but which had been mistreated and neglected in Mississippi. Many townships failed to sell their sixteenth sections, so that no revenue accrued to support schools, while many that had sold their sections failed to use the money generated to hire a teacher or operate a school. In other areas, squatters inhabited the land or illegally cut and sold the timber thereon, with no benefit to the school fund whatsoever. Brown wanted the state to take charge of the various sixteenth sections and the money they generated and to appoint local officials who would report to a state education officer to ensure compliance with the laws. He urged the election of school commissioners in each county who together would serve as a board that would oversee the sixteenth section lands, and he urged the appointment of a state school commissioner who would supervise and direct the work of local officials. The county commissioners would meet quarterly and use the proceeds from the sixteenth section lands to contract a teacher for the county.[20]

Governor Brown proposed additional revenue to aid in the establishment of schools, including 5 percent of the amount of state and county taxes collected. Also, all fines and forfeitures "other than legitimate taxes on property [would] be relinquished to a fund to be established and called the 'school fund.'" Brown wanted the money in the Literary Fund to be transferred to the school fund, which, with the additional revenue he suggested, he estimated would yield $75,000 annually that could then be used to aid in the establishment of free schools. The money would be apportioned to each county based on its white population and the school commissioners would be responsible for establishing schools. If a particular county fell short of the funds needed to maintain its school, the deficiency would be made up out of the general fund, so that every township would be able to support a free school for at least a portion of the year.[21]

The governor's plan was quite comprehensive and reveals his interest and determination to see schools established in his state that would be accessible to all children. He continued to lobby for free schools following the close of the legislative session and invited Judge John B. Thacher to propose a plan for education in the state. As in Louisiana where state officials looked to New Orleans when establishing a statewide school system, Mississippi politicians likewise looked to Natchez. Thacher, judge of the high court of errors and appeals, was a prominent resident of that town and was intimately familiar with the public school system established there. In response to Brown's request, in 1845 Thacher wrote an open letter to the governor, which Brown presented to the legislature and which many newspapers in Mississippi published. Thacher devoted a considerable portion of his missive to the need for normal schools to train teachers, partly attributing the lack of schools in the state to the dearth of such institutions. It is interesting that Thacher would use this opportunity, meant to solicit his advice on establishing a statewide school system, to lobby for what education proponents in Natchez most wanted for their urban school system—a normal school.[22]

The impetus for politicians to urge education reform came from demands by average citizens who grew tired of watching the government squander public money to support schools with so few tangible benefits for the educational needs of their children. Mayes cites a Democratic Party meeting in June of 1845 where "elaborate resolutions in favor of the establishment of public free schools were adopted," to argue that Mississippians begin to demand a system of free schools during the mid-1840s. Delegates to the state Democratic convention that year were instructed to push education measures through the convention. Whigs, the party traditionally associated with education reform, likewise spoke out in favor of public schools during the legislative campaign that year. That both parties felt compelled to come out in favor of school reform during the campaign reveals its popularity with the state's voters. Likewise, the debate unfolding in Natchez newspapers in 1845 over the best method to establish a public school system reveals the level of interest among the state's voters. Such demands could not be ignored and forced the legislature to act in 1846. The school act of that year instructed the boards of supervisors to appoint five school commissioners for each county, who bore the responsibility of organizing schools and licensing, paying, and supervising instructors. The statute gave control of the sixteenth section funds to the county commissioners and ordered them to lease any remaining lands, as well as requiring them to make semiannual reports to the secretary of state, who was named general commissioner of schools. An initial glance at the 1846 school law may give the impression that the legislature heeded the pleas of public education proponents by allowing a county tax to be levied to support schools. However, the law itself ensured that provision would come to naught by requiring the written consent of a majority of the heads of households in each county for the tax to be levied. Furthermore, the act went on to allow any county to exempt itself from the law altogether if a majority of the heads of households issued a written protest before March of each year. Such a provision no doubt astounds the modern reader. The law required written consent in order to levy a local tax to support public schools. Imagine the difficulty in complying with such a provision, even in areas where support for public schools was high. It boggles the mind that with both parties pledged to assist education, their "support" amounted to so little.[23]

Very soon after the passage of the law, complaints began to surface over the nature of the legislation. In his annual message to the next legislative session, Governor Brown went so far as to request that it be repealed immediately and that an entirely new law be crafted to take its place. Others complained it was "a law which is no law, for it contains within its own bosom the seeds of destruction. It is made a suicide, holding in its own hand the knife to cut its own throat." A protest nullified the law in any given county, and the express written consent had to be garnered before a tax could be levied, leaving the law inoperable in most of the state. Furthermore, the law failed to repeal all previous education statutes, leaving room for discrepancy and conflict.[24]

Governor Brown left for Congress shortly after his message requesting the repeal of the law, and the legislature acted on its own. On March 4, 1848, it passed four statutes on education, each of which applied to a different set of counties. Those counties not encompassed by the special acts of 1848 remained under the 1846 act, leaving five distinct school laws in operation, each of which only applied to a portion of the state. Like governors before him, in his 1850 message to the legislature, Governor Joseph Matthews pleaded for a revamped system of public schools. Basing his comments on the report of the general school commissioner, Matthews assured the state's politicians "that the results of the common school system adopted by the legislature of 1846, if not a total failure, has fallen far short of the expectations of its friends. It is apparent that a more efficient system must be adopted, or the permanent interests of education must languish."[25]

Mississippi's school system remained completely localized throughout the remainder of the antebellum period. Unlike Louisiana, where a state system was instituted, Mississippi allowed local areas to run their public schools as they chose. In the legislative session of 1859–1860, twenty-six different school laws were passed, which pertained to different counties. According to historian Charles William Dabney, "This legislation was local government run riot and it destroyed every trace of a system." Despite the trouble arising from the different laws governing schools in different parts of the state, education nonetheless progressed in Mississippi in the decade leading up to the Civil War. In 1840 the Magnolia State housed 382 common schools with more than eight thousand students. In 1850 the number of schools had increased to 762 with 826 teachers and nearly 19,000 students, while in 1860 it housed 1,116 schools with 1,215 teachers and 30,970 students.[26]

The number of public schools, teachers, and students in Mississippi all increased in the decades preceding the Civil War, but no system of education was adopted by the state as a whole. Legislators catered to local desires and exempted entire swaths of the state from laws to which they objected. Although Mississippi governors tried to offer leadership and guidance, the legislature stifled progress with its pandering. No legislative reformer emerged to champion the cause of education in the state, leaving Mississippi with a broken system as war descended upon the South in 1861.

As with Louisiana and Mississippi, in Alabama the 1840s brought agitation in favor of free public schools. Democratic governor Arthur P. Bagby assumed office in 1837, pledging to support both education and internal improvements. In his message to the legislature in 1840, he urged it to work on behalf of education, if nothing else, arguing that "I have no hesitation in expressing the opinion that Education should be put in advance of every other interest." Despite his urging, action on public schools continued to be put on hold due to the economic depression, while the legislature devoted state funds to other projects. Legislation aimed at raising a school fund or aiding areas with valueless sixteenth sections was continually postponed or reported out of committee as inexpedient during the 1840s. In the legislative session of 1844, politicians debated asking Congress for permission to use the 2 and 3 percent fund for the establishment and support of primary schools. At the time of Alabama's entrance into the Union, Congress set aside 5 percent of the net proceeds of the land it sold within the Alabama Territory for making roads, building canals, and improving river navigation. Three-fifths of this fund was designated for use within the state and two-fifths for roads leading to the state. These moneys were referred to as the 2 and 3 percent funds. Some politicians wanted to use these funds for the support of primary schools rather than other internal improvements. The committee charged with drafting a resolution to petition Congress requesting that the funds be diverted to education reported negatively on the proposal. Their report claimed that the timing was not right, although it included a passionate minority perspective from Democratic state senator Tandy W. Walker. Walker carefully elucidated the large amounts accruing in the accounts for the 2 and 3 percent funds and then made a fervent appeal that the money would garner much more tangible results if spent on education rather than being squandered to improve navigation on remote rivers. The state senate rejected his proposal nineteen to ten, with the votes cast in favor coming from mostly Democratic counties made up of smaller farms. According to historian Forrest Mathews, "The farmers who elected Walker's ten allies cared little for roads, which would assist the planters in marketing their cotton, but favored state educational aid, which would help them build schools in their less prosperous townships."[27]

As late as 1846 the committee on sixteenth sections, while debating how best to fund schools across the state, felt compelled to acknowledge that "the whole system of common schools demands a thorough revision." Throughout the decade legislators debated transferring the sixteenth section funds from individual townships into a general school fund for distribution by the state. The dispute raged throughout the 1840s, with legislators arguing over whether the sixteenth sections had been awarded to the state or to the townships, and whether the state could legally take over the sixteenth sections of the various townships and consolidate the funds into one general account. The topic came up continually, with legislators, governors, and impassioned citizens all coming down on different sides of the argument.[28]

Throughout the 1840s, Alabama governors such as Arthur P. Bagby, Benjamin Fitzpatrick, Joshua Martin, and Reuben Chapman spoke of their support for public schools but insisted that the economic climate prevented them from urging additional funding for schools or from making suggestions for a revamped school system. A few legislators committed to education reform within the state did more, proposing a complete system of schools across Alabama. Not long after Senator Walker made his plea to spend available funding for education rather than internal improvements, state representative Benjamin Porter lobbied for a comprehensive state system of public schools. In 1847 the senate committee on sixteenth sections proposed that the sixteenth section funds that remained in the state bank, then in the process of being liquidated, be distributed back to the individual townships. Mathews points out that this committee was dominated by planters, whose counties enjoyed valuable sixteenth sections and would not be harmed by this decentralization scheme. Poorer counties, however, which needed state aid in order to run their schools, would be devastated. Porter's proposals to create a permanent common school fund, which he introduced in the late 1840s, were, according to Mathews, an attempt to avoid this decentralization. Porter echoed previous reformers in lobbying for the state to compensate townships with worthless sixteenth sections in order to equalize school funding and urging that a general tax be instituted to support the state's education system.[29]

Notwithstanding the few proposals from legislators, little was done on behalf of public education in Alabama during the 1840s. Unlike in

Louisiana and Mississippi where the late 1840s witnessed the passage of state laws to attempt to establish public school systems, Alabama did little to bolster education in the same period. As late as 1849 Governor Reuben Chapman, no education crusader, lamented to the legislature that despite his belief that "the subject of common schools deserves all the consideration and encouragement it is in the power of the General Assembly to bestow. . . . Unfortunately for our State, her financial condition will not allow her to do more than to make a faithful application of the fund granted by Congress for that important object." In fact, one scholar goes so far as to blame Governor Chapman for the lack of action on education during his term, calling his education ideas "insensitive," "antiquated," "questionable," and "unimaginative."[30]

Chapman's successor, however, would be more involved in the crusade for public schools in the state. Henry Collier, Democratic governor who served from 1849 to 1853, began agitating for a revamped system of schools immediately upon taking office. Collier insisted on the need for a state superintendent to oversee the entire system, visit schools, inspect teachers, and help wage a public opinion campaign to get Alabamians to support schools. The governor assured the legislature, "Such an officer would not only exercise a healthful influence over the schools committed to his watch-care, but he would awaken the people to the importance of education—give an interest and impetus to the cause, not only in the lower but in the higher branches also." Under the state superintendent the governor lobbied for county officers who would be charged with overseeing school trustees and teachers and reporting regularly to the state superintendent.[31] Mathews credits Governor Collier with helping to "shift the attention of the popular school enthusiast from financial injustices, stemming from the variations in the value of the sixteenth section grants, to a larger vision of a 'system' of public schools with effective administrative leadership." Education committees in both houses of the legislature echoed Collier's insistence on the appointment of a state superintendent to oversee schools and lobbied for the hiring of qualified teachers and the establishment of local school taxes in order to effectively conduct public schools across the state.[32]

Much of the discussion over school reform in Alabama continued to center around the disparity of the sixteenth section funds allotted to each township. The sixteenth section grants made by the federal government formed the cornerstone of financial support of schools for the southern state governments. They attempted to use these funds to support schools, but in Alabama the funds remained in the hands of the individual townships rather than a consolidated state fund. Many believed that consolidation would allow the funds to be distributed more equitably and alleviate the tension created by the disparate values of these lands in different areas. Politicians could not agree over the legality of consolidation, so after years of debate, they finally sent the question to the voters to decide in 1853. Out of the forty-five counties that voted on the proposition, only six registered a majority of voters against consolidation. Seven hundred ninety-three townships voted in favor of consolidation, with 227 voting against. Yet enough townships failed to vote at all, that less than a majority cast ballots in favor of the proposition, thus defeating it.[33]

The table in the Appendix (p.171) reveals the results of the 1853 vote on consolidating the sixteenth section funds by county. It also includes agricultural, manufacturing, education, and population statistics to explore the differences between counties that voted for and against consolidation, revealing some fascinating characteristics. Only six of the forty-five counties participating in the election voted against consolidating the funds. One of those, Simesstone, is not found in the 1850 census. The other five counties, Greene, Lowndes, Montgomery, Russell, and Sumter, share some striking similarities. In 1850 those five counties produced an average of 22,006 bales of ginned cotton. The thirty-nine counties that voted against consolidation only produced an average of 8,788 bales in the same year. This trend continues when examining the number of acres owned, the value of farmsteads, and the number of slaves—the counties that voted against consolidation enjoyed greater prosperity on average than those voting in favor of it. The anticonsolidation counties owned an average of 180,729 improved acres and 245,657 unimproved acres, versus 67,708 improved acres and 127,215 unimproved acres in those areas voting in favor of the proposition. The value of farmsteads in the proconsolidation counties averaged $990,221, while the value of farms in areas on the other side of the issue was more than double that—$2,375,028.

The Appendix table also includes population figures for each Alabama county voting in the 1853 referendum. It is interesting to note that the number of school-age children does not differ drastically in the counties voting for or against consolidation, revealing that it does not seem to have been a factor influencing the vote. Likewise, the number of public schools listed in the 1850 census does not differ largely between the two groups.

The population figure that does reveal a pattern, however, is the average number of slaves owned by the two groups. The proconsolidation counties owned an average of 5,017 slaves, with the anticonsolidation areas possessing more than three times that—an average of 16,429 slaves per county. The areas opposing consolidation on average owned more slaves and more land, and produced more cotton, than those areas favoring it.

Yet not all wealthy counties opposed the proposition. There were five counties with cotton production above 20,000 bales that voted in favor of consolidation. Especially notable is Tuscaloosa, the wealthiest county by far with an output of 73,561 bales, more than double the number of bales ginned in the next highest producing county. In fact, excluding Tuscaloosa's high output brings the average number of bales produced in the remaining counties favoring consolidation down to 6,988. Tuscaloosa, of course, had housed the state university since 1831 and many education reformers called it home. Those factors helped influence the 1853 vote in that county, leading Tuscaloosa to favor consolidation.

Another difference visible between the two sides is the amount of public money devoted to state schools. While the figures for many counties are missing from the 1850 census, the counties that are included show that those favoring consolidation spent an average of $996 on their public schools, while those that opposed the scheme spent more than twice that—about $2,363. The latter counties would have less to gain from consolidating the money devoted to individual townships. If they already enjoyed large sixteenth section funds, they would likely lose part of that fund to other townships that had less. Therefore it is not surprising that they would oppose the referendum.

The 1853 popular vote on consolidating the sixteenth section funds of the various townships in Alabama reveals a split between wealthier areas of the state, which voted against consolidating the funds, and less affluent areas, which tended to favor consolidation. The counties that voted against the proposition were wealthy and enjoyed large sixteenth section funds, which they stood to lose to offset smaller funds in other areas. Not all wealthy areas opposed consolidation, but the areas that did oppose consolidating the school funds consisted of counties that enjoyed better than average wealth.

Perhaps even more important than the trends visible in the 1853 vote is the fact that the debate over consolidation garnered such interest and excitement among the state's inhabitants that the following year the legislature enacted provisions to establish a statewide public school system. The agitation on the question of consolidation helped to arouse inhabitants' interest in education, forcing the legislature to act soon thereafter. According to J. Mills Thornton, "The issue was now sufficiently before the public so that ambitious politicians were beginning to seize upon it as a possible means to secure approval." There is a discernible correlation between public interest in education and action on the part of the state legislatures.[34]

Following the defeat of the consolidation proposal, instead of continuing to debate how best to equalize the sixteenth section funds, the legislature concentrated on establishing a system of schools for the state. In addition to the demand coming from voters, many in the 1853–1854 legislature, in part due to agitation for internal improvements from the Know Nothing Party in the 1853 legislative campaign, took office pledged to internal improvements. Thus, it is not surprising that like efforts to aid railroads, public education would finally be created by this legislature. That session the house appointed Alexander B. Meek to head the chamber's committee on education. As in Louisiana and Mississippi where politicians leaned on officials from New Orleans and Natchez when establishing their state school systems, Meek hailed from Mobile and was well known as a writer and reformer. In his presentation of the education committee's report, Meek lamented that the promise made in the state constitution to support education had not been fulfilled: "No general system of public schools—no provision for the means of popular education—has ever been adopted."[35]

Meek's bill would change that. It set out to establish at least one free primary school in each township of the state based on the principle that "every child in our state, of suitable age, is entitled to a sufficient sum to give him the elementary branches of knowledge, free of cost." The committee proposed to solve the unequal sixteenth section funding by giving state money to those townships without enough sixteenth section funds to support a school. According to the committee, "There is no subject of more momentous and vital importance to any State than that of common school education." The report carefully elucidated an argument for state government support of free schools and the importance of an educated populace in a democracy. Not only was education necessary in a republic, but it helped avoid crime and contributed to economic success, according to the committee. In his argument in favor of free schools Meek did not concentrate on charity and pauperism—the need for those of means to assist the less fortunate. Instead he considered universal education to be the responsibility of the state and necessary for its protection and safety.[36]

The bill introduced by Meek's committee first established an education fund made up of revenue from various sources, including $100,000 from the state treasury, all escheats, and an annual tax on banks, insurance companies, and railroads. The federal government gave Alabama an additional land grant to aid townships with valueless sixteenth sections, and the interest from those land sales also went into the fund. The bill created the office of state superintendent of education to be elected by the assembly for a two-year term and paid $2,000 annually. Each county would have three commissioners of free public schools to be elected by the voters, who would generally supervise schools, control all school funds, and provide any supplies they deemed necessary. Each township would elect three school trustees who would establish schools and license and hire teachers.[37]

The law designated that children between five and eighteen years of age would be eligible to attend public school. It instructed the state superintendent to equalize sixteenth section funds by using the Educational Fund to aid those townships with less money. The law authorized the county commissioners to consolidate weak townships and ordered the township trustees to divide pupils into grades. The primary grade would focus on reading, writing, and simple arithmetic and would be free to all students, and the higher grades would be free of tuition if funding allowed. The law allowed moderate tuition charges in the higher grades if necessary in order to give teachers fair compensation.[38]

In addition to the sixteenth section money and the Educational Fund, each county could establish an annual tax on real and personal property "for the support of common schools therein and for providing suitable houses and purchasing libraries and apparatus for such schools." These funds would be collected and deposited into the county treasury and used for schools, provided that at least 50 percent of the fund went to pay teachers' salaries.[39]

Historian David Mathews contends that "the alignments that occurred when the Meek Bill came to the floor of the legislature suggest that most of the state's political leaders favored education reform in the 1850's, that only a few of the wealthier planters objected to a state system of public schools, and that the opponents of the bill were prompted by economic self-interest." The bill passed both houses by large majorities—seventy-two to twelve in the house and twenty-three to six in the senate. Legislators who voted for the bill came from counties across the economic spectrum, but those who voted against it came solely from wealthy counties with sufficient sixteenth section funds to support schools. The opposition, however, was no match for the supporters of the bill.[40]

Reactions to the new school law varied, with both supporters and critics coming forward to comment on its effects. In his message to the legislature the following session, Governor John A. Winston, a Democrat, reported "the results of the School Bill of the last session, have not been so favorable as were hoped for by its friends. In some parts of the State it has worked well, in others it has not been well received, and not been productive of good." Although the governor signed the bill into law and pledged his support to the system in his first inaugural address, Winston's conservatism led him to become one of the main opponents of the state school system. He did not just oppose public education; he opposed all state aid for any sort of internal improvements. The legislative journals are filled with the governor's vetoes and objections. When in 1857 the legislature acted to create the much needed office of county superintendent of education to oversee local public schools, Winston objected to the expenditure, although his criticism did not damn the measure.[41]

Despite Governor Winston's opposition, public schools began to appear across Alabama as a result of the 1854 law. To serve as first state superintendent, the legislature chose William F. Perry, an experienced educator who would go on to serve as brigadier general in the Confederate Army. Perry explained in his reminiscences, published at the end of the century, the troubling situation he encountered when he first assumed his post. Commenting on the school fund, he explained the trouble with the sixteenth section scheme where plantation counties in the Tennessee Valley and the Black Belt with the most valuable land enjoyed the largest sixteenth section funds. Filled with large plantations, these counties had a small white population and often supported no school, for planters could afford to send their children elsewhere for education. The poorer counties with the largest populations and the least wealth enjoyed very little support from their sixteenth section funds. Perry explained how many counties and townships had no schoolhouses at all, and how many he encountered, "but for the rude benches visible through the cracks, and the broken slates and tattered spelling books scattered around them, any one would have been at a loss to determine for what purpose connected with civilized life they were designed."[42]

But the superintendent explained how things improved once the new school law took effect. Although it took some time to get the people acquainted with it and to get public schools up and running across the state, Perry boasted, "In my tour through the State, I found the schools generally in operation and the people pleased and hopeful, especially in those counties which were most benefited by the system; and returned to my office feeling fully assured that the public educational system of Alabama, though still crude and imperfect, had come to stay."[43]

The main complaint of the superintendent was the county supervision of the schools. The 1854 law required the county probate judges to take on the duties of school commissioners for the county without any increase in pay or reduction of other duties. According to Perry, "The judges of probate, not without good reason, regarded the imposition of new and onerous duties upon them without compensation, as a great hardship; and while many of them were faithful and efficient, they could not give the amount of attention that was absolutely essential to the prompt and efficient inauguration of a united system."[44]

Although the Alabama legislature's commitment to establishing and supporting a public school system for the state had been late in coming, it proved lasting when in 1856 it responded to Perry's complaints about county administration of the schools. That year the legislature passed an act "to render more efficient the system of free public schools in the State of Alabama," which created the office of county superintendent, increased the interest paid on the sixteenth section fund as well as the sources of school income, increased the sum given by the state to each child, and extended the age range for attending school.[45]

These changes, resulting from experience gained during the first two years of operation, improved the system overall and helped to bring more schools into existence and to educate more children across the state. In his 1857 report to the governor, Perry commented on the "continued and even increased prosperity and usefulness of our system of Public Schools." From the county reports he received, he calculated 2,262 public schools in operation in forty-six counties, where 89,013 students attended for an average of just over six months out of the year. A year later, with an increase in the number of schools and children attending, 52.1 percent of Alabama's young people were enrolled in school. In 1858 there were 180,160 school-age children in the state and 54.5 percent of them were enrolled in school. The entire system continued to expand up until the outbreak of war.[46]

Opponents, however, remained. To the dismay of education proponents, in the 1859–1860 legislative session a proposal came to the floor to abolish the offices of county and state superintendent. Yet despite opposition from certain planter counties, the public school system could boast many converts to its cause in the previous years. Governor Andrew B. Moore decried the efforts to abolish the state and county superintendencies, arguing the state bore the responsibility to provide schools as pledged in the constitution. He praised the wise measure of instituting a system of common schools, and warned against any policy that would cripple or retard its progress, and the 1856 adjustments to the law remained.[47]

The progress of Alabama's public education system during the 1850s is impressive, and it is important to note that these achievements came as a result of the demands of the voters, a fact that previous historians have overlooked. In *Politics and Power in a Slave Society,* historian J. Mills Thornton argued that Alabama did not have a comprehensive state public education system prior to 1854 because the residents did not want one. Thornton contends that, following the establishment of that system in 1854 and its financial reform in 1855, legislators dropped the issue of schooling because voters failed to respond to it politically by casting their ballots for or against education candidates. He argues, "The point is that the state at large not only had not had such a [public school] system; it had not really wanted one. The politicians quickly discovered that the issue aroused no great enthusiasm. It was not the hobby they sought, and they dropped it."[48]

More focused research suggests otherwise. The action taken in 1856 to create county superintendents, as suggested by the state superintendent, reveals a commitment by Alabama legislators to help the school system succeed. While Alabama was the last of the Gulf South states to institute statewide public schools, lawmakers there continued to improve their legislation so as to bring more order and success to the school system in response to demands from the voters. Creating the office of county superintendent indicated their support of public schools, and those officials would prove vital in ensuring the success of local school systems.

Legislators acted in response to demands from voters. The southern population in general did in fact desire and lobby for public schools.

Southerners took advantage of opportunities to avail themselves and their families of schooling and, in the 1830s and 1840s, began to demand that their states provide learning institutions. Once those schools were established, southerners sent their children to them. It took time, unsurprisingly, for the kinks to be worked out of the system, and all the public schools did not flourish immediately. But inhabitants embraced every possible avenue for learning, public as well as private. A local official from rural Louisiana reported in 1851: "There is a strong desire manifested on the part of the parents and guardians to have their children educated."[49]

In contrast to the actions of Alabama lawmakers, the Louisiana legislature took the exact opposite step. Rather than continuing to tweak the education system there in order to bring more children into it, Louisiana legislators altered the school law in ways that hampered the progress of public education. When the Louisiana legislature abolished the office of parish superintendent, they dealt a devastating blow to the state's school system.

Under Louisiana's 1847 law, public schools began functioning across that state and brought praise to legislators for their beneficent work. Yet it was not long before there was a change in the democratic tide that brought in the state's new constitution and the public school system. In 1852 voters saddled the state with a much more restrictive constitution that resembled the stringent 1812 document more than the democratic 1845 one. Alarmed by the impressive reforms realized through the 1845 document, wealthy planters sought to reassert their control through a new constitution. Allowing monopolies and granting the wealthy parishes dominance of the legislature through the apportionment of legislative seats, the new constitution reflected the prevailing mood of state officials. Thus it is not surprising that the legislature significantly altered the school law that year in ways that did irreversible damage to public education in the state. The legislature cut the salary of the state superintendent by two-thirds, from the generous amount of $3,000 annually to a mere $1,000, and also relieved him of the duty of visiting individual parishes. Even more appalling to public school proponents, the legislature abolished the office of parish superintendent, claiming that the meager $300 annual salary cost the state too much. With this provision, the legislature recalled the most effective education officer functioning on behalf of the school system, and hope for public education in the state soon dissipated. In addition, lawmakers replaced the parish superintendents with unpaid boards of district directors, whose apathy and ineptitude would soon prove detrimental to the school system. The legislature also burdened the parish treasurer with the additional duty of obtaining information from the school directors and reporting annually to the legislature, a task which few treasurers accomplished satisfactorily.[50]

The adjustments made to the school law in 1852 were among many legislative measures passed during the 1850s that caused hardship for Louisiana's plain folk and retarded social progress. Planters reasserted their control of the state with the 1852 constitution, which based representation in both houses on total population, including slaves. This measure allowed plantation parishes with their large slave populations to dominate both houses, and many contemporaries decried it as a glaring injustice that put slaves on the same footing with free white men. An examination of the legislative measures passed following the new apportionment scheme does indeed seem to reveal an advance toward planter hegemony—a general assembly that acted in favor of the wealthy few at the expense of the masses. During the 1850s, aside from stripping funding and supervision of public schools, the legislature passed bills that exempted slave property from taxation, appropriated state funds to repay owners whose slaves were convicted of crimes, denied protection to families whose property was seized by sheriffs, and refused to extend the time for payment for lands bought from the state. Additional measures removed restrictions on rates of interest money lenders could charge and continually privatized roads, allowing wealthy planters to control access to market. These bills served the planters at the expense of the plain folk. The retrenchment on education is symptomatic of this larger trend: public free schools served those who could not afford private schools. Once planters regained control of the legislature, they stripped the education system of needed funding and supervision. These measures stand in stark contrast to the actions taken by the Alabama legislature in the 1850s to strengthen and improve their public school system. Louisiana's legislation proved detrimental to public schools in the state, which, up to that time, had been improving dramatically each year.[51]

These adjustments generated a passionate outcry from public school proponents. State Superintendent of Education Robert Carter Nicholas and his successor John N. Carrigan both admonished the legislature for its actions and explained the detrimental effects the change immediately had upon the school system. As the schools began to function under the adjustments of 1852, many parishes reported unhappily back to the legislature. One parish superintendent complained to the state superintendent that he had not even heard of the abolition of his own office. Explaining that the auditor refused to release his parish's funds, and so no money could be drawn to support the schools, he requested information about the abolition of his post, and asked, "Let me know at what time it is considered that I went out of office." He also went on to condemn the legislature's actions, adding, "I want it distinctly understood, however, that I do not recognize the power of the Legislature to abolish an office when the individual filling it has been duly and constitutionally elected by the people, and has himself complied with all the requirements of the law creating such an office." One historian explained that, because of the alterations, "in some instances where half the children of educable age had attended public school in the years before 1852, less than a third attended in 1858. For example, in one parish where there were thirteen public school-houses in 1851, there were only three in 1860."[52]

One of the most important factors determining the success of a given school was the competence of local officials charged with overseeing the school system. Just as in the private realm where the owner often made crucial decisions that impacted the welfare of the school, in the public sphere those decisions fell to parish or county officials. While the principal and teachers impacted a school's functioning in vital ways, the public officers were tasked not only with determining whom to employ, but also resolving questions such as when the school should meet, what classes should be taught, and what books and materials would be used.

As early as 1822, the Alabama legislature charged the judge of the county court along with the commissioners of revenue and roads to choose three freeholders from each township to act as school commissioners who would serve for four years. The same legislation charged the school commissioners with employing a teacher, negotiating his salary, having a schoolhouse built and kept in repair, purchasing books and stationery for the school, making rules regarding the use of materials and the admittance of students, and determining which students' tuition expenses would be paid by the state. Commissioners were to certify instructors for employment by reviewing both their qualifications and their moral character before they could begin teaching. It is easy to see why local officials with these types of responsibilities played such a critical role in determining the success of public schools.[53]

Louisiana provides a powerful example of the importance of local officials. In New Orleans, the school boards actively administered and supervised the public schools of the city. Rather than just handing out funds, school administrators met with teachers, visited schools, and attended annual exams of students. A committee of administrators carefully examined all teaching applicants and tested their ability and knowledge before hiring, ensuring that the instruction offered in the city's public schools remained exceptional. The school board also decided how the schools would function, determining what classes would be taught, when the school term would commence and end, and where school would be held, carefully procuring schoolhouses in which to conduct classes. During the year, supervisors continued to monitor the progress of the public schools and took an active part in their administration. New Orleans city officials established the necessary urban government institutions to administer and supervise its schools. In the absence of such municipal institutions, rural residents depended upon their legislatures to provide the supporting framework, but the states' elected officials often failed to do so.[54]

In the absence of state institutions, local administration proved to be the key to overcoming the inefficiencies of state guidance and conducting successful public schools. Where public schools did succeed, those areas, like New Orleans, boasted of competent and dedicated local administrators. In 1855 when De Soto Parish officials reported that "the cause of education is in a good condition in our parish," they also explained that the police jury regularly appointed school directors who then carefully interviewed all teaching applicants. In 1857 J. L. Generes summarized conditions in his area: "In regard to the condition of the Free Public Schools in the parish, I can truly state that great improvement has been effected since my last report, and our schools are now filled with competent and efficient teachers. This is to be attributed to a desire on the part of the Directors generally to obtain men of capacity, and also from the effect of some ordinances of the Police Jury relative to Public Schools." Where competent administrators ran public schools, the public education system worked.[55]

Given the importance of local administration to the success of public schools, it remains surprising that state legislatures took so little action to institute standards or regulations for the officials who supervised the system. Reports continually flowed into the Louisiana legislature noting the incompetence of local administration and often blaming the school supervisors for the problems of the system, yet state lawmakers neglected to address this tremendous hindrance to public education in the state. In parish after parish, administrators proved completely unconcerned with the functioning of the school system. After the legislature abolished the office of parish superintendent in 1852, held by someone widely regarded as "the only responsible agent" of public schools, local supervision fell to an unpaid board of district directors. In most areas these directors quickly became regarded as incompetent administrators and apathetic agents of the public school system. Year after year parish officials attributed the chronic problems that plagued their schools to the district directors, like R. H. Cuny, who blamed the poor condition of the schools on "the entire neglect of most of the School Directors to perform their duty. They never visit and examine into the condition of their respective schools." Years later another official explained, "the school directors take no interest in the discharge of the duties of their offices." Such failures of local administration helped to condemn Louisiana's public school system in the years leading up to the Civil War. As early as 1851, state education officials acknowledged the necessity of competent local administrators for the system to succeed, pointing out to the legislature that "where the Parish has been favored with a zealous and able Superintendent . . . the schools seem to be attended with the greatest benefit," but the state's elected officials still took no steps to ensure competent administration. Few parishes in Louisiana could claim to have efficient local supervisors, unlike New Orleans where observers continued to praise the conscientious administrators of its public schools, commenting, "Few cities in the Union, if any, have more energetic, more vigilant, or more able Directors of Public Schools than New Orleans." In contrast, the rest of the state continued to suffer from incompetent administration; as the state superintendent reported to the legislature, "The complaint of the negligence of local officers in the performance of their duties has been uniform throughout"—a grievance that lawmakers ignored.[56]

Ultimately the burden of establishing quality control guidelines for education rested with the legislature. Although the success of Louisiana's public school system greatly depended on local supervision, the only way to ensure competent administrators throughout the state required legislative action, a responsibility state lawmakers shunned. Aside from providing inadequate sums of money, legislators did little else to support the school system. As the state superintendent chided in 1854, "The providing of funds for education is an indispensable means for attaining the end; but it is not education. The wisest system that can be devised, cannot be executed without human agency." But legislators provided little guidance for rural areas attempting to comply with state laws in establishing schools and made no requirements to ensure the proper functioning of the system. The state's elected officials offered no solutions to the problems of sparse rural settlements, refused to increase the inadequate amount of state funding, made no suggestions for how or where schools should be organized, and set no regulations or standards for such basic concerns as the quality of schoolhouses, the literacy of teachers, the courses of instruction offered, or the length of the school term. The state required nothing of local administrators who directly controlled the schools, not even mandating that the supervisors themselves be literate, much less requiring them to visit schools or interview teaching applicants. As the St. Landry Parish treasurer reported, "The Directors [are] uneducated, and consequently incompetent to judge of the acquirements of applicants, and are regardless of their social standing and moral character." One state official insisted that for the public school system to function effectively, "a rigorous and vigilant central influence must be brought to bear upon it, in order to insure concert of purpose and of action throughout the various members of the system," but state officers offered no such guidance.[57]

Indeed, rather than helping to correct the inadequacies of the system, most observers agreed that the actions of the legislature only served to further hamper public education in Louisiana. In 1856, one education official commented, "Our Public Schools are some ten years old, and the laws governing them have been changed and altered to but little purpose, if not with decided detriment." Most officials familiar with the school system noted "the inadequacy of the law," or as an official from Winn Parish explained, "The school law, as carried out here, is all a humbug." Local officers continually pleaded with the legislature to adjust the failings of the school law, but state lawmakers did little to address their grievances. Parish officials as well as state superintendents made numerous suggestions, such as stiffer requirements for assessors and parish treasurers, increased funding, and changes in the basis for the distribution of funds. Even the most basic standards were not applied, so that local leaders asked lawmakers to pass rules as simple as requiring school boards to examine teaching applicants and mandating that at least two of three school directors be literate.

Aside from suggestions, local officials pointed out contradictory sections of the law, such as those that referred to collecting taxes, drawing interest on school lands, and paying teachers, and asked the legislature to clarify discrepancies. Most often officials asked the legislature to address issues not mentioned in the school law, such as requiring school directors to visit schools and examine teachers, and allowing the police jury to appoint directors in areas where none had been elected. But to these pleas the legislature did not respond. As one disgusted local official commented, "The present condition of the Public Schools of this parish calls loudly upon the legislature for some revision and modification of the present system. If the members of that body would only devote one-half of their time which is consumed in useless and idle discussions upon party issues, and devote the same to the examination of the Public School system, the system would ere long be improved, and the children of the State thereby benefited." But state officials did not address the problems of Louisiana's public education system. Their negligence in making the necessary adjustments to the school law and their failure to institute specific requirements and guidelines for local administrators reveal the apathy that state legislators exhibited in regard to public education.[58]

The comments by local officials are invaluable when considering the opinion of middling southerners who themselves often left no documentary record behind concerning education. Local officials were in everyday contact with residents who utilized the public schools, so their reports contain a wealth of detail about how they viewed the schools. Through the correspondence from Louisiana officials, a refrain emerges whereby residents embraced the schools but criticized the legislature for its neglect of the system. Many reported that the public schools instituted in 1847 brought education to children whose parents would not have been able to afford to pay tuition for them to attend a private school. But many officials also complained of the harm done by the legislature beginning in 1852. While public schools had been progressing prior to that time, the retrenchment of that year seriously hampered public education in the state, which continued to decline in the succeeding years. As reported in 1853 by John Carrigan, "Had the motto, 'Let us alone' been adhered to more strictly from the first organization of the system, the schools in the country parishes might have been in an equally flourishing condition with those in the city . . . of New Orleans."[59]

Many of the flaws in Louisiana's school system were in part attributable to lack of funding. In addition to income from sixteenth section lands, the state also assessed a mill and poll tax that was added to the school fund. The state superintendent was charged with apportioning the funds to each parish based on the number of school-age children residing therein. Knowing that the combination of these sources of revenue might still prove insufficient to support a school year-round, the Louisiana legislature authorized local taxes for the support of schools, with many parishes also relying on voluntary contributions to keep classes in session. In areas that levied no local taxes and did not receive donations, schools operated only as long as money from the state lasted. As explained by the treasurer of Avoyelles Parish, "Generally, as long as a district has a sufficient school funds, its school works; when the funds are exhausted, the school stops, until a new supply comes to call it again into activity." To sustain the operation of schools, many parishes accepted private contributions or raised local funds to pay teachers for the remainder of the year. In 1854 a Plaquemines Parish official suggested tripling the amount of the state appropriation, noting that its school system, "without the generous aid derived from personal contribution, would remain sadly inoperative in most of the School Districts." Another official succinctly concluded, "Were all the districts in the parish to rely wholly upon the Public School Fund, the condition of our schools would be deplorable."[60]

Regrettably, due in part to the inadequacy of state funding, many residents began to view the public school system as onerous rather than beneficial. An official from Plaquemines Parish explained that the apathetic nature of parents in his parish was directly related to the insufficient amount of state funding, which "would not support a school for more than one month, and that in most all the Districts the schools are supported more by private subscription than by public funds." Concordia Parish residents registered similar complaints, noting that state appropriations supported public schools for only a few months despite the large amounts they paid into the state fund. Residents from parishes that contributed large amounts into the state's school fund became disgruntled when their share equaled less than their contribution and proved insufficient to sustain their schools. An 1859 report bitterly declared, "The defects I believe exist in the general apathy of the people, brought about in a great measure *in this parish,* by the utter inadequacy of the amount of money appropriated compared with the amount collected in the parish." Such sentiment resonated throughout the state, as an official from Livingston Parish commented, "The funds apportioned to this parish will hardly keep a school three months, and parents think they are oppressed, that they have to pay their taxes and receive no benefit of any importance from it; what their children learn in one school, they forget before there is another school in operation." He concluded, "One thing is certain, this system of apportionment has reduced the number of schools materially, and retarded the progress of education."[61]

Such an assertive denunciation from a Livingston Parish official proves instructive. Similar to the case in Alabama where the unequal sixteenth section funds led to much consternation, so in Louisiana the apportionment of school funds created friction among parishes. Complaints concerning the amount of money paid into the school fund and the disproportionate share a given parish received back echoed throughout the state. At first glance, one might assume that such complaints came from wealthier areas that paid large amounts into the fund but, because of the large number of plantations and the small number of white inhabitants, received less money back when funds were distributed based on the number of school-age children. That certainly seemed to be the case in Alabama, where counties in the Black Belt with ample sixteenth section funds to support their educational needs bristled at attempts to supplement the meager funding of poorer areas. But that trend did not hold true in Louisiana. Livingston farms produced an average of less than three bales of cotton annually with very little rice and had an average land holding of 390 acres. Compared with the surrounding plantation parishes, which boasted average landholdings around 1,800 acres and produced an average of two hundred bales of cotton annually, Livingston is easy to identify as a poorer, piney woods area. Yet the complaint remains, revealing that not all such objections stemmed from wealthier areas trying to hang on to their money. In this case, the official's comments reveal that his constituents valued education and sought to have their children instructed in the public school, but the funding system the state put in place did not meet their educational needs. They required a better school than one that operated haphazardly for a few months each year while the state funding held out. It is not surprising that such conditions led to frustration with the system, and that constituents came to see the situation as oppressive. Paying taxes into the fund but not receiving enough back to support a school helped to erode confidence that the state could effectively operate a school system.[62]

The money in Louisiana's school fund came from several sources—the income from sixteenth section lands donated by the federal government for education purposes, a mill tax, and a poll tax. The parishes collected this money locally and then sent it to the state office, which controlled the entire fund. There the state superintendent of education allocated the money based on the number of white children of school age in each parish.

That the amount of money appropriated from the state to support public schools would not keep the institutions in operation year-round engendered many problems, but the legislature expected that local initiative would supplement state aid. In many cases such local financing simply failed to materialize. One parish official summed up the situation in his annual report: "In short, take the Free Public School system as a whole, it does not—here, at least—work well. It supposes that in each School District the citizens shall tax themselves, and thus establish a school; and that they shall be *aided* therein from the State School Fund. But how does the matter operate here? It is thus: the people rely wholly upon the State, instead of relying mainly upon themselves. Not a tax has ever been laid in any district, that I have ever heard of."[63]

Those parishes that relied only on the state appropriations operated schools for an average of three months a year, while parishes that added to the state fund either through taxes or voluntary contributions managed to keep their schools running longer and more successfully. Parishes faced with insufficient funding from the state gratefully accepted personal donations to assist in running the schools. These contributions came in different forms; many residents donated buildings to be used as school rooms, provided money to rent classrooms, or offered their time, materials, and labor to help build schoolhouses. Others provided supplies such as fuel, furniture, and stationery, or contributed funds to prolong the length of the school term or to pay a teacher when the amount for which he was contracted did not materialize. In 1851 fifteen parish officials explicitly mentioned voluntary contributions as a means to pay for or procure schools in their parishes. As the Plaquemines Parish superintendent explained that year: "Besides the sum accruing from the State (which is here too small to keep up the schools) I have obtained in each district, small voluntary contributions which will for the present keep them in operation. In several instances these contributions have been received from persons who are not parents, but who have been prompted to this course by a sincere and praiseworthy desire to advance the cause of education."[64]

In other parishes, officials attempted to levy local taxes to supplement the state appropriation. Nineteen parishes levied local taxes in 1851, when Ascension Parish officials reported $5,916.50 raised through local taxes and Avoyelles Parish reported $4,133.37. Some of the parishes raised much less, so that the amount collected through taxation ranged from $172 to more than $5,000, equaling a total of $29,598.92 in fifteen parishes that year. Yet even these diverse and sometimes disappointing results proved more successful than the failed attempts at local taxation experienced in some areas. As the parish superintendent for Pointe Coupee recounted, "The directors in the district where I lived, levied a tax to build a schoolhouse. Some of the planters refused to pay, a suit was the consequence. The directors lost." Similarly, St. Tammany Parish officials reported that in 1849 their district tried to collect a local tax for school purposes but many refused to pay, "and as the law is rather vague with regard to the manner of assessing the tax, the directors did not like to attempt to enforce the collection, but have relied upon voluntary contributions." While inhabitants paid both a mill and poll tax assessed by the state, which benefited the school fund, many refused to pay more, defeating efforts at local taxation. In the words of an official from St. Helena, "Our schools have not advanced as well as they should have done, owing to the fact that the citizens have been divided—all think because it is a public thing that they are to labor under no disadvantage whatever."[65]

Besides contributing additional resources, the way in which parishes employed the funding appropriated from the state often differed drastically. As already mentioned, some parishes used the state allotment to run their schools for as long as the fund allowed, which most often amounted to a few months each year. In contrast, rather than supporting free schools for such a short period, other parishes used the state funds to offset tuition. This meant that the state provision for "free schools," outlined in the constitutions of 1845 and 1852, was ceasing to function in many parishes. Local officers from one parish reported, "The public money is either applied for a stated length of time, where all can attend free, or each scholar is allowed to draw his pro-rata share of the public money as part payment of his tuition." In 1861 a Bossier Parish official offered this observation: "Most of our schools partake in some measure of both public and private character, the teachers being employed by the Directors, and the public funds paid to him, and the remainder paid by private subscription. Tuition ranges from $2.50 to $5.00 per month, owing to the grade of school and of the branches taught." Since the state funding proved insufficient to support satisfactory public schools, in 1858 an official from De Soto Parish explained that in his parish, "Strictly speaking there are but very few public schools in this parish. . . . The people of the district generally employ one or more teachers as they may require, to suit the convenience of the particular neighborhood, and at the termination of the school or schools, the Directors divide the funds of the district, proportionately with the number of scholars in the district and the number taught by each teacher respectively, reserving such amount as may be due those who did not attend."[66]

This official believed that his parish had found the most productive use of the state appropriations, that "this arrangement seems much more satisfactory, as by this means all the children receive a benefit from the public fund, which is not the case as in some districts, where the Directors employ a teacher to teach a public school, and the whole fund of the district is consumed in paying him, when, perhaps, not half the children of the district are in reach of the school, and do not attend." Many parishes echoed this arrangement of employing the state appropriations for public schools to offset the cost of private schools in their areas, as in Union Parish where almost all the schools charged tuition despite receiving state funds. This trend toward using public money to offset tuition costs followed the trend in Alabama, showing that in both states the inadequacy of state funding meant that provisions for "free" schools proved unworkable.[67]

Few Louisiana legislators publicly admitted their disregard for education, but their actions clearly reveal their disinterest in providing public schools for the children of the state. According to one historian attempting to explain the problems haunting public education in the state, "Their apathy was chiefly responsible for the failure of free schools in Louisiana before the Civil War. . . . But they did not scruple to appropriate public money for private institutions at their own plantations."[68] The state superintendent of education in 1864 provided a synopsis of the school system of the antebellum period, concluding that "the whole plan was admirably adapted to hurt the feelings of the poor and pamper the pride of the rich—the slaveholders. They, we have no doubt, were quite satisfied with the system."[69] An interested party reported to the state superintendent that "members of the Legislature, composed of rich men only, always made laws *in order to prevent the light to spread over the poor.* The funds for the schools were few and badly appropriated." Legislators, like planters across the South who paid for the private education of their children, took little interest in the success of the public schools of the state. Though mandated in Louisiana's 1845 constitution and unanimously endorsed, the lack of concern for the collapsing system of public education clearly reveals the attitude of the state's elected officials.[70]

Without the necessary provisions put in place by state lawmakers requiring local school administrators to attend to their jobs in an effective manner, Louisiana's public education system deteriorated in the decade leading up to the Civil War. Rather than suggesting solutions to the problems encountered in rural areas of Louisiana, such as sparsely settled regions, inadequate schoolhouses, and incompetent teachers, the legislature ignored such problems and continued to fund an inefficient school system inadequately. Comments from local residents reveal that rather than assisting languishing school districts, state legislators altered the school law in ways that often caused more problems, such as their abolition of the office of parish superintendent in 1852. Although in some cases efficient local supervision could overcome the obstacles facing rural education, without central guidance most areas of the state would continue to house failing public schools. State administrators could have used New Orleans's successful school laws to formulate regulations for the rest of the state, instituting requirements, such as committees to certify teachers before employment, and offering guidelines to establish schools, but legislators continued to neglect public education. Without a more aggressive centralized control of the system and without stringent requirements that would combat the apathy and indifference of many school administrators, public education in the rest of Louisiana fell far short in comparison with the New Orleans school system. As the state superintendent fatalistically remarked to the legislature less than a decade before the outbreak of war, "You may extend your fields of sugar and cotton—erect your palatial mansions—establish manufactories—construct your magnificent floating palaces, expend millions for railroads, and accumulate illimitable wealth, but if you neglect to educate the people, you are but making a richer prize for some bold and crafty Cataline, some Santa Anna, or Louis Napoleon, who may ultimately, be hailed as a welcome deliverer from anarchy and confusion."[71]

In contrast to the actions of the Louisiana lawmakers, Alabama legislators continued to tweak their system, established in 1854, to bring better success to their schools. When Alabama enacted a statewide system of common schools in 1854, the first man to serve as state superintendent of education, William F. Perry, undertook the office with "serious misgivings" due to the difficulties associated with creating a statewide school system. Perry knew at the outset that "the building up of an efficient educational system, adapted to the various wants and circumstances of a large community, has never been accomplished, hitherto, but by the patient unremitting efforts of successive years." Despite initial obstacles, Perry believed that Alabama residents embraced the idea of public schools and would prove ready to support the legislature in whatever measures it deemed necessary to make the system function effectively. Townships across the state began to establish schools immediately once the law was passed. From 1856 to 1857, there were 175 additional schools established, with an increase of 6,008 pupils. Such increases reveal the desire of local communities to institute schools and the willingness of parents to utilize them.[72]

Alabama legislators took pride in their public schools. After establishing the school system in 1854, they adjusted the law in 1855 and 1856 to make it more effective and bring more schools into operation—measures that did achieve success. In 1858, 54.5 percent of the state's residents of scholastic age were attending school. Contrary to Thornton's premise that Alabama lawmakers dropped the issue of public education once the school system was established, the legislative record reveals that they continued to take an interest in expanding access to education and took positive measures toward that goal prior to the Civil War.

The record for Louisiana and Mississippi is not so positive. In Louisiana, after establishing a system that succeeded in bringing more schools with increasing enrollments to rural areas in desperate need of such institutions, in 1852 the legislature was recaptured by conservative elements who drastically cut state spending on schooling, cutting the salary of the state superintendent by two-thirds and abolishing the office of parish superintendent. Why the governmental body that created such a system would then take steps that would greatly harm its functioning is clear—the legislature of 1847 that created the state's school system did so because of the constitutional mandate of 1845. That munificence was overturned in a few short years when conservative planter politicians regained control of the legislature. Despite the argument espoused by republican political philosophy that the entire society benefited by having well-educated children, planters could afford to pay for their children to attend private schools. They were not directly benefited by the public schools—their children did not utilize them—so when they sought to cut state expenditures, public education was an easy target. The state itself, like most of the South, was prospering during the 1850s. Yet legislators denuded the public school system of provisions necessary for its successful functioning.

Unlike Louisiana's system, in which schools were administered through a statewide officer, Mississippi's school system remained completely localized until the Civil War. After attempting to institute a statewide school system in 1846, the legislature enacted special legislation pertaining to schools in particular counties, so that different portions of the state operated under different laws. Governors and numerous secretaries of state (ex-officio general school commissioners) continually urged the legislature to change this policy and insisted upon the institution of a statewide official charged with overseeing the school system, but to no avail.[73] As late as 1859 Governor William McWillie urged the establishment of such an officer, noting that almost every other state in the Union employed such an official and insisting, "This office is so absolutely necessary to any system of public education." Unlike in Alabama where legislators amended the state school law to make the system more successful, lawmakers in Mississippi failed to heed the advice of officials intimate with the school system and to enact legislation to improve education in the state.[74]

Mississippi and Louisiana established statewide public school systems in 1846 and 1847 respectively, yet the legislation that followed the initial laws proved more detrimental than beneficial, retarding public school progress in both states. Alternatively, Alabama's lawmakers made provisions that improved the functioning of its school system after it was established. Legislators there heeded the advice of the state superintendent and instituted measures to improve school administration, funding, and access, revealing a trend in that state divergent from those of its sister states to the west.

If residents in all three states desired greater access to education through public schools, why was Alabama the only state to continually improve its school system prior to the Civil War? One might expect that political partisanship played a role in determining each state's educational policy, since the national Whig party was openly committed to state aid for public education. In some instances, there is evidence of a split between Democrats and Whigs in the Gulf South when it came to state support for education. Such a divide between the parties occurred, for instance, in the debates of the Louisiana constitutional convention of 1845. Likewise, when Alabama politicians sparred about accepting their share of the distribution of the federal surplus, the state senate split along party lines. But in other instances, the divide is not so clear. There were plenty of cases of loyal Jacksonian Democrats supporting increased state action on education. For example, Democratic Mississippi governor John J. Pettus argued in 1859, "The education of the youth should then be regarded as an object of the first magnitude, to be promoted by the untiring efforts of those who govern the State." Likewise, Alabama, which made the most positive educational progress in the last decade of the antebellum era, was largely dominated by the Democratic Party, although they did house a large Whig presence that succeeded in affecting some legislation. In Louisiana, where there was a visible divide in 1845 with Whigs calling for more support to education, in 1852, when the state retrenched education spending with detrimental consequences, the legislature was controlled by Whigs. Such evidence reveals that one cannot simply attribute the educational progress of the southern states to the strength of a particular political party.[75]

The divergent trends in the three states can be more fully explained by looking at the governmental structures in each. Power was divided among the branches of government differently in Alabama than in Louisiana and Mississippi. In both of those states, the governors exercised a considerable amount of power, including the privilege of appointing numerous state officials. Governor Thomas B. Robertson of Louisiana went so far as to argue in 1824, "The people have no right to say who is to govern them. The constitution places the power in my hands." In Alabama, by contrast, the governor enjoyed very little power. Instead, the office was merely a "salaried honor," which allowed him to address the legislature annually on issues he deemed important, but then fade into the background for another twelve months. Not only did the legislature have all the power in the Cotton State, but those lawmakers were closer to the voters than in the other states. Alabama instituted white manhood suffrage in its first constitution in 1819, ensuring that a broader segment of the population had a say in electing officials, making lawmakers there more responsive to the masses than in other states with more restrictive suffrage requirements. These characteristics ensured that Alabama would prove most sensitive to the demands of the populace. Though tardy in its enactment of a state school system, the legislature continued to improve the system even as the sectional crisis diverted attention from such domestic issues. Louisiana and Mississippi did not. There, planter political dominance allowed officials to act with impunity against the public interest. Such disregard for the public would have certainly caused rumbling among the voters, but the planter control was such that few suffered politically for their behavior. One Louisiana resident reported in 1851 of the trouble in his parish stemming from the operation of the school system, reporting, "Parents think they are oppressed, that they have to pay their taxes and receive no benefit of any importance from it."[76]

The southern population at large valued learning and sought out every possible opportunity to have their children educated. Wealthier families employed tutors or sent their children to private schools both inside and outside the South. Other families utilized relatives to teach youngsters inside the home, and many children attended schools in their neighborhood when a teacher was available to teach class. Most such schools, however, operated erratically, and in the 1840s residents began to demand that their state governments do more to improve access to education. It is this yearning among the masses which is most significant. Previous scholars have failed not only to recognize the number of schools and the amount of learning going on in the antebellum Gulf South, they have failed to notice its centrality in southern culture. The establishment of statewide public school systems did not come from the benevolent charity of enlightened leaders. Legislators were forced to act by their constituents, who demanded that their governments uphold the promises made in their state constitutions to foster education. Public schools were established because the people demanded them. Such agitation, along with the evidence that southern families throughout the socioeconomic ladder embraced avenues for learning when available, reveal that the previous historiographical consensus that there were few schools in the South because southerners did not value education demands revision. Residents in the Gulf South embraced learning and demanded that their state governments step in to do more to extend access. While politicians in the three states responded with differing levels of action, the impulse was the same among the people. Southerners embraced, valued, and demanded education.

Despite the trouble with running the schools year-round and allowing children to attend for free, Louisiana, Mississippi, and Alabama all managed to support and extend education and learning across their states. The number of schools and the children attending them increased in the decade before the Civil War. The following table is based on the US census figures from 1840, 1850, and 1860. The figures include all schools in the state, since the line between private and public schools was so blurry during the time period under study. Rather than showing the number of schools in operation that could be considered "public," the table reveals the prevalence of schooling in the Gulf South states. These numbers differ from the reports of the various state superintendents, offering lower attendance ratios than the officials reported to their legislatures. In 1858, for example, Alabama state superintendent of education reported 98,274 children attending school across the state, while the 1860 census showed far fewer attending—72,529.[77] Nonetheless, the figures clearly reveal the spread of schools across the Gulf South in the decades before the Civil War.

In all three states, circumstances emerged that forced the hand of legislators in the 1840s and 1850s. Governors had been urging action on public education and the establishment of statewide school systems for decades to little effect. As the Lower South economies began to recover from the Panic of 1837 and were able to fund other forms of internal improvements, legislators could no longer hide behind lack of money as an impediment to action on public schools. Furthermore, the successful schools instituted in New Orleans, Natchez, and Mobile all stood as evidence that inhabitants in those states could and would support public institutions rather than patronizing private academies. Despite the different conditions in rural and urban areas, the successful systems in the major cities led folks living in the country to demand schools where they lived as well. These demands from the voting public proved to be the most important factor in prodding legislative action. All three states provided some sort of funding to support schools, but the money expended prior to the establishment of statewide systems did very little to help advance learning. Residents grew weary of watching their politicians spend public moneys nominally for education, yet gaining so little benefit from the expenditure. The fact that both parties felt compelled to speak out in favor

Table 5.2: Number of Schools, Students, and Teachers
in the Gulf South States

	1840	1850	1860
ALABAMA			
# of Schools	755	1,323	2,109
# of Students	21,413	37,237	72,529
# of Teachers	—	1,630	2,438
% of White School-Age Children Attending School	17%	21%	34%
LOUISIANA			
# of Schools	243	813	865
# of Students	6,557	31,003	43,087
# of Teachers	—	1,217	1,302
% of White School-Age Children Attending School	13%	37%	35%
MISSISSIPPI			
# of Schools	560	964	1,285
# of Students	19,149	26,230	38,944
# of Teachers	—	1,168	1,645
% of White School-Age Children Attending School	28%	22%	27%

Source: *Sixth Census,* 1840, 52–63; *Seventh Census,* 1850, 141–59; *Eighth Census,* 1860, 503–11.

of public education in the 1840s and 1850s reveals the demand from their constituents.

The public school systems in all three states suffered from problems that would linger until after the Civil War, yet those troubles did not condemn public schools entirely. Local inhabitants worked to overcome obstacles facing their schools, including lack of direction from state agencies and vague and contradictory legislation. Even inadequate funding from the state did not defeat local schools. Residents struggled to keep classes in operation, whether by passing local taxes, soliciting private donations, or charging tuition to keep teachers employed. Such local initiative reveals that parents in the Lower South valued education and would labor to secure lessons for their children. The establishment of statewide school systems came as a result of the demands of residents, and the systems were sustained only by the sheer determination of local inhabitants to keep the schools in operation. The importance of education to residents in the antebellum Gulf South proves undeniable.

## CHAPTER SIX

Within the Schoolroom Walls

STUDENT LIFE IN THE ANTEBELLUM GULF SOUTH

With the establishment of statewide school systems in Louisiana, Mississippi, and Alabama, more Gulf South children than ever before enjoyed access to education. A majority of families chose to take advantage of the opportunity for scholastic advancement, with over 250,000 white children enrolled in schools throughout those three states in 1860. School life differed for students and teachers based on the type of school they patronized, but certain patterns emerge that shed light on the experience of southerners within the schools themselves.[1]

Although census statistics as well as reports from local and state government officials reveal a large number of southern children attending school in the late antebellum period, it is quite likely that those figures greatly underestimate the number of students in the South. When employing attendance patterns to examine the breadth of schooling in the South, one must keep several facts in mind. For one thing, such reports rarely contain reliable information about private schools also serving children in the area. Additionally, as James Leloudis points out in his study of education in postbellum North Carolina, attendance figures are misleading because of the fluid nature of school attendance in the South. He explains, "Parents placed little value on regular attendance. Between the ages of six and twenty-one, children moved in and out of school according to family needs, often attending when they were very little, then remaining at home for several years, and finally returning when younger brothers and sisters were old enough to relieve them of field work and household duties. For that reason, nineteenth-century school census figures could be quite misleading."[2]

Joseph B. Lightsey was a young yeoman farmer in southeastern Mississippi who worked with his brother on their father's 150-acre farm alongside eight slaves. Lightsey began working at the age of sixteen, and he records the drudgery of daily farm life in his diary. Along with notes on crops, fishing, and local happenings, Lightsey records occasional stints doing coursework at a local school. In 1852 at the age of twenty, he attended a school conducted by James Smith with twenty-six other students. He went to school throughout the summer, from June through September, when the school concluded and Lightsey returned to the fields.[3]

In addition to Lightsey's accounts of his own school experience, he composes an essay on education that has been noted by previous historians as representative of the attitude of southerners toward schooling. The essay presents a dialogue between a young man, Tom, and a more educated friend. The friend wonders why Tom is not attending the local school, and Tom explains that his father pulled him out of school after six months, believing that amount of schooling was sufficient for a farmer. Tom's father then enters and the friend sets out to convince the father to send his son back to school. The father, a farmer himself, explains that his son's time at school had already surpassed his own tenure of only three months, and he worried that Tom might learn far-fetched theories like the rotation of planets, when "this earth is as flat as a pancake and don't no more turn round than nothing." So as not to offend the father, the friend carefully couches his argument in favor of Tom's schooling, successfully convincing the father, who enrolls Tom in school at the end of the dialogue.[4]

The essay offers an important glimpse into rural education. The fact that Tom had received such minimal schooling and had been pulled out at his father's insistence certainly reveals one attitude that existed in the antebellum South. But perhaps even more important than what the dialogue says is who wrote it. Lightsey himself was the son of a farmer who we know spent most of the year in the fields, not inside a classroom. Yet his composition reveals a cultivated mind, both learned and creative. On the days he was not in school he composed such work during his leisure time. His explanation of planetary rotation and orbits reveals a level of knowledge that might surprise someone who sees in his same diary that he only attended school for three months out of the year. When school was in session, Lightsey's enthusiasm for it leaps off the pages of his diary.

Previous scholarship that has used his essay to argue that the bumpkin father frightened by advanced study is representative of the South misses the point entirely. It is Lightsey's clever observations, disciplined labor, and creative endeavors that reveal the true character of young southerners, aware of the value of education and eager to participate whenever possible.

As Lightsey's experience reveals, perhaps even more important to understanding the place of education in the South than the fluidity of school attendance is the recognition that a child's absence from a formal classroom does not mean a total lack of learning. The prevalence of home schooling is unmistakable, despite the difficulty of quantifying such instruction. A majority of southerners received some sort of instructional support within their own homes, whether from a private tutor or by a family member or through independent study, and such experiences show up nowhere in census figures or education statistics for the antebellum period. Therefore, the number of children attending formal public or private schools does not accurately reflect the total number of young people actually receiving instruction in the antebellum Gulf South.[5]

Students receiving lessons inside their own homes often studied basic elementary subjects commonly known as the "3 Rs"—reading, writing, and arithmetic. One family instructor reported working with his younger siblings on arithmetic, geography, grammar, and music, although he noted in his diary that it was "rare" for him to act as a math teacher. Some family teachers might include more complex subjects, but in general, lessons offered by relatives remained basic.[6]

Often teaching done by family members merely served to prepare children to attend a formal school at a later date, so they did not need more advanced classes. This type of home instruction served as a sort of preschool for young southerners. Alternatively, tutors hired to provide lessons for children at a family's home taught more advanced subjects. Rather than preparing students to enter school, tutors often replaced either elementary or high school altogether, so the curriculum reflected that fact accordingly. Most tutors promised to teach all branches "belonging to a finished English education." One couple who advertised in a Mobile newspaper under the title "Teachers in Want of a Situation" offered classes by the husband in German and Music while his wife taught English and French as well as "every variety of Ornamental work; including shell, worsted and wax work."[7]

In private schools, pupils could take classes in more advanced subjects. The Silliman Female Collegiate Institute, located in Clinton, Louisiana, and headed by Sereno Taylor and his family during the 1850s, offered students courses in reading, elementary arithmetic, English grammar, geography, writing, ancient and modern languages, mathematics, natural science, philosophy, history, government, the fine arts, and music instruction in the harp, piano, guitar, and organ. The Boys High School of Dauphin Way Academy in Mobile promised that students would "receive thorough instruction in the various branches of an English, Mathematical and Commercial education, and in the Latin, Greek, and Modern languages. French and Spanish will be taught by able native Professors in connection with the Principal." The Clinton Academy, a primary school, offered a more modest curriculum, including classes in spelling, writing, arithmetic, English literature, and the Latin and Greek languages. The Baton Rouge High School for Boys promised that "no institution in the South offers greater advantages for the successful prosecution of a thorough and liberal course of studies, both civil and military." It offered classes in the "ordinary branches of an English education," including the higher branches of mathematics, natural philosophy, astronomy, French, Spanish, Italian, military engineering, drawing, painting, fencing, straight sword, broad sword, and instrumental music.[8]

The addition to the curriculum of drawing, painting, and music is slightly unusual in a boys' school. Female academies often offered more classes in the "ornamental" branches, which included painting, drawing, singing, instruction in musical instruments, sewing, and needlework. Schools offered these courses to supplement the standard curriculum, and students took them as extra classes in addition to the regular course load. Instruction in these polite arts served to prepare girls to act as a wife and hostess. Schools offered classes in composition and letter writing to students of both genders, but often emphasized it more for females. "Belles letters," as it was often called, required pupils to write weekly letters home to their families, which would be scrutinized by parents as evidence of their academic progress.[9]

Male students also had the opportunity to take courses specifically offered to their gender. Military exercises obviously served only the male student population, as did courses in surveying and engineering. Yet aside from these supplemental courses, the basic curriculum remained almost identical for both male and female students. In elementary schools or the primary department, students took classes in English grammar and composition, geography, and arithmetic. As students progressed to secondary school, classes accordingly became more varied and more complex, including instruction in European and American history; modern languages such as French, Italian, Spanish, and German as well as the ancient languages of Latin and Greek; advanced mathematics, including algebra, geometry and trigonometry; sciences such as botany, astronomy, and chemistry; and moral and natural philosophy. Boys might be offered classes in political economy, while both genders could enroll in bookkeeping, and schools always emphasized the study of geography for both sexes.[10]

Most public schools instituted in the rural South offered a basic primary school instruction, focusing on English grammar and composition, arithmetic, and geography, although some schools did provide instruction in advanced mathematics. Rural Claiborne Parish in northern Louisiana in 1851 boasted of eight public schools that taught rhetoric, philosophy, astronomy, geography, algebra, and the higher sciences. Most public schools were primary, but there were many high schools as well. In Louisiana, De Soto Parish housed five high schools in 1851, Iberville Parish supported three, Morehouse Parish touted four, and West Baton Rouge Parish housed two high schools.[11]

Thriving public institutions in the urban centers unsurprisingly offered the most varied public school curriculum. The Natchez Institute offered both its boys and girls primary department classes in "Learning, Letters, and Spelling," as well as arithmetic and geography. After passing the primary department exams, students then advanced to the next level of schooling, which the Natchez Institute labeled secondary but more closely aligned to the modern conception of middle school. Students in that department took more advanced classes in reading, spelling, grammar, geography, and arithmetic, with the boys also receiving instruction in writing and declamation. The Junior Department served as the next highest level in the Natchez Institute, in which girls studied reading, spelling, geography, arithmetic, anatomy, physiology, and US history, with the boys studying those courses as well as writing, declamation, English history, and grammar. In the Senior Department, girls took classes in reading, natural philosophy, moral philosophy, arithmetic, algebra, grammar, composition, and writing. To those studies, the boys' Senior Department also added classes in bookkeeping, Latin, Greek, English history, and the study of Cicero, Virgil, and Anabasis. In all types of schooling—home, public, and private—instructors offered their students a classical education rather than practical instruction.[12]

Annual examinations, where instructors tested the students on the subjects they had studied, served as a huge public event for both private and public schools. The community took an interest in these exams, with announcements in local newspapers letting residents know when and where they would take place. Parents, family friends, and interested observers gathered to watch the students display their knowledge acquired throughout the school year. Newspaper editors often attended and carried a description of the events in their publications. Oakley Academy held its annual examination on July 23, 1845, with very satisfactory results. As reported in the *Mississippi Free Trader and Natchez Gazette,* the students deeply impressed the audience, who left feeling certain that "the pupils are not confined in their education to the mere gleaning of knowledge, but that they are led, by an able guide into the full harvest of learning." Aside from the prepared questions, the editor reported that on numerous instances throughout the exam spontaneous exchanges occurred between students and examiner, allowing the pupils to display their wit and intelligence in a very unrehearsed fashion. The editor himself left the exam most impressed by "the affectionate and respectful confidence with which the pupils regarded their instructor and the happiness and cheerfulness of home that beamed in their eyes and appeared in their actions."[13]

Similarly, the *Mobile Advertiser* carried a report of the annual exams of the Bethel Free School. Reporting his regrets that he had not been able to attend the examination himself, the editor nonetheless provided readers with an account of the event, noting that a large crowd had attended, all of whom seemed exceedingly pleased with the students' performance. The editor noted specifically, "The beautiful and impressive scene of 'the reception of General Washington and Staff at Trenton Bridge' was very well represented by the little soldiers of the school." Several leading citizens spoke at this examination, revealing the interest in such activities by the local community. Once the students completed their examination to everyone's satisfaction, "The pupils marched to the pic-nic table, the contents of which they seemed to enjoy as heartily as they ever had their books."[14]

Such exams would cause great anxiety for students as well as for teachers who felt intense pressure to make sure everything went perfectly and that the students represented their school in a positive manner. Pupils often dreaded annual exams, like Nannie Cage, who attended the Bethany Institute in Mississippi in 1864. She wrote to a cousin about how preparing for the examination kept everyone busily engaged for weeks—the schoolchildren preparing their recitations and the teachers getting the schoolhouse ready. The exam took place in the parlor of the schoolhouse, which became so crowded with visitors that the audience had little room for movement, forcing many of the schoolchildren to sit in the hall. Nannie related to her cousin, "You never saw a party of such badly embarrassed girls in your life." She went on to recount how "most of us had to read two compositions—when I read my first I had to stop twice to get my breath. I never was so badly frightened in my life." Like Nannie, most students registered some anxiety about their public examination. One schoolboy from Louisiana wrote home to his mother about the results of his recent annual exam, in which upon completion, the president of the school announced the students' standings in all their classes. The prospect of having the entire audience aware of one's class standing caused grief for many pupils, but William Jackson was pleased to report that he placed eleventh out of thirty-five students in Greek, seventh out of thirty in Latin, and first out of twenty-eight in English. He recounted with pride that most of the other boys had been attending school for much longer than he and that the president made a point of talking to him about his impressive progress after such a short period of time.[15]

In addition to annual exams, schools sometimes held various sorts of expositions throughout the year to showcase their students' progress. Lucy Fisher's school in Baton Rouge held such an exhibition to highlight the musical accomplishments of her students. Fisher invited prominent members of the community, so that many of the city's social elite attended, including future president Zachary Taylor and other high-ranking army officers. Fisher decorated the music room and parlor for the occasion and all the students dressed in their best clothes, making quite an impression on the audience. Despite all of Fisher's careful planning, things did not go quite as she hoped. Just before the recital began, Fisher's sister arrived with two young women brought from New England to teach at the school. The "plainly dressed" women stood in contrast to the festively decorated parlor and the impeccably attired students. Fisher's sister brought these women at her request from their native Connecticut in order to teach for Fisher in Baton Rouge. Fisher hired the women to teach music, so as the recital came to a close, the audience insisted on hearing the new instructors perform. According to Fisher, the two "shy awkward" teachers tried to excuse themselves, but to no avail. An onlooker led one of the women to the piano, and when she began to play, Fisher recounted, "She did not play as well as the youngest of our pupils." The proprietor was horrified. She remembered decades later that "the mortification of that evening almost killed me." She did not blame the teachers, noting that "they were good girls but incompetent to fill the positions required. For months the new teachers had been expected and now neither was capable of filling the situation for which they were desired." Fisher blamed her sister for bringing the women without verifying their qualifications. She bemoaned, "Nothing ever sickened me of teaching or standing at the head of an institution as much as that." Despite her carefully laid plans for the music exhibition, the night ended with her embarrassment, as the new teachers revealed to the prominent audience their utter lack of skill and competence to teach at the school.[16]

Most events went off more successfully. In addition to annual examinations and exhibitions, schools held other parties throughout the year. May Day proved one of the most common celebrations. The girls attending Mr. Merrill's school in Mobile hosted a lavish event attended by a large crowd of onlookers. The celebration took place on a Wednesday evening inside the schoolhouse, which was "brilliantly illuminated, and most beautifully and tastefully dressed and adorned with every variety of flowers . . . in the richest and most lavish profusion." Flower arches filled the room, so that the young girls moving about in procession "were literally surrounded and covered with flowers. It was in truth a fairy scene." William Jackson, a student from Louisiana, recalled the celebration he and his schoolmates participated in to commemorate Washington's birthday. The boys got two days off from studies for the celebration, which included a march into town by the rifle company, who played several pieces of music and discharged their rifles numerous times.[17]

Most social activities for students took place on school grounds, with few schools allowing their pupils to attend events off campus. Most teachers did not allow their boarders to attend balls. Lizzie Connell, attending school at Silliman Female Collegiate Institute in Clinton, Louisiana, received an invitation to a grand ball in 1861, but wrote to her cousin that the principal would not allow her go because she was "only a schoolgirl." Other girls did manage to gain permission to leave campus for such occasions. In 1816 Mary Baker, who attended boarding school in Lexington, Kentucky, did not return home to Natchez, Mississippi, for winter break, in part because she planned to attend the winter balls in town. Interestingly, a few years later Mary had changed her mind about the appropriateness of schoolgirls attending such fêtes. She related to her brother that a cousin had recently gone to a ball but that she did not approve of young girls attending such affairs, which distracted them from their schooling, causing them to worry more about their appearance than their studies. One schoolboy, Richard Ellis, promised his sister that "If I was to go to a dozen balls a month it would never interfere with my studies."[18]

Students attending boarding school away from their families needed some social engagement as an occasional diversion from their constant studies. But such celebrations remained peripheral to the task at hand, and while schools organized amusements for their students, administrators remained focused on providing pupils with the requisite learning to allow them to prosper once leaving the institution. Administrators and teachers made grand promises to parents when admitting students into their school, such as J. A. Ringe, who ran a school for young gentlemen in Mobile and assured patrons that pupils "will possess every facility to prepare for College, as well as to acquire a complete education for Mercantile Pursuits." The Mobile Collegiate Institute promised, "The united attention of Messrs. Blackburn & Walshe will be devoted to the moral as well as the literary improvements of their pupils while under their charge, and will enable them to offer such inducements to parents and guardians as shall merit their patronage."[19]

Morality remained a constant concern for both teachers and parents, who expected that their children would be instructed not only in strictly academic subjects, but also in how to conduct themselves in a manner appropriate for a proper southern gentleman or lady. R. M. Brumby wrote to his daughter Ann Eliza attending school in Tuskegee, Alabama. His affection for his daughter is immediately apparent, for he addressed her as "my very dear little one," and admitted that although she had been gone for less than a week, he missed her every day. Brumby then instructed his daughter in the appropriate behavior for a young woman, and advised her on her studies. He wrote of the value of books, literature, and science, but went on to insist, "The great object of female education should be, the development of the girl into a *lady,* healthy in person, refined in feeling, pace in morals, humble in religion." Brumby wanted his daughter to be constantly mindful of that fact, and allow it to dictate her behavior in all aspects of school life, from her interactions with teachers and classmates to her recitations and studies. Brumby also had more specific instructions for his daughter, including to bathe regularly, not to remain seated constantly, and to be "careful & exact in personal neatness, as well as cleanliness." He also wanted his daughter to "dress always as becomes a lady, plainly attired." Brumby's instructions, offered affectionately but authoritatively, reveal that he concerned himself not only with his daughter's academic achievements but her socialization and deportment as well.[20]

Teachers strove to meet the high expectations of parents, who expected them to look not only after the intellectual welfare of their pupils, but their social and moral well-being as well. One man in Mississippi, when recommending Dr. Thornton's school in Jackson, made sure to mention, "The Doctor is one of the best disciplinarians we have ever known, besides his other qualifications for teaching youth and conducting an institution of this kind." When offering instructions to teachers in a Natchez newspaper column entitled "Advice to Instructors of Youth," one writer stressed the importance of the profession and the careful balancing act instructors must maintain. He insisted that teachers must be both patient and steady while at the same time managing to encourage the shy and repress the insolent. He argued that while teachers needed to challenge their students intellectually, they had to do so without overburdening their delicate minds. But most importantly for teachers, the writer emphasized that "it is their bounden duty to be ever on the watch, like a good soldier on his sentinel, in order to check the first dawnings of vice, for valuable as knowledge may be, virtue is infinitely more valuable." He went on to warn that "worse than useless are mental accomplishments if accompanied with dissipation of manners and a heart goaded with depravity."[21]

To ensure that teachers met this challenge, administrators needed to interview teaching applicants carefully and then continually monitor their progress throughout the course of the semester. That is one reason why public examinations became such an important component of school life—they served as a means for teachers to showcase their ability by publicly displaying the accomplishments of their students. In the public school systems of the Gulf South, urban administrators carefully chose teachers from a pool of applicants who they felt confident could perform the requisite duties, not only instructing students, but watching out for their welfare as well as managing the classroom. The board of visitors for the Natchez Institute created a committee of examination who "thoroughly examined every applicant in his literary attainments and capacity for government of schools, before his name was presented for election as a teacher." As in Natchez, New Orleans school administrators carefully selected and monitored the instructors they hired to teach in Crescent City schools. City administrators typically reported to the state superintendent that their teachers proved "capable, faithful and attentive," and explained that "the moral and intellectual qualifications of the teachers, and the general character and condition of the schools, justify the confidence and affection of the community." Every year New Orleans school administrators praised the teachers employed in public schools for their intellectual ability and dedication. New Orleans school board members explained in their very first report the care and consideration that went into choosing public school instructors, carefully examining applicants on a wide range of subjects.[22]

In the rural areas, administrators did not always monitor the qualifications of teachers so carefully. Some rural schools hired exceptional instructors who conducted the schools with great efficiency and success. Most school administrators in rural Louisiana related in 1851 that they employed well qualified teachers of good moral character. A. J. Moss from Lafayette promised that "only those teachers who possess the highest literary qualifications and unexceptionable character are employed in the Lafayette public schools." L. D. Brewer, reporting on the condition of teachers in West Feliciana Parish, informed his audience, "I have regarded men of intemperate habits as not qualified as respects moral character to instruct in our schools, and have consequently refused to give certificates to such as were known to me of such habits."[23]

Such comments reveal the importance of local administration in conducting public schools. While some local officials in Louisiana reported unfavorably on the qualifications of teachers in 1851, many more did so after the adjustments of the 1852 school law took effect. That law, which cut the salary of the state superintendent by two-thirds and abolished the office of parish superintendent, caused great harm to the school system of the state by taking away the most important local official charged with overseeing the schools. The reports of local residents on the qualifications of teachers became decidedly more negative after that law took effect, as a result of the lack of care taken in hiring. R. H. Cuny, reporting on the quality of teachers in Catahoula Parish, revealed that "in reference to their qualifications, I have to admit, that in most cases they are not good, and are not at all qualified to teach." This fact he directly attributed to the lack of local supervision, arguing that the unpaid district directors who replaced the parish superintendent proved incompetent themselves, unaware of their responsibility in overseeing the schools and uninterested in performing their duty. Unsurprisingly, Cuny closed out his report by noting, "I find very general dissatisfaction with the system."[24]

While most private schools lauded the accomplishments of their faculty and staff, plenty of evidence exists showcasing incompetence in private schools as well. In fact, one public school proponent used the lack of qualified teachers in the private realm to advance his argument in favor of state-supported institutions. In 1845 Natchez resident and newspaper editor T. A. S. Doniphan lamented that "the province of education has hitherto opened a wide field for the knavery of quacks and charlatans who have made a practice of plundering the community." Doniphan argued that too often young men from the North traveled south and commenced teaching school with no real commitment to enlightening young minds, but only to raise as much money as possible to set themselves up in some other profession. Rather than cultivating knowledge in their young wards, they busied themselves with preparations for their future business ventures and planned how they would spend their earnings. Doniphan believed that creating public institutions under the supervision of government officials would allow a more careful screening process and ensure more qualified instructors who catered to the city's youth.[25]

The quality of instruction offered in both private and public schools depended upon the action administrators took to employ competent teachers. Unsurprisingly, larger towns and cities enjoyed access to a greater population and accordingly a better applicant pool from which to choose teaching candidates. So for both private and public institutions, usually those located in larger towns found it easier to attract qualified teachers, though such a statement should not impugn the quality of instructors in rural areas. Many rural schools employed excellent teachers who earned the praise of their local community. R. M. Sawyer reported that in St. Mary Parish bordering the Gulf of Mexico in extreme southern Louisiana, seventeen public schools operated in 1851 with extremely well-qualified teachers. Several of the men employed could have taught higher level grades, while the others conducted their primary classes impeccably, doing "very good justice to their schools," and proving themselves to be "all men of good moral character, and have well earned the money they have received."[26]

Families took a sincere interest in their children's educational progress and sought out such qualified teachers to instruct their sons and daughters. Parents continually kept abreast of their children's progress in their studies. John Palfrey of Louisiana wrote to a friend in January of 1811 about his sons' education. The two boys attended two different schools— one went to a French school to learn the language, and the other attended an English school conducted by a local pastor. The father noted with pride that both boys improved quickly, and the "expense is very great, but the advantages resulting from the situation will amply compensate." One of the boys had received more than one job offer for positions in counting houses, but Palfrey preferred that his sons continue to concentrate on their schooling full-time. Palfrey's oldest son, Gorham, was finishing high school in Boston and let his father know that he wanted to start college there. Although Palfrey expressed concern about his ability to pay for his education, he committed to finding a way to do so, writing his son's guardian, "with regard to Gorham his mind appears to be so strongly bent upon his studies. I will by any sacrifice I can make endeavor to carry him thro[ugh]."[27]

Palfrey continued to take an interest in the educational pursuits of his family long after his own children finished school. Once his son William had children of his own, the grandfather kept abreast of his grandchildren's intellectual progress, continually corresponding with his son and his daughter-in-law regarding their studies. In August of 1832 Palfrey wrote to William concerning his children's education. Palfrey worried about his granddaughter Mary, who was just beginning school. He feared she would struggle at first, writing to his son, "Her trouble is now commencing in the road of education. She will find it rough at times but it will become more smooth as she progresses & eventually useful & delightful." He went on to suggest that Mary's younger brother Willy also start school, so that the two children could be together. While Willy was younger, his grandfather thought he should also enroll in classes to help lessen Mary's anxiety about being separated from her family.[28]

Like Palfrey, who not only concerned himself with his children's education but also his grandchildren's, the intellectual well-being of their children remained a central theme in the writing of parents across the

South. Martha Batchelor kept her children in schools throughout the antebellum period, even as the invasion of Union troops forced the family to move and separate. Brothers Charles, James Madison, and Albert all attended the Kentucky Military Institute before joining the ranks of the Confederate Army. Younger siblings Kate, Mollie, Iverson, and Tommy continued to attend school even after the outbreak of war. Martha wrote to Albert while she was away at school in 1861: "All that I want in the way of wealth is enough to make my children and give them good educations." Her commitment to keep her children in school despite her anxiety over separation and her concerns about money is evident throughout her correspondence with her daughters and sons.[29]

Another southern mother, Anne Jackson, sent her daughter from Camden, Mississippi to Kentucky in 1864 to live with her grandmother so that she could attend school, noting that the war had disrupted schools in Mississippi. Jackson hoped that the school's proprietor, Mother Columba, might allow her to hold off paying the girl's tuition until the close of the war. Jackson assured the principal that she had "notes enough on land estate to ensure the payment, which under no circumstances will be confiscated." She wrote that she had plenty of Confederate money but very few greenbacks. The few greenbacks she did have she sent with her daughter to pay for her passage and to "buy her a few plain clothes for school." Jackson refused to allow the war to interfere with her children's education, writing to her mother, "I can't bear the thought that my children will be deprived of an education, it will be more to them than fortune." Jackson missed her daughter terribly, but asserted that she did not regret sending her away to go to school. She only regretted that she could not do the same for her young son, Frank. She pleaded in an 1864 letter, "God grant we may have peace and that [Frank] may yet go to school." Even the fog of war did not keep southern parents from trying to secure an education for their young children.[30]

Aside from parents who carefully monitored the educational progress of their children, schooling remained a central issue for students themselves. Personal correspondence and diary entries are full of details about their schoolwork, and letters to schoolchildren from home regularly contain advice about how to handle a particular course or a certain teacher and often return to the familiar refrain of the importance of education and the necessity of applying oneself completely to the task at hand. While Charles Batchelor attended Oakland College in Mississippi, he kept up a steady stream of correspondence with his younger brother Albert at home in Pointe Coupee Parish, Louisiana. Charles constantly reminded Albert of the importance of intellectual pursuits and stressed the necessity of studying hard while young so that he would not be at a loss when he entered college. In 1857 the older brother opined, "let me advise you to try to improve your talent while young and as you grow older your mind will expand and perhaps when you become a man you will be a talented man." Charles insisted, "The younger you begin the better. The only way you can improve yourself is by constant study and reading." He clearly used his own experience as a guide and wanted his younger brother to be better prepared for college than he himself had been, noting, "now as I grow older I will have to work the harder." Charles constantly chided his little brother about studying, warning that he did not want to have to start college in the "scrub school," or remedial class. He warned that every year applicants improved so that requirements for bypassing remedial classes increased annually. Such comments reveal that Charles not only worried for his own intellectual development, but for that of his family as well.[31]

Perhaps the goading from his older brother made an impact, for when Albert finally did begin college classes at the Kentucky Military Institute, he thrived. He did not have to enter the remedial class as Charles had feared but instead entered as a freshman, although a former teacher registered some concern about this fact. T. W. Mieure, upon hearing that his former student would be starting college as a freshman, responded, "I must confess that I was somewhat flattered when I read that you had entered the freshman class although I fear lest they have been over indulgent." Mieure nonetheless believed that Albert would excel at school as long as he studied diligently. Throughout his tenure in Lexington, Albert continued to get advice from friends and family concerning his studies just as he had as a young child while attending school closer to home.[32]

Students themselves reported to family and friends at home about their trials and triumphs while away at school. One schoolgirl in Clinton, Louisiana, kept her brother informed of how her studies progressed, stressing that "I am so busily engaged with my studies during the week I don't get home sick much." She continually wrote her family regarding her schoolwork, noting her concentration on specific subjects and reporting her thoughts on her teachers and other students. Mary Lancaster told her parents that she awoke everyday at five in the morning to be able to study for two hours before breakfast. Daniel Gorham confided in his diary at the start of the 1856 school term that he and most of his fellow male classmates felt happy to be back at school after summer break. Unlike the girls, none of whom seemed anxious to begin school, Daniel believed that the boys "on the contrary, have grown heartily tired of vacations, and manifest some anxiety to study."[33]

Isaac L. Baker attended school in Lexington, Kentucky, in the 1800s and wrote to his cousin in the Mississippi Territory regarding his scholastic endeavors. Isaac boasted, "it is with pleasure I inform you I am making great proficiency in my studies and if attentive (which I am resolved to be) I will have studied all the arts and sciences usually taught in the academies and colleges of the United States with the Latin language by the 1st of October 1810." His correspondence to family in Mississippi updated them on his schooling and revealed his commitment to furthering his own intellectual development. The boy admitted that he missed home, but would channel his energy into working harder at his studies so that he could finish and get home all the quicker. Several years later, Isaac's younger siblings Mary, Lewis, and Joshua followed in their brother's footsteps and also attended school in Lexington. The three siblings kept up a lengthy correspondence with Isaac, telling him of their studies, boarding, and social outings.[34] Joshua reported with pride that he was taking classes in natural philosophy, astronomy, composition, and Euclid and studied eight to ten hours a day. Mary likewise informed her sister how hard she studied and that she had risen to the head of all her classes except one, which she determined to excel in as well. She had not received a single infraction for whispering, and had been "as studious as I possibly could." The Baker children took their studies very seriously and worked hard to succeed in all their classes.[35]

The routine for schoolchildren differed drastically depending on whether they attended a local school, traveling from home every day, or took classes out of town where they boarded at or near the school. Nannie Cage attended schools in Louisiana, Mississippi, and Alabama in the early 1860s, and she constantly informed her friends of how hard she studied. While attending the Bethany Institute in Mississippi, she related to a relative that her cousin, Lizzie Connell, struggled to adjust to the workload, and that "she is going to beg her Ma not to send her out here next session for she has to *study too* hard." Lizzie did manage to make it through the program, however, and her correspondence makes it clear how much effort and time she put into her studies. In 1864 she bemoaned that it had been weeks since she had written a letter because she was too busy studying for annual exams. Nannie Cage likewise immersed herself in schoolwork. In 1864 we find Nannie "so deeply absorbed in her Algebra that she can neither see or think of anything else," while Lizzie took a break from her studies to write a letter to a friend. But the schoolgirls did enjoy some free time as well, noting days off from school and day trips to visit family and friends. Nannie lived close enough to the school that she could go home on the weekends, and sometimes brought school friends home with her. She gushed about one such weekend that she and her friends "have been having a splendid time ever since—been just as wild and bad as could be." While attending the Silliman Institute in Clinton, Louisiana, students frequently played games in the afternoons thanks to the large number of children and the spacious house and grounds that offered plenty of room to play. Ann Morancy, studying in Kentucky in 1841, wrote home to her mother about a party and supper the schoolgirls attended the previous evening, in which they "danced in the study room" and enjoyed themselves thoroughly.[36]

While away at school, students kept abreast of events at home and informed about national affairs. Many students discussed politics with their family and friends, and registered opinions about the controversies of the day. One female student wrote home about how her classmates all identified strongly with the national political parties. She told her parents, "There is no place where politics are more warmly ascribed than at Nazareth. The young ladies here are either violent Whigs or violent Democrats, and argue warmly on political topics, of which they are profoundly ignorant." The schoolgirls all took an active interest in the approaching 1840 presidential election and even held a mock election, which the Whigs handily won. "We have already had one Whig dinner, at which enthusiastic toasts to the Harrison cause were drank," the schoolgirl wrote home, explaining that they enjoyed "plentiful glasses of color water! And Mother Catherine, who is a Whig, says when the election of Harrison is confirmed, we will have another dinner."[37]

While students often found themselves consumed by the world within their schoolhouse walls, teachers who committed their entire lives to educating young southerners likewise became absorbed by the developments surrounding their school, as evidenced by the experiences of the Taylor family of southern Louisiana. Sereno Taylor served as a minster, teacher, and principal of the Silliman Female Collegiate Institute. His wife and children, along with other family members, assisted him in running the school, and the entire family seemed to revolve around the world of education and learning. Taylor's school became well known throughout the South for its achievements. One gentleman, Mr. T. O. Sully, even reportedly told an acquaintance in 1856 that he only remained in Clinton to patronize Taylor's school, and that once Taylor left the area, he would as well.[38]

Taylor's wife Mary and his daughter Stella both taught at his school during the 1850s, where they offered a wide range of courses. According to the school catalog for 1854–1855, classes included reading, defining, elementary arithmetic, English grammar, geography, writing, languages, mathematics, natural science, philosophy, history, government, and fine arts. Taylor commented that he had plenty of teaching applicants from whom to choose the most qualified, telling his daughter, "I was as choice of my teachers as a young man in the selection of a wife." The proprietor tried to get his son-in-law, Colonel Eugene Hunter, to come teach military exercises for the school, which he promised would allow them to charge at least $300 a year and would be the main attraction of a boys department he wanted to add to the school.[39]

When running the Silliman Institute, Taylor promised his patrons that the school did not serve as a prison nor a hospital nor a showroom for jewelry and fashion, but instead as a place for "the cultivation of every truthful sentiment and noble feeling." He recited the school's motto as "feel well—work briskly—recreate judiciously—avoid every meanness of your mis-schooled nature—reverence your Maker—honor you parents, and cultivate, vigorously and perseveringly, all your physical, mental and moral capabilities for the glory of your Redeemer, and the benefit of your entire race."[40]

In 1855 Taylor resigned his post as principal of Silliman during a bout of bad health. He was unable to leave his room for a week and his weight dropped to only 106 pounds. Despite health concerns, Taylor opened a new school on the Mississippi Gulf Coast. Referring to it as the Sereno Taylor Cottage College and Academy of Music and Painting, he contacted some of his former patrons at Silliman to inquire if they would want to enroll their children in his new school. He offered former students a discount on tuition, charging them $300 for a ten-month term while charging other students $400. A few years later, a rumor began that

Taylor would be returning to Silliman, and several families enrolled there because of his reputation. But Taylor did not return to Clinton. Instead, after his sixty-fifth birthday he began pursuing a position in a small school or with an individual family that would allow him to teach during the week and preach on Sundays.[41]

Taylor and his wife moved around the South as he took charge of different schools or opened his own institutions, but he never lacked employment. Rather, Taylor managed to dictate the terms upon which he would teach quite effectively, a product, no doubt, of his reputation as an excellent teacher and school manager. Sereno and Mary enjoyed their lives and lived quite comfortably. Mary Taylor wrote to her daughter in 1855 that her son had tried to convince her to go to a political barbeque put on by the Democratic Party in Biloxi, but that "when people live as well as we do at home, they never care about going elsewhere."[42]

Teachers like Sereno Taylor, who earned a superb reputation for themselves, could expect the respect of the community and the gratitude of the families they served. In 1853 Joseph Reynes received a thank-you note from girls attending public school in the first district of New Orleans, thanking him for serving as the librarian and expressing their regrets at his resignation. Many students fondly remembered teachers in later years. One young man who attended the University of Alabama in 1850, ran into a former student of his mother's whom she taught decades earlier. The former student, now grown and a business owner himself, emotionally related the impact of her instruction, which still resonated so many years later.[43]

Most students fondly remembered their time at school as a happy occasion. Schoolchildren offset the hours spent studying by time spent playing with friends and celebrating with classmates. During this stage of their lives, young southerners began exercising their independence before the full weight of responsibility fell upon them. The years spent at school served as a formative period in their lives, when attitudes took shape and personalities emerged. Whether receiving lessons inside one's own home, attending a local public school, or boarding away from their families at a prestigious private school, the time spent as a schoolchild usually had a determining effect on young southerners and helped shape them into the men and women they would become.

The experiences of young people in the Gulf South help to reveal the important place ascribed to learning in southern culture. It is obvious when looking through the archival legacy of southerners that education and intellectual pursuits remained a central theme in their lives. Letters to family and friends, diary entries, newspaper clippings, old report cards, and diplomas reveal how education factored into their thinking in a central way. Families consistently concerned themselves with ensuring that younger members received instruction, and continually monitored progress to make sure students advanced as expected. The commitment of parents to ensure that their children had access to learning and the devotion to their studies revealed by so many students help to elucidate the central place of learning in the lives of southerners before the Civil War.

CONCLUSION

Punctuated Progress

THE PLACE OF EDUCATION IN THE
ANTEBELLUM GULF SOUTH

The trend of educational development in the Gulf South states of Louisiana, Mississippi, and Alabama is not a straight trajectory of progress over time. Although the first Americans to occupy the region did concern themselves with the intellectual welfare of the younger generations, it took decades before all the obstacles in the path of southern education would yield to successful schools throughout the region. But in spite of those early impediments, southerners committed themselves to the intellectual well-being of their children. Using various avenues to scholastic achievement, residents managed to ensure that their children did not grow up in ignorance, as some previous scholars have suggested.

The absence of studies exploring learning in the South before the Civil War has led many to conclude that there were few schools in the South and that residents there did not value education. The evidence presented here suggests otherwise. Early citizens sought the means to provide learning to their children, whether this meant patronizing a private school, hiring an instructor to teach their children in their own home, or appointing a family member to look after their intellectual development. Aside from the obvious commitment of parents to educational pursuits, the state early became involved in fostering learning. As soon as the areas bordering the Gulf of Mexico came under American control, the governments there began legislating to foster education. In the 1820s and 1830s, these efforts focused on aiding private schools already in operation. State aid helped support schools so they could reduce tuition costs and offer free instruction to children from poor families.

A few southern politicians consistently lobbied that the state do more to extend learning, and governors regularly came down on this side of the issue. Executives in all three states urged legislators to take action to extend access to learning for residents. But when true public schools finally came into existence in the South, they emerged not as a result of legislation, but from the dedication of local residents.

The Panic of 1837 created a serious obstacle to educational progress in the South as it wiped out much of the money set aside by state governments to support schools. The economic recovery of the 1840s, however, coincided with the maturation of Jacksonian democracy there. This political philosophy, which assaulted vestiges of privilege within the political system and demanded greater democracy, led southerners to demand access to privileges formerly reserved for the elite, including schooling. Voters began to demand government-supported free schools just as prosperity returned to the region, making such ventures possible.

While Jacksonian democracy motivated voters to demand schools from their legislators, the desire for education stemmed from other sources. The political philosophy of republicanism, which argued that democracies needed educated voters to survive, led many to believe that access to schooling must be extended along with suffrage. In addition, southerners exhibited an innate desire to have their children educated, stemming in part from a hope for upward social mobility. Parents believed that schooling would help their children prosper and contribute to their later success in life.

The urban areas of the South led the way in establishing successful public schools. In New Orleans, Natchez, and Mobile, city leaders took the necessary measures to create public institutions. These schools thrived, evidence of the support they received from the surrounding community. Residents in rural areas took notice of the achievements of urban schools and began to demand similar schools in their own neighborhoods. The successful example provided by schools in the cities, along with the financial recovery following the Panic of 1837 and the spread of Jacksonian democracy, combined to lead southerners to insist that their state governments do more to foster opportunities for learning. The agitation by voters forced their state legislatures to act, so that before 1860, Louisiana, Mississippi, and Alabama all housed statewide public school systems.

The story of educational development in the Gulf South reveals that southerners valued education. While the statewide school systems there did lag behind the accomplishments of New England states, this fact does not indicate a disregard for the intellectual well-being of young southerners. When considering the achievements of southern education, one must jettison the historiographical bias that measures all academic progress in relation to the establishment of public schools in Massachusetts. When one considers the South in context, including its frontier-like setting, the low population density, and the informal modes of learning available, it is obvious that education remained an ambition of southern society throughout the antebellum era. This fact helps to shed light on the people who inhabited the region in the nineteenth century, and demands inclusion in the larger narrative of southern history.

APPENDIX

Alabama: 1853 Vote on Consolidating Sixteenth Section Funds, by County

County	Townships voting for consolidation	Townships voting against consolidation	Ginned cotton bales produced in 1850s	# of improved acres in 1850	# of unimproved acres in 1850	Value of farmsteads in 1850	Value of home manufactures in 1850	Total white population	Total slave population	# of school-age children	Amount of public funds allotted to schools
Autauga	22	9	12,016	108,172	175,604	1,308,113	93,348	6,274	8,730	2,578	2144
Barbour	27	5	628	6,098	40,254	120,476	31,830	12,842	10,780	5,762	
Benton	25	4	5,995	74,991	131,603	1,301,603	65,308	13,307	3,763	5823	1246
Bibb	22	4	4,643	53,411	129,744	621,944	22,431	7,097	2,601	3037	816
Blount	24	2	248	27,915	43,255	240,056	21,480	6,941	426	2996	
Butler	22	6	4,094	46,551	102,751	400,170	16,855	7,162	3,639	3019	190
Chambers	20	2	17,442	171,290	225,261	2,274,261	40,714	12,784	11,158	5483	2503
Cherokee	9	4	2,717	55,158	126,277	1,182,308	76,111	12,170	1,691	5148	214
Choctaw	11	7	4,435	43,367	128,318	649,395	13,461	4,620	3,769	1916	142
Clarke	34	7	4,881	47,927	165,126	675,460	28,301	4,991	4,876	1985	195
Coffee	16	0	1,408	24,820	36,433	232,001	25,406	5,380	557	2312	
Conecuh	31	2	4,628	55,076	94,615	426,965	21,281	4,925	4,394	2104	701
Coosa	20	4	5,524	67,081	161,822	819,211	98,118	10,414	4,120	4337	1700
Covington	12	0	416	9,201	17,901	90,751	14,890	3,077	480	1314	
Dale	18	0	2,158	33,565	68,344	291,522	26,045	5,622	757	2386	
DeKalb	16	3	260	31,972	47,054	464,967	27,573	7,730	506	3422	67
Fayette	26	1	2,920	46,641	99,789	409,649	80,087	8,451	1,221	3681	564
Franklin	20	2	15,045	105,461	296,370	2,196,209	42,333	11,308	8,197	4823	922
Greene*	4	20	25,680	239,307	287,560	3,705,218	66,016	9,265	22,127	3663	33
Hancock	7	1	26	6,829	5,258	40,139	9,032	1,480	62	677	
Henry	28	5	5,235	52,919	85,004	603,240	43,178	6,776	2,242	2985	1205
Jackson	7	3	2,382	73,353	158,696	952,486	42,600	11,754	2,292	5034	497
Jefferson	28	6	2,451	51,921	85,438	580,808	37,692	6,714	2,267	2996	1089
Lauderdale	10	6	10,606	98,646	141,602	1,637,935	47,844	11,097	6,015	4650	562

County										
Lowndes*	6	9	23,872	157,560	244,447	1,800,772	20,041	7,258	14,649	2980	2850
Macon	16	8	29,080	186,014	292,729	2,490,003	35,962	11,286	15,596	5567	2064
Madison	12	6	20,888	165,024	163,982	3,276,203	43,449	11,937	14,326	4898	5470
Marengo	12	8	32,295	174,097	246,556	3,604,083	25,115	7,101	20,093	2816	
Marshall	19	3	1,966	27,826	34,389	416,170	22,655	7,952	868	3422	219
Mobile	18	0		5,152	39,544	495,660	240	17,303	9,356	5435	1850
Monroe	21	5	6,977	67,188	191,523	842,285	48,513	5,648	6,325	2250	169
Montgomery*	11	17	25,326	203,045	284,804	2,864,322	31,869	10,169	19,427	3877	550
Morgan	10	4	4,777	64,123	102,821	805,597	28,569	6,657	3,437	2920	14
Perry	11	3	24,524	159,822	207,448	2,618,994	20,211	8,342	13,917	3422	1850
Pike	25	2	8,679	93,431	165,234	963,742	52,311	12,102	3,794	5170	146
Randolph	27	1	1,986	41,477	111,572	607,907	61,225	10,616	936	4624	
Russell*	10	11	21,088	148,947	223,857	1,724,187	25,000	8,405	11,111	3608	
St. Claire	26	3	1,434	31,841	71,849	377,090	48,651	5,501	1,321	2349	72
Shelby	20	4	3,737	41,402	107,147	646,448	63,091	7,153	2,376	3123	795
Simesstone*	5	8									
Sumter*	5	16	14,066	154,785	187,816	1,780,640	24,524	7,369	14,831	2967	
Talladega	16	2	8,509	96,999	182,645	1,607,153	42,489	11,617	6,971	5016	752
Tallapoosa	19	3	6,589	76,207	194,950	1,017,801	46,759	11,511	4,073	4323	
Tuscaloosa	25	10	73,561	97,833	241,605	1,087,655	23,947	10,571	7,477	3937	724
Walker	20	1	592	19,831	44,905	244,154	27,532	4,857	266	2070	

COUNTIES VOTING FOR CONSOLIDATION

795 | 6,968,884 | 227 | 8,788 | 67,708 | 127,215 | $990,221 | $38,888 | 8,540 | 5,017 | 3,585 | $996

COUNTIES VOTING AGAINST CONSOLIDATION

4,995,362 | 227 | 22,006 | 180,729 | 245,657 | $2,375,028 | $20,300 | 8,493 | 16,429 | 3,419 | $2362.80

Source: Compiled from Alabama Secretary of State, Election Files—state and national, 1823—ongoing, ADAH; U.S. Census, 1850, 414–33. The counties marked with an asterisk are the six counties that registered a vote against consolidation.

NOTES

INTRODUCTION

1. Frederick Law Olmsted, *A Journey in the Seaboard Slave States: With Remarks on Their Economy* (New York: Dix and Edwards, 1856), ix–x (first quote); William J. Cooper Jr. and Thomas E. Terrill, *The American South: A History,* 4th ed., 2 vols. (Lanham, MD: Rowman and Littlefield, 2009), 1:273 (second quote).

2. Martin Luther Riley, "The Development of Education in Louisiana prior to Statehood," reprinted from *Louisiana Historical Quarterly* 19 (1936): 6; *Eighth Census, 1860,* 503–11; "Report of the Alabama State Superintendent of Education, 1858;" "Report of the Secretary of State on Public Education," *Louisiana Legislative Documents,* 1859. State education officials often report higher figures than those in the census returns.

3. Lawrence A. Cremin, *A History of Education in American Culture* (New York: Holt, 1953); *The Genius of American Education* (Pittsburgh: University of Pittsburgh Press, 1965); *American Education: The Colonial Experience, 1607–1783* (New York: Harper and Row, 1970); *Public Education* (New York: Basic Books, 1976); *Traditions of American Education* (New York: Basic Books, 1977); *American Education: The National Experience* (New York: Harper and Row, 1980); *American Education: The Metropolitan Experience, 1876–1980* (New York: Harper and Row, 1988); *Popular Education and Its Discontents* (New York: Harper and Row, 1990); Bernard Bailyn, *Education in the Forming of American Society: Needs and Opportunities for Study* (Chapel Hill: University of North Carolina Press, 1960; reprint, New York: Norton, 1972); Michael B. Katz, *The Irony of Early School Reform: Educational Innovation in Mid-Nineteenth Century Massachusetts* (Cambridge, MA: Harvard University Press, 1968).

4. John Hardin Best, "Education in the Forming of the American South," *History of Education Quarterly* 36, no. 1 (1996): 44 (first quote); James L. Leloudis, *Schooling the New South: Pedagogy, Self, and Society in North Carolina, 1880–1920* (Chapel Hill: University of North Carolina Press, 1996); Charles William Dabney, *Universal Education in the South,* 4 vols. (Chapel Hill: University of North Carolina Press, 1936); Edgar W. Knight, *Public Education in the South* (Boston: Ginn, 1922); J. Mills Thornton III, *Politics and Power in a Slave Society: Alabama, 1800–1860* (Baton Rouge: Louisiana State University Press, 1978); Steven M. Stowe, *Intimacy and Power in the Old South: Ritual in the Lives of the Planters* (Baltimore: Johns

Hopkins University Press, 1987); Catherine Clinton, *The Plantation Mistress: Woman's World in the Old South* (New York: Pantheon, 1982); Christie Anne Farnham, *The Education of the Southern Belle: Higher Education and Student Socialization in the Antebellum South* (New York: New York University Press, 1994); Mary Kelley, *Learning to Stand and Speak: Women, Education, and Public Life in America's Republic* (Chapel Hill: University of North Carolina, 2006); Forrest David Mathews, "The Politics of Education in the Deep South: Georgia and Alabama, 1830–1860" (PhD diss., Columbia University, 1965), 3 (second quote); see also Loyce Braswell Miles, "Forgotten Scholars: Female Secondary Education in Three Antebellum Deep South States" (PhD diss., Mississippi State University, 2003); Julia Huston Nguyen, "Molding the Minds of the South: Education in Natchez, 1817–1861" (Master's thesis, Louisiana State University, 1997).

CHAPTER ONE

1. Céline Frémaux Garcia, *Céline: Remembering Louisiana, 1850–1871*, ed. Patrick J. Geary, foreword by Bertram Wyatt-Brown (Athens: University of Georgia Press, 1987), 29–31.

2. Lawrence A. Cremin, *Traditions of American Education* (New York: Basic Books, 1977), 19–20, 28–29, 55–56; Catherine Clinton, *The Plantation Mistress: Woman's World in the Old South* (New York : Pantheon, 1982), 49–50; Emily Bingham and Penny Richards, "The Female Academy and Beyond: Three Mordecai Sisters at Work in the Old South," in *Neither Lady nor Slave: Working Women of the Old South,* ed. Susanna Delfino and Michele Gillespie (Chapel Hill: University of North Carolina Press, 2002), 174–97; Thomas C. W. Ellis Diary, Buck-Ellis Family Papers, Mss. 4820, Louisiana and Lower Mississippi Valley Collections, LSU Libraries, Baton Rouge, Louisiana, hereafter cited as LLMVC; Garcia, *Céline*; John D. Pulliam and James J. Van Patten, *History of Education in America,* 7th ed. (Upper Saddle River, NJ: Merrill, 1999), 58; Julia Huston Nguyen, "Molding the Minds of the South: Education in Natchez, 1817–1861" (Master's thesis, Louisiana State University, 1995), 4–5.

3. Garcia, *Céline,* 31.

4. Clinton, *Plantation Mistress,* 50, 126; see also Nguyen, "Molding the Minds of the South," 4–5; Jean A. Friedman, *The Enclosed Garden: Women and Community in the Evangelical South, 1830–1900* (Chapel Hill: University of North Carolina Press, 1985), 99.

5. Bertram Wyatt-Brown, foreword, and Patrick J. Geary, introduction, to Garcia, *Céline,* ix–xxxix.

6. Garcia, *Céline,* 28–29, 50.

7. Ibid., 24, 28, 29.

8. Richard Parkinson, *A Tour in America* (London, 1805), 2:474, quoted in Ulrich B. Phillips, *Life and Labor in the Old South* (New York: Grosset and Dunlap, 1929; reprint, Boston: Little, Brown, 1963), 361.

9. Thomas C. W. Ellis Diary, entries of January 1–June 25, 1856, Buck-Ellis Family Papers, Mss. 4820, LLMVC.

10. Martha L. Batchelor to Albert A. Batchelor, March 2, 1861, Albert A. Batchelor Papers, Mss. 919, 1293, LLMVC.

11. Garcia, *Céline,* 149.

12. Clinton, *Plantation Mistress,* 126.

13. Garcia, *Céline,* 21 (first quote); Wyatt-Brown, foreword to Frémaux, xiii (second quote); Geary, introduction to Garcia, *Celine,* xxix (third quote).

14. Bingham and Richards, "Female Academy and Beyond," 174–97; Emily Bingham, *Mordecai: An American Family* (New York: Hill and Wang, 2003), 59–60, 63, 140.

15. Clinton, *Plantation Mistress,* 126.

16. William J. Cooper Jr. and Thomas E. Terrill, *The American South: A History,* 2nd ed. (New York: McGraw Hill, 1996), 68; Phillips, *Life and Labor in the Old South,* 234; Annie Beatrice Barnett, "A History of Education in the City of Montgomery, Alabama, from 1818 to 1860" (MS thesis, Alabama Polytechnic Institute, 1949), 22; Clement Eaton, *The Growth of Southern Civilization, 1790–1860* (New York: Harper and Row, 1961), 113.

17. *Mississippi Free Trader and Natchez Gazette,* February 18, 1845; Cooper and Terrell, *American South,* 68; Barnett, "History of Education in the City of Montgomery," 60–61; Clinton, *Plantation Mistress,* 127; Fletcher M. Green, *The Role of the Yankee in the Old South* (Athens: University of Georgia Press, 1972) 39; William Kauffman Scarborough, *Masters of the Big House: Elite Slaveholders of the Mid-Nineteenth-Century South* (Baton Rouge: Louisiana State University Press, 2003), 66, 75; Ngyuen, "Molding the Minds of the South," 37.

18. Joseph G. Tregle Jr., *Louisiana in the Age of Jackson: A Clash of Cultures and Personalities* (Baton Rouge: Louisiana State University Press, 1999), 44 (first quote); D. Clayton James, *Antebellum Natchez* (Baton Rouge: Louisiana State University Press, 1968), 217; Charles B. Galloway, "Thomas Griffin: A Boanerges of the Early Southwest," 161, cited in James, *Antebellum Natchez,* 217 (second quote).

19. *The Weekly Advocate* (Baton Rouge), March 1, 1848.

20. William T. Palfrey Plantation Diary, entry of January 3, 1848, Palfrey (Family) Papers, Mss. 334, LLMVC; Scarborough, *Masters of the Big House,* 75; Eaton, *Growth of Southern Civilization,* 113–14; Isaac L. Baker to Dr. John Ker, March 8, 1821, Ker Family Papers #4656, Southern Historical Collection, Louis Round Wilson Special Collections Library, University of North Carolina at Chapel Hill, hereafter cited as SHC; John Wager Swayne to Henry R. Slack, March 24, 1856, Slack Family Papers, #3598, SHC.

21. *Alabama Journal,* January 1, 1840, cited in Barnett, "History of Education in the City of Montgomery," 61.

22. Seargent Smith Prentiss to his mother, October 4, 1827, April 20, 1828, November 18, 1828, quoted in George Lewis Prentiss, ed., *A Memoir of S. S. Prentiss* (New York: C. Scribner's Sons, 1881), 59.

23. William T. Palfrey Plantation Diary, entry of January 3, 1848, Palfrey (Family) Papers, Mss. 334, LLMVC; Scarborough, *Masters of the Big House,* 75; Eaton, *Growth of Southern Civilization,* 113–14; Isaac L. Baker to Dr. John Ker, March 8, 1821, Ker Family Papers #4656, SHC; John Wager Swayne to Henry R. Slack, March 24, 1856, Slack Family Papers, #3598, SHC; Seargent Smith Prentiss to his mother, October 4, 1827, April 20, 1828, November 18, 1828, quoted in Prentiss, ed., *Memoir of S. S. Prentiss,* 59 (first quote); *Alabama Journal,* January 1, 1840, cited in Annie Beatrice Barnett, "A History of Education in the City of Montgomery," 60–61 (second quote); see also Phillips, *Life and Labor in the Old South,* 359.

24. James, *Antebellum Natchez,* 142; Barnett, "History of Education in the City of Montgomery," 60.

25. Abraham Hagaman Memoir, 32–49, Mississippi Department of Archives and History, Jackson, MS, hereafter cited as MDAH.

26. Clinton, *Plantation Mistress,* 128–29.

27. Ibid. (quote); Mary E. Taylor to Stella Hunter, February 7, 1859, in Hunter-Taylor Papers, Mss. 3024, LLMVC. For a discussion of the feminization of the teaching profession prior to the Civil War, see Kim Tolley and Nancy Beadie, "Socioeconomic Incentives to Teach in New York and North Carolina: Toward a More Complex Model of Teacher Labor Markets, 1800–1850," *History of Education Quarterly* 46, no. 1 (March 2006): 36–72.

28. Barnett, "History of Education in the City of Montgomery," 60 (first quote); John Davis, *Travels* (London, 1803), 84, 85, cited in Phillips, *Life and Labor in the Old South,* 359–60 (second quote); Tregle, *Louisiana in the Age of Jackson,* 44 (third quote); Nguyen, "Molding the Minds of the South," 54.

29. Alma H. Peterson, "A Historical Survey of the Administration of Education in New Orleans, 1718–1851" (PhD diss., Louisiana State University, 1962), 21.

30. Julius A. Reed to Henry Watson Jr., February 11, 1832, cited in James, *Antebellum Natchez,* 139–40.

31. Julius A. Reed to Henry Watson Jr., April 14, 1832, ibid.

32. Ibid.

33. Hagaman Memoir, MDAH, 35; Nguyen, "Molding the Minds of the South," 52–53.

34. Barnett, "Education in the City of Montgomery," 60 (first quote); Charles M. Conrad to William G. Walton, October 2, 1854, Charles M. Conrad Letter, Mss. 3377, LLMVC (later quotes).

35. "Report of the State Superintendent of Public Education," *Louisiana Legislative Documents,* 1857, 9, 55.

36. Barnett, "History of Education in the City of Montgomery," 60.

37. Scarborough, *Masters of the Big House,* 75.

38. Margaret Batchelor to Albert Batchelor, March 2, 1861, in Albert A. Batchelor Papers, Mss. 919, 1293, LLMVC.

39. Cooper and Terrill, *The American South,* 245. The authors note, "Virginia had only 14 white inhabitants per square mile and North Carolina but 12. Massachusetts, in contrast, had 127 inhabitants for each square mile."

40. Phillips, *Life and Labor in the Old South,* 359; Anna Dunbar Smith to Thomas Affleck, March 3, 1842 (quote); Sarah Walworth to Douglas Walworth, October 15, 1851, both in Nguyen, "Molding the Minds of the South," 5.

41. Lizzie Connell to "Pet" [Cornelia Randolph Stewart], April 17, 1863, Albert A. Batchelor Papers, Mss. 919, 1293, LLMVC.

42. Buck-Ellis Family Papers, Mss. 4820, LLMVC.

CHAPTER TWO

1. United States Census Bureau, *Sixth Census,* 1840, 55–63; *Seventh Census,* 1850, 142; *Eighth Census,* 1860, 506.

2. Frank Lawrence Owsley, *Plain Folk of the Old South,* with an introduction by John B. Boles (Baton Rouge: Louisiana State University Press, 1949; updated edition, 2008), 147 (quote); John D. Pulliam and James J. Van Patten, *History of Education in America,* 7th ed. (Upper Saddle River, NJ: Merrill, 1999), 58; Clement Eaton, *The Growth of Southern Civilization, 1790–1860* (New York: Harper and Row, 1961), 115.

3. School Article for 1828, Clinton School Papers, Mss. 925, Louisiana and Lower Mississippi Valley Collections, Louisiana State University Libraries, Baton Rouge, Louisiana, hereafter cited as LLMVC.

4. School Article for 1827, Clinton School Papers, Mss. 925, LLMVC.

5. Loyce Braswell Miles, "Forgotten Scholars: Female Secondary Education in Three Antebellum Deep South States" (PhD diss., Mississippi State University, 2003), 11 (quotes); *Eighth Census,* 1860, 506.

6. Fisher (Lucy Maria W. F. P.) Memoir, [typescript] Mss. 2497, LLMVC, 13–15.

7. Ibid., 13–14.

8. "Silliman Female Collegiate Institute," Hunter-Taylor Papers, Mss. 3024, LLMVC.

9. Harriet B. Ellis, "Mobile Public School Beginnings and Their Background" (MS thesis, Alabama Polytechnic Institute, 1930), 18, 21 (quote); *History of Education in Alabama,* Bicentennial Intern Project conducted by the Alabama State Department of Education in cooperation with the Southern Regional Education Board, Bulletin 1975, no 7, 7; Forrest David Mathews, "The Politics of Education in the Deep South: Georgia and Alabama, 1830–1860" (PhD diss., Columbia University, 1965), 348.

10. Maggie Lea Causey, "A Study of Education in Alabama prior to Statehood" (MEd thesis, University of Alabama, 1938), 16–17.

11. Caroline Lee Hentz Diary and Finding Aid, Hentz Family Papers, #332, Southern Historical Collection, the Louis Round Wilson Special Collections Library, University of North Carolina at Chapel Hill, hereafter cited as SHC; "Silliman Female Collegiate Institute" [brochure for 1854–55 school session], Sister to [Stella Hunter Taylor], October 19, 1855 [Mary Emerson Taylor to Stella Hunter Taylor], September 30, 1859, Hunter-Taylor Family Papers, Mss. 3024, LLMVC; Fisher Memoir, 13–14, LLMVC.

12. Fisher Memoir, 13; Contract between John T. Faulk and William J. Henderson, February 7, 1833, John Faulk Papers, Mss. 877, LLMVC (quote).

13. Mary L. Baker to Isaac L. Baker, May 20, 1816; Mary L. Baker to Sarah Metcalfe, July 23, 1818, Ker Family Papers, #4656, SHC. Mary Baker alternately refers to this family as Hosmer, Hasmer, and Hesmer; Mollie Batchelor to Albert A. Batchelor, February 18, 1861, Albert A. Batchelor Papers, Mss. 919, LLMVC; John Palfrey to Rezin D. Shepherd, August 16, 1815, Palfrey Family Papers, Mss. 333, LLMVC (quote).

14. "Baton Rouge High School for Boys," Baton Rouge *Democratic Advocate,* June 5, 1847 (first quote); Elizabeth Norton to [Sarah] Robinson, July 18, 1822, Ker Family Papers, #4656, SHC (second quote).

15. Sr. Mary Bernard Graham to Judge Palfrey, August 8, 1852, Palfrey Family Papers, LLMVC.

16. Eaton, *The Growth of Southern Civilization, 1790–1860,* 116; Caroline Lee Hentz Diary, entry of March 19, 1837, Hentz Family Papers, #332, SHC (quote).

17. Annie Beatrice Barnett, "A History of Education in the City of Montgomery, Alabama, from 1818 to 1860" (MS thesis, Alabama Polytechnic Institute, 1949), 26–28.

18. Thomas Millsaps to Thomas Ellis, September 14, 1855, Buck-Ellis Family Papers, Mss. 4820, LLMVC (first quote); Fisher Memoir, 15, LLMVC (second quote).

19. E. L. Ellis to "Father," April 1, 1857, Buck-Ellis Family Collection, Mss. 4820, LLMVC; T. W. Mieure to Albert A. Batchelor, August 30, 1860, in Albert A. Batchelor Collection, Mss. 919, LLMVC (quote); Joseph B. Lightsey Diary, June 25, 1852, Mississippi Department of Archives and History, Jackson, MS, hereafter cited as MDAH.

20. William Lacey to Thomas Butler, June 25, 1847, Ellis-Farar Papers, Mss. 1000, LLMVC (first quote); Caroline Lee Hentz Diary, entry of February 11, 1836, Hentz Family Papers #332, SHC (second quote).

21. Lawrence Daily to James Williams, November 11, 1803, Ker Family Papers #4656, SHC.

22. James J. Lemon Letter, June 29, 1861, Mss. 3245, LLMVC.

23. E. Mazureau to H. Holley, December 4, 1824, Joseph Reynes Family Papers, Mss. 1038, LLMVC.

24. Philip H. Dunbar to "My dear little cousin," November 4, 1857, Albert A. Batchelor Papers, Mss. 919, LLMVC (first quote); Nannie Cage to [Cornelia Randolph Stewart], April 1864, ibid. (second quote).

25. Fisher Memoir, 44, LLMVC.

26. George Leidigh to Jacob Leidigh, September 1, 1859, November 26, 1859, January 30, 1860, Jacob M. Leidigh Correspondence, Mss. 1598, LLMVC.

27. Edward Palfrey to William T. Palfrey, September 8, 1848, Palfrey Family Papers, Mss. 333, LLMVC (first quote); Charles Batchelor to Albert Batchelor, December 10, 1856, Albert A. Batchelor Papers, Mss. 919, LLMVC (second quote).

28. Nannie Cage to [Cornelia Randolph Stewart], January 31, 1864, Albert A. Batchelor Papers, Mss. 919, LLMVC.

29. Nannie Cage to [Cornelia Randolph Stewart], January 31, 1864, Albert A. Batchelor Papers, Mss. 919, LLMVC (quote); William Hooper, *Lecture on the Imperfections of Our Primary Schools,* cited in Ulrich B. Phillips, *Life and Labor in the Old South* (New York: Grosset and Dunlap, 1929; reprint, Boston: Little, Brown, 1953), 358.

30. This is a different Thomas Ellis than the Thomas C. W. Ellis mentioned in the first chapter who tutored his siblings.

31. H. Peugnet to Mss. Howaland and Aspinwall, May 11, 1846; Thomas Ellis to Thomas Butler, August 3, 1846, Ellis-Farar Papers, Mss. 1000, LLMVC.

32. S. S. Morris to Joseph Embree, February 12, 1861, Joseph Embree Family Papers, Mss. 692, LLMVC.

33. James F. Gayle to [Albert Batchelor], May 4, 1860, Albert A. Batchelor Papers, Mss. 919, LLMVC (first quote); J. F. Gayle to [Albert Batchelor], November 14, [1860], ibid. (second quote).

34. [Edward] Palfrey to [William T. Palfrey], September 2, 1848, September 8, 1848, September 11, 1848, Palfrey Family Papers, Mss. 333, LLMVC.

35. Ibid.; W. Gordon McCabe, "Graduates of West Point Serving in the CSA Army," *Southern Historical Society Pages* 30 (1902): 34–76.

36. E. A. Bonner to John M. Bonner, December 5, 1850, Samuel C. Bonner Family Papers, Mss. 1472, 1507, LLMVC (first quote); Charles Batchelor to [Martha L. Batchelor], January 16, 1860 (second quote); James Madison Batchelor to Albert A. Batchelor, February 5, 6, 1858, Albert A. Batchelor Papers, Mss. 919, LLMVC (third quote).

37. Laura May Gayden to "Cousin," October 1, 1858, Albert A. Batchelor Papers, Mss. 919, LLMVC.

38. Thomas Ellis to [Ezekiel Parke Ellis], January 10, 1853, Buck-Ellis Family Papers, Mss. 4820, LLMVC; William T. Palfrey Jr. to William T. Palfrey Sr., November 22, 1844, Palfrey Family Papers, Mss. 333, LLMVC; James Madison Batchelor to Albert A. Batchelor, February 6, 1858, Albert A. Batchelor Papers, Mss. 919, LLMVC.

39. Martha L. Batchelor to Albert A. Batchelor, December 11, 1860, Batchelor Papers, LLMVC.

40. Sister Columba Morancy to Anne Morancy, November 9, 1852, Honore P. Morancy Family Papers, Mss. 2430, LLMVC.

41. Laleah G. Pratt to Eliza Lancaster, August 4, 1841, Sister Columba to Eliza Lancaster, September 19, 1841 (quote), ibid.

42. Eliza A. Bonner to John M. Bonner, May 5, 1851, Samuel C. Bonner and Family Papers, Mss. 1472, 1507, LLMVC; Martha L. Batchelor to Albert A. Batchelor, April 13, 1861 (quote), James Madison Batchelor to Albert A. Batchelor, February 5, 1858, Albert A. Batchelor Family Papers, LLMVC.

43. Bettie Morancy to "Sister," August 1860, Honore P. Morancy Family Papers, Mss. 2430, LLMVC.

44. Lizzie to Albert A. Batchelor, February 18, 1861, Albert A. Batchelor Papers, Mss. 919, LLMVC.

45. Jessie M. Menzies to Albert A. Batchelor, March 15, 1861, Albert A. Batchelor Papers, Mss. 919, LLMVC.

46. John Palfrey to "Sir," December 29, 1810, Palfrey Family Papers, Mss. 334, LLMVC; Richard G. Ellis to Thomas Butler, September 27, 1837, Ellis-Farar Papers, Mss. 1000, LLMVC.

47. Bettie Morancy to "Sister," August 1860, Honore P. Morancy Family Papers, Mss. 2430, LLMVC (first quote); Martha L. Batchelor to Albert A. Batchelor, December 11, 1860, Albert A. Batchelor Papers, Mss. 919, LLMVC (second quote).

CHAPTER THREE

1. Dunbar Rowland, ed., *Official Letter Books of W. C. C. Claiborne, 1801–1816,* 6 vols. (Jackson, MS: State Department of Archives and History, 1917), 4:293.

2. *Alabama House Journal,* First Annual Session, 1819, 8–9 (first quote); *Mississippi House Journal,* Twelfth Annual Session, 1829, 15 (following quotes).

3. *Mississippi House Journal,* Seventeenth Annual Session, 1833, 13 (quote); *Journal of the Senate of the State of Alabama,* Third Biennial Session, 1851–1852, 29–39.

4. *Alabama Legislative Documents,* 1818–1860.

5. *Alabama Senate Journal,* Called Session, December 1841, 94.

6. *Mississippi House Journal,* Regular Session, 1850, 20–21.

7. *Mississippi Constitution* (1817), art. 6, sec. 16 (first quote); *Alabama Constitution* (1819), art. 3, sec. 5 (second quote); Walter I. Trattner, "The Federal Government and Needy Citizens in Nineteenth-Century America," *Political Science Quarterly* 103, no. 2 (1988): 350.

8. Oscar W. Hyatt, "The Development of Secondary Education in Alabama prior to 1920" (DEd diss., George Peabody College for Teachers, 1933), 7; "An Act to establish an Academy in the town of Sparta, and for other purposes," approved December 8, 1821, *Acts passed at the Third Annual Session of the General Assembly of the State of Alabama* (Cahawba: Wm. B. Allen and Co., State Printers, 1822), 84–85 (first quote); "An Act to incorporate the Montpelier Academy, and to make an appropriation for said Academy and for the College of Alexandria, approved March 30, 1833," Henry A. Bullard and Thomas Curry, *A New Digest of the Statute Laws of the State of Louisiana, From the Change of Government to the Year 1841, Inclusive* (New Orleans: E. Johns, 1842), 1:317–18 (second quote).

9. *Alabama Senate Journal,* Fifth Biennial Session, 1855–1856, 13–14, 103. The legislatures of other Gulf South states likewise tended to enact special legislation rather than general statutes that applied to the entire state. J. Mills Thornton points out that in 1851 the Alabama legislature passed 452 laws, only 42 of which were general laws; see Thornton, *Politics and Power in a Slave Society: Alabama, 1800–1860 (Baton Rouge: Louisiana State University Press, 1978),* 85.

10. "An Act to provide for leasing for a limited time the Lands reserved by the Congress of the United States, for the support of Schools, within each township in this State; for a Seminary of Learning, and for other purposes," *Acts of the General Assembly of the State of Alabama, Passed at Its First Session* (Huntsville, AL: John Boardman, 1820; reprint, Washington, DC: T. L. Cole, 1912), 60–64 (first and second quotes); "An Act to provide for leasing the Sixteenth Sections, and for the application of the funds arising therefrom to the purposes of Education," *Acts passed at the Fourth Annual Session of the General Assembly of the State of Alabama* (Cahawba: William B. Allen, 1823), 73–78 (third quote). For the use of sixteenth section land, see also George Duke Humphrey, "Public Education for Whites in Mississippi, A Historical and Interpretive Study" (DEd diss., Ohio State University, 1939), 16; Earl Wayne Adams, "The History of Public School Finance in Mississippi" (DEd diss., University of Mississippi, 1980), 21–23; Forrest David Mathews, "The Politics of Education in the Deep South: Georgia and Alabama, 1830–1860" (PhD diss., Columbia University, 1965), 231; William C. Reavis, "Federal Aid for Education," *Annals of the American Academy of Political and Social Science* 265 (1949): 56; Walter I. Trattner, "The Federal Government and Needy Citizens in Nineteenth-Century America," *Political Science Quarterly* 103, no. 2 (1988): 350; Paul W. Gates, "An Overview of American Land Policy," *Agricultural History* 50, no. 1 (1976): 219; Charles H. Judd, "Federal Support of Public Education," *The Elementary School Journal* 36, no. 7 (1936): 498; Edgar W. Knight, *Public Education in the South* (Boston: Ginn, 1922), 172.

11. A county was a large territorial unit, composed of parishes.

12. Knight, *Public Education in the South,* 172; Adams, "The History of Public School Finance in Mississippi," 24; Humphrey, "Public Education for Whites in Mississippi," 16–17; William Henington Weathersby, *A History of Educational Legislation in Mississippi from 1798 to 1860* (Chicago: University of Chicago Press, 1921), 26; Sarah E. Lipscomb, "A Crisis of Opportunity: The Example of New Orleans and Public Education in Antebellum Louisiana," (MA thesis, Louisiana State University, 2005), 46–47; "An Act to extend and improve the system of Public Education in the State of Louisiana, approved February 16, 1821," Bullard and Curry, *A New Digest,* 357–62.

13. *Alabama Senate Journal,* Tenth Annual Session, 1828, 8.

14. Raleigh A. Suarez, "Chronicle of a Failure: Public Education in Antebellum Louisiana," *Louisiana History,* no. 12 (1971): 115.

15. The fifth section of the 1821 law stipulated, "That the trustees shall admit in the school or schools of their respective parishes, eight day scholars, taken from those families who are indigent, which day scholars shall be apportioned in the different schools by said trustees, and shall receive instruction gratis, and be moreover furnished with classical books, quills and paper, at the cost of said school or schools." "An Act to extend and improve the system of Public Education in the State of Louisiana, approved February 16, 1821," Bullard and Curry, *A New Digest,* 358.

16. *Louisiana Senate Journal,* First Session, 1833, 4 (first quote); *Louisiana Senate Journal,* Second Session, 1833, 2 (second quote); *Louisiana Senate Journal,* Second Session, 1842, 4.

17. *Louisiana Senate Journal,* First Session, 1823, 7.

18. "An Act to provide for the support and administration of Parish Schools, and for other purposes, approved March 14, 1827," Bullard and Curry, *A New Digest,* 360; "An Act supplementary to an act entitled, 'An Act to provide for the support and administration of parish schools and for other purposes, passed and approved March 14, 1827,' approved March 21, 1828," Bullard and Curry, ibid., 362–63 (quote).

19. *Louisiana Senate Journal,* First Session, 1833, 4; "An Act supplementary to the several acts relative to public education, approved April 1, 1833," Bullard and Curry, *A New Digest,* 289–91 (quote).

20. *Louisiana Senate Journal,* Second Session, 1834; *Louisiana Senate Journal,* First Session, 1835, 25; *Louisiana Senate Journal,* Second Session, 1836, 33.

21. *Louisiana Senate Journal,* Second Session, 1833, 38–39. There were thirty-two parishes in Louisiana in 1833, but only twenty-seven reported school conditions to the secretary of state; "Report of the Secretary of State on Public Education," *Louisiana Senate Journal,* Second Session, 1836, 34.

22. "Report of the Secretary of State on Public Education," *Louisiana Senate Journal,* Second Session, 1842, 48.

23. Charles William Dabney, *Universal Education in the South,* 4 vols. (Chapel Hill: University of North Carolina Press, 1936), 1:363; T. H. Harris, *The Story of Public Education in Louisiana* (New Orleans: by the author, 1924), 10; *Louisiana Senate Journal,* Second Session, 1833, 2 (first quote); *Louisiana Senate Journal,* First Session, 1835, 25 (second quote); "Report of the Secretary of State on Public Education," *Louisiana Senate Journal,* Second Session, 1842, 48.

24. *Louisiana Senate Journal,* Second Session, 1833, 40 (first quote); Suarez, "Chronicle of a Failure," 115–16; "Report of the State Superintendent of Public Education," *Louisiana Legislative Documents,* 1847, 7–9 (second quote).

25. Suarez, "Chronicle of a Failure," 116; James William Mobley, *The Academy Movement in Louisiana* (n.p., reprinted from *The Louisiana Historical Quarterly,* 1947), 13.

26. "Report of the Secretary of State on Public Education," *Louisiana Senate Journal,* Second Session, 1842, 48 (first quote); "Report of the Secretary of State on Public Education," *Louisiana Legislative Documents,* 1844, vi (second quote); "Report of the Secretary of State on Public Education," *Louisiana Senate Journal,* 1846, 56 (final quotes).

27. Adams, "The History of Public School Finance in Mississippi," 34–38; Humphrey, "Public Education for Whites in Mississippi," 30–32; Weathersby, *A History of Educational Legislation,* 28.

28. Adams, "The History of Public School Finance in Mississippi," 20, 217; Weathersby, *A History of Educational Legislation,* 9–10, 28–29.

29. *Mississippi House Journal,* Twelfth Annual Session, 1829, 15; *Mississippi House Journal,* Thirteenth Annual Session, 1830, 11, 169–70 (quote).

30. *Mississippi House Journal,* Thirteenth Annual Session, 1830, 170.

31. Ibid.

32. *Mississippi House Journal,* Fourteenth Annual Session, 1831, 9.

33. *Mississippi House Journal,* Sixteenth Annual Session, 1833, 13 (first quote); *Mississippi House Journal,* Seventeenth Annual Session, 1834, 186–87 (second quote).

34. *Mississippi House Journal,* Seventeenth Annual Session, 1834, 186–87; *Mississippi House Journal,* Regular Session, 1836, 23–24, 325; *Mississippi House Journal,* Twelfth Annual Session, 1829, 14; *Mississippi House Journal,* Sixteenth Annual Session, 1833, 13; *Mississippi House Journal,* Adjourned Session, 1837, 52–53; *Mississippi House Journal,* Adjourned Session, 1839, 7–10; *Mississippi House Journal,* Regular Session, 1840, 17–19; *Mississippi House Journal,* Regular Session, 1844, 14–20.

35. Humphrey, "Public Education for Whites in Mississippi," 32–34; Adams, "The History of Public School Finance in Mississippi," 36–37.

36. *Alabama Senate Journal,* Eighth Annual Session, 1826–1827, 6.

37. Mathews, "The Politics of Education in the Deep South," 251 (first quote); *Alabama Senate Journal,* Twelfth Annual Session, 1830, 7–8 (final quotes).

38. *Alabama Senate Journal,* Twelfth Annual Session, 1830, 7–8.

39. Mathews, "The Politics of Education in the Deep South," 254–60.

40. *Alabama Senate Journal,* Seventeenth Annual Session, 1835, 41.

41. Mathews, "The Politics of Education in the Deep South," 261 (first quote); *Flag of the Union* (Tuscaloosa), November 8, 1837, cited in Mathews, "The Politics of Education in the Deep South," 261 (second quote).

42. *Alabama Senate Journal,* Regular Session, 1838–1839, 13.

43. Hyatt, "The Development of Secondary Education in Alabama prior to 1920," 12; Mathews, "The Politics of Education in the Deep South," 271–73; Stephen B. Weeks, *History of Public School Education in Alabama* (Washington, DC: Government Printing Office, US Bureau of Education Bulletin, no. 12, 1915; reprint, Westport, CT: Negro University Press, 1971), 49; *Alabama Senate Journal,* Annual Session, 1840–1841, 14–15 (quote).

44. *History of Education in Alabama,* Bicentennial Intern Project conducted by the Alabama State Department of Education in cooperation with the Southern Regional Education Board, Bulletin no. 7, 1975, 6; Mathews, "The Politics of Education in the Deep South," 271; Weeks, *History of Public School Education,* 50. George Duke Humphrey argues in his 1939 study that "a planter-controlled Legislature was selling Mississippi down the river, and in so doing squandering educational funds, and every other kind they could get their hands on." He goes on to surmise that the history of Mississippi's early banking system reveals that "the planter class, who for a long time dictated legislative policies, actually did much to retard the development of public education in the State by getting control and squandering the funds that had been intended for educational purposes." In Humphrey, "Public Education for Whites in Mississippi," 38–39.

45. Richard E. Ellis, *The Union at Risk: Jacksonian Democracy, States' Rights, and the Nullification Crisis* (New York: Oxford University Press, 1987), 176.

46. *Alabama Senate Journal,* Twenty-Sixth Session, 1844–1845, 207.

CHAPTER FOUR

1. "Eleventh Annual Report of the Board of Visitors of the Natchez Institute: made to the President and Selectmen of the City of Natchez" (Natchez, MS: printed at the *Courier* Office, 1856), 11; *Mississippi Free Trader and Natchez Gazette,* February 18, 1845, February 20, 1845.

2. Martin Luther Riley, "The Development of Education in Louisiana prior to State-hood" (n.p., reprinted from *Louisiana Historical Quarterly* 19, 1936:, 39; Raleigh A. Suarez, "Chronicle of a Failure: Public Education in Antebellum Louisiana," *Louisiana History* 12 (1971), 111; Alma H. Peterson, "A Historical Survey of the Administration of Education in New Orleans, 1718–1851" (PhD diss., Louisiana State University, 1962), 32; *Louisiana Senate Journal,* Second Session, 1816, 7; *Louisiana Senate Journal,* First Session, 1817, 43 (quotes); *Louisiana Senate Journal,* First Session, 1819; *Louisiana Senate Journal,* First Session, 1820.

3. "Annual Report of the Central and Primary Schools," *Louisiana Senate Journal,* First Session, 1833, 24–25 (quote); *Louisiana Senate Journal,* First Session, 1823; *Louisiana Senate Journal,* First Session, 1825; *Louisiana Senate Journal,* Second Session, 1826, 92; Joseph G. Tregle Jr., *Louisiana in the Age of Jackson: A Clash of Cultures and Personalities* (Baton Rouge: Louisiana State University Press, 1999), 45; Joel L. Fletcher, *Louisiana Education since Colonial Days* (Lafayette: Southwestern Louisiana Institute, 1948), 5; Donald E. Devore and Joseph Logsdon, *Crescent City Schools: Public Education in New Orleans, 1841–1991* (Lafayette: Center for Louisiana Studies, University of Southwestern Louisiana, 1991), 9; Peter J. Hamilton, *Mobile of the Five Flags: The Story of the River Basin and Coast about Mobile from the Earliest Times to the Present* (Mobile: Gill Printing, 1913), 210; T. H. Harris, *The Story of Public Education in Louisiana* (New Orleans: by the author, 1924), 7; Peterson, "Historical Survey," 33–34; Suarez, "Chronicle of a Failure," 113; John B. Robson, *Education in Louisiana* (Natchitoches, LA: Northwestern State College, 1957), 1; Edwin Whitfield Fay, *The History of Education in Louisiana* (Washington, DC: Government Printing Office, 1898), 33.

4. *Louisiana Senate Journal,* Second Session, 1826, 92; Peterson, "Historical Survey," 38–39; "Report of the Central and Primary Schools," *Louisiana Senate Journal,* First Session, 1833, 24–25 (quote).

5. [First] *Annual Report of the Council of Municipality Number Two, of the City of New Orleans, on the Condition of its Public Schools* (New Orleans: printed at the Office of the *Picayune,* 1845), 5; "Report of the Committee on Education," *Louisiana Senate Journal,* First Session, 1823, 53; *Report of the Board of Directors of the Public Schools of the Second Municipality* (New Orleans: Die Glocke Office, 1848); Peterson, "Historical Survey," 40–41; see also *Third Annual Report of the Council of Municipality Number Two* (New Orleans: printed at the office of the *Commercial Bulletin,* 1844).

6. Peterson, "A Historical Survey of the Administration of Education in New Orleans," 40–41; Mel Leavitt, *A Short History of New Orleans* (San Francisco: Lexikos, 1982), 88; John Smith Kendall, *History of New Orleans* (Chicago: Lewis Publishing, 1922), 134–35.

7. Robert C. Reinders, "New England Influences on the Formation of Public Schools in New Orleans," *Journal of Southern History* 30 (1964): 181, 183; *Louisiana Senate Journal,* First Session, 1841.

8. [First] *Annual Report of the Council of Municipality Number Two,* 6; *Second Annual Report of the Council of Municipality Number Two,* 25; "Report of the State Superintendent of Education," *Louisiana Legislative Documents,* 1847, 12; Robert W. Shugg, *Origins of Class Struggle in Louisiana: A Social History of White Farmers and Laborers during Slavery and After, 1840–1875* (Baton Rouge: Louisiana State University Press, 1939), 68–69; Peterson, "Historical Survey," 53–54; Devore and Logsdon, *Crescent City Schools,* 22, 23 (quote); Rein-

ders, "New England Influences," 190–91; Charles William Dabney, *Universal Education in the South,* 4 vols. (Chapel Hill: University of North Carolina Press, 1936), 1:363.

9. Kendall, *History of New Orleans,* 172; Reinders, "New England Influences," 186.

10. [*First*] *Annual Report of the Council of Municipality Number Two,* 5–6 (quotes); Jonathan Messerli, *Horace Mann: A Biography* (New York: Knopf, 1972), xi; Reinders, "New England Influences," 183; Peterson, "Historical Survey," 122.

11. [*First*] *Annual Report of the Council of Municipality Number Two,* 5–6, 12.

12. Peterson, "Historical Survey," 193, 206.

13. [*First*] *Annual Report of the Council of the Second Municipality,* 6 (quotes); Peterson, ibid., 55, 119; Fay, *The History of Education in Louisiana,* 71.

14. *Second Annual Report of the Council of Municipality Number Two,* 15.

15. [*First*] *Annual Report of the Council of Municipality Number Two,* 7–8 (quotes); *Second Annual Report of the Council of Municipality Number Two,* 18; Annual Report of the Treasurer of the Parish of Orleans, First–Fourth Districts, to the State Superintendent," included in "Report of the State Superintendent of Public Education," *Louisiana Legislative Documents,* 1859, 84–91; Reinders, "New England Influences," 189; Peterson, "Historical Survey," 141–45; *Report of the Board of Directors of the Public Schools of the Second Municipality,* 1848, 4.

16. [*First*] *Annual Report of the Council of Municipality Number Two,* 8; *Third Annual Report of the Council of Municipality Number Two,* 37 (quote).

17. Devore and Logsdon, *Crescent City Schools,* 29; "Report of the State Superintendent of Public Education," *Louisiana Senate Journal,* 1847, 43.

18. *Second Annual Report of the Council of Municipality Number Two* reports their schools were only closed during the month of August, although most reports, such as those included in the State Superintendent of Education Reports, document a ten-month term. See also "Report of the State Superintendent of Public Education," *Louisiana Legislative Documents,* 1858, 96–102.

19. Peterson, "Historical Survey," 131, 147, 224, 244; *Annual Report of the Board of Directors of the Public Schools of the First District of New Orleans, for the Year ending June 30, 1856* (New Orleans: printed at the office of the *Creole,* 1856); "Annual Report of the Treasurer of the Parish of Orleans, First District, to the State Superintendent," included in "Report of the State Superintendent of Public Education," *Louisiana Legislative Documents,* 1859, 84.

20. Reinders, "New England Influences," 184; *Annual Report of the Board of Directors of the Public Schools of the First District of New Orleans, for the Year ending June 30, 1856.*

21. Peterson, "Historical Survey," 58; Thelma Welch, "Salary Policies for Teachers in New Orleans Public Schools, 1841–1941" (unpublished Master's thesis, Tulane University, 1942), 17, cited in Peterson, "Historical Survey," 58.

22. *Second Annual Report of the Council of Municipality Number Two,* 17; "Report of the Second District of New Orleans," included in the "State Superintendent of Education Report," *Louisiana Legislative Documents,* 1854, 95; [*First*] *Annual Reports of the Council of Municipality Number Two,* 10; *Annual Report of the Board of Directors of the Public Schools of the First District of New Orleans, for the Year ending June 30, 1856;* see also "Report of the State Superintendent of Public Education," *Louisiana Legislative Documents,* 1847, 10.

23. "Report of the State Superintendent of Education," *Louisiana Legislative Documents,* 1859, 89, 91 (first and second quotes); [*First*] *Annual Report of the Council of Municipality Number Two,* 8 (third quote); *Second Annual Report of the Council of Municipality Number*

Two, 21. For typical comments on the qualifications of teachers, see reports of the municipalities, included in "Report of the State Superintendent of Education," *Louisiana Legislative Documents,* 1854, 92–97; 1858, 96–102; 1859, 84–91; 1861, 41–49.

24. *Second Annual Report of the Council of Municipality Number Two,* 17 (first quote); "Report of the State Superintendent of Education," *Louisiana Legislative Documents,* 1858, 9; "Report of the Normal School," included in "Report of the State Superintendent of Education," *Louisiana Legislative Documents,* 1859, 101 (second quote); "Annual Report of the Treasurer of the Parish of Orleans, Fourth District, to the State Superintendent," included in "Report of the State Superintendent of Public Education," *Louisiana Legislative Documents,* 1858, 102 (third quote). For examples of requests to the legislature for a normal school, please see "Report of the State Superintendent of Education," *Louisiana Legislative Documents,* 1857, 12; 1856, 10.

25. [*First*] *Annual Report of the Council of Municipality Number Two,* 11–12 (first quote); *Report of the Board of Directors of the Public Schools of the Second Municipality,* 1848; *Second Annual Report of the Council of Municipality Number Two,* 25 (second quote).

26. [*First*] *Annual Report of the Council of Municipality Number Two,* 6 (first quote); *Second Annual Report of the Council of Municipality Number Two,* 24 (second quote); *Third Annual Report of the Council of Municipality Number Two,* 34 (third quote).

27. *Report of the Board of Directors of the Public Schools of the Second Municipality,* 1848 (first quote); *Third Annual Report of the Council of Municipality Number Two,* 34 (second quote); *Report of the Board of Directors of the Public Schools of the Second Municipality,* 1848; [*First*] *Annual Report of the Council of Municipality Number Two,* 10; "Report of the State Superintendent of Education," *Louisiana Legislative Documents,* 1861, 42.

28. "Report of the State Superintendent of Education," *Louisiana Legislative Documents,* 1854, 92, 95, 96, 97; 1859, 84; 1861, 47.

29. [*First*] *Annual Report of the Council of Municipality Number Two,* 10 (first quote); *Second Annual Report of the Council of Municipality Number Two,* 18 (second quote); Reinders, "New England Influences on the Formation of Public Schools in New Orleans," 186.

30. [*First*] *Annual Report of the Council of Municipality Number Two,* 11; "Report of the State Superintendent of Education," *Louisiana Legislative Documents,* 1857, 6 (quote).

31. Reinders, "New England Influences," 183 (quote); Peterson, "Historical Survey," 73, 110–11, 209.

32. *Second Annual Report of the Council of Municipality Number Two,* 22.

33. Peterson, "Historical Survey," 49, 98, 196; "Report of the Secretary of State on the Public Education of Louisiana," *Louisiana Legislative Documents,* 1843, vi ; *Third Annual Report of the Council of Municipality Number Two,* 34, 38; *Second Annual Report of the Council of Municipality Number Two,* 20; "Annual Report of the Treasurer of the Parish of Orleans, Second District, to the State Superintendent," included in "Report of the State Superintendent of Education," *Louisiana Legislative Documents,* 1861, 44.

34. Leavitt, *A Short History of New Orleans,* 94–95.

35. [*First*] *Annual Report of the Council of Municipality Number Two,* 14; *Second Annual Report of the Council of Municipality Number Two,* 19–20; *Third Annual Report of the Council of Municipality Number Two,* 34.

36. *Second Annual Report of the Council of Municipality Number Two,* 24; *Third Annual Report of the Council of Municipality Number Two,* 38.

37. [*First*] *Annual Report of the Council of Municipality Number Two,* 14.

38. *Acts Passed at the Seventh Annual Session of the General Assembly of the State of Alabama, begun and held in the Town of Cahawba, on the Third Monday in November, 1825* (n.p. [1826?]), 35.

39. Forrest David Mathews, "The Politics of Education in the Deep South: Georgia and Alabama, 1830–1860" (PhD diss., Columbia University, 1965), 243–44; Willis G. Clark, *History of Education in Alabama 1702–1889* (Washington, DC: Government Printing Office, 1889), 222 (quote); Peter J. Hamilton, *Mobile of the Five Flags: The Story of the River Basin and Coast about Mobile from Earliest Times to the Present* (Mobile, AL: Gill Printing, 1913), 229; T. C. Fay, *Mobile Directory, or Stranger's Guide for 1839: Embracing Names of Firms, the Individuals Composing Them, and Citizens Generally; together with their Professions, Residence & Number, Alphabetically Arranged, with a Cross Index* (Mobile, AL: R. R. Dade, 1839), IV; Harriet Amos Doss, *Cotton City: Urban Development in Antebellum Mobile* (University: University of Alabama Press, 1985), 37, 162, 171–72, 181.

40. *Acts Passed at the Seventh Annual Session of the General Assembly of the State of Alabama, 1825,* 35; Harriet B. Ellis, "Mobile Public School Beginnings and their Background" (MS thesis, Alabama Polytechnic Institute, 1930), 12; Doss, *Cotton City,* 179–80; Doss, *Cotton City,* 180 (quote).

41. Oscar W. Hyatt, "The Development of Secondary Education in Alabama prior to 1920" (DEd diss., George Peabody College for Teachers, 1933), 13; Doss, *Cotton City,* 181–82; Ellis, "Mobile Public School Beginnings," 21–24.

42. Doss, *Cotton City,* 182; Ellis, "Mobile Public School Beginnings," 23–24; Nita Katharine Pyburn, "Mobile Public Schools before 1860," *Alabama Historical Review* 11, no. 3 (July 1958): 181.

43. Pyburn, "Mobile Public Schools before 1860," 180–82; Doss, *Cotton City,* 182–83; Ellis, "Mobile Public School Beginnings," 24–25; R. P. Vale, *Mobile Directory, or Strangers' Guide, for 1842: Embracing the Names of Firms, the Individuals Composing Them, and Citizens Alphabetically Arranged; together with a Variety of Miscellaneous Information, and Advertisements* (Mobile, AL: Dade and Thompson, 1842), ix, 15, 39, 65; *Mobile Directory and Commercial Supplement, for 1855–6, Embracing the Names of Firms, the Individuals Composing Them, Householders & Freeholders Generally, within the City Limits, Alphabetically Arranged* (Mobile, AL: Strickland, 1855), 83; *Mobile Directory, Embracing the Names of the Heads of Families and Persons in Business, Alphabetically Arranged* (Mobile, AL: M. McGuire and T. C. Fay, 1837), 37; E. T. Wood, *Mobile Directory, and Register, for 1844: Embracing the Names of Firms, the Individuals Composing Them, and Householders Generally Within the City Limits, Alphabetically Arranged* (Mobile, AL: Dade and Thompson, 1844), 35, 43, 52.

44. Doss, *Cotton City,* 183–84.

45. Mathews, "The Politics of Education in the Deep South," 348–49.

46. Ibid., 349; Doss, *Cotton City,* 186–87; Clark, *History of Education in Alabama 1702–1889,* 221 (quote).

47. *Daughdrill & Walker's General Directory for the City and County of Mobile, for 1856* (Mobile, AL: Book and Job Printers, 1856), 1, 99; Pyburn, "Mobile Public Schools before 1860," 185; Mathews, "The Politics of Education in the Deep South," 350–51; Stephen B. Weeks, *History of Public School Education in Alabama* (Washington, DC: Government Printing Office, 1915), 44–45; Hamilton, *Mobile of the Five Flags,* 266; Clark, *History of Education in Alabama,* 222;.

48. Clark, *History of Education in Alabama 1702–1889,* 221–23; Mathews, "The Politics of Education in the Deep South, 351–52 (quote); Pyburn, "Mobile Public Schools before 1860," 185.

49. Pyburn, "Mobile Public Schools before 1860," 186; Clark, *History of Education in Alabama 1702–1889,* 224 (quote).

50. Clark, *History of Education in Alabama 1702–1889,* 224–25 (quotes); William F. Perry, *Report of William F. Perry, Superintendent of Education of the State of Alabama, Made to the Governor, for the year 1857* (Montgomery, AL: N. B. Cloud, State Printer, 1858), 57.

51. Perry, *Report of William F. Perry, 1857,* 4, 57 (quote); Pyburn, "Mobile Public Schools before 1860," 186–87.

52. John Hebron Moore, *The Emergence of the Cotton Kingdom in the Old Southwest: Mississippi, 1770–1860* (Baton Rouge: Louisiana State University Press, 1988), 198–99.

53. William Moore Dalehite, *A History of the Public Schools in Jackson, Mississippi: 1832–1972* (Baton Rouge: TJM, 1974), 8–10.

54. D. Clayton James, *Antebellum Natchez* (Baton Rouge: Louisiana State University Press, 1968), 220 (first quote); *Mississippi Free Trader and Natchez Gazette,* February 11, 1845; February 18, 1845 (second quote); February 25, 1845 (third quote).

55. *Mississippi Free Trader and Natchez Gazette,* February 18, 1845.

56. Ibid., February 20, 1845.

57. Ibid., February 20, 1845; February 22, 1845; February 25, 1845.

58. *Mississippi Free Trader and Natchez Gazette,* February 27, 1845.

59. *Fourth Annual Report of the Board of Visitors of the Natchez Institute: Also, the Report of the Board of Examiners. July 4th, 1849* (Natchez, MS: printed at the Courier Book and Job Office, 1849), 4–5.

60. Ibid, 7.

61. Ibid., 11.

62. Ibid., 15–16.

63. "Eleventh Annual Report of the Board of Visitors of the Natchez Institute" (n.p., 1856), 5–17.

64. "Twelfth Annual Report of the Board of Visitors of the Natchez Institute," *Annual Reports of the Board of Visitors and the Board of Examiners of the Natchez Institute* (Natchez, MS: printed at the *Daily Courier* Office, 1857), 16.

65. "Report of the State Superintendent of Public Education," *Louisiana Legislative Documents,* 1864, 19; Reinders, "New England Influences on the Formation of Public Schools in New Orleans," 190; Devore and Logsdon, *Crescent City Schools,* 22–23.

66. "Eleventh Annual Report of the Board of Visitors of the Natchez Institute," 11 (quotes); "Fifteenth Annual Report of the Board of Visitors," *Annual Reports of the Board of Visitors, and the Board of Examiners, of the Natchez Institute* (Natchez, MS: printed at the *Daily Courier* Office, 1860), 4.

CHAPTER FIVE

1. *Weekly Courier and Journal* (Natchez, MS), June 18, 1838.

2. *Mississippi Free Trader and Natchez Gazette,* February 11, 1845; February 20, 1845; March 4, 1845; April 10, 1845; May 15, 1845; June 28, 1845; September 9, 1845; September 20,

1845; September 30, 1845; October 11, 1845; October 18, 1845; November 1, 1845; November 9, 1845; January 15, 1846; January 17, 1846; January 22, 1846; January 24, 1846.

3. *Mississippi Free Trader and Natchez Gazette,* February 11, 1845.

4. Samuel C. Hyde Jr., *Pistols and Politics: The Dilemma of Democracy in Louisiana's Florida Parishes, 1810–1899* (Baton Rouge: Louisiana State University Press, 1996), 56–59; John M. Sacher, *A Perfect War of Politics: Parties, Politicians, and Democracy in Louisiana, 1824–1861* (Baton Rouge: Louisiana State University Press, 2007), 109–10; *Proceedings and Debates of the Proceedings of the Convention of Louisiana. Which assembled at the City of New Orleans, January 14, 1844* (New Orleans: Besancon, Ferguson, 1845).

5. Hyde, *Pistols and Politics,* 58–59 (first quote); Sacher, *Perfect War of Politics,* 115; Richard Loucks, *An Exposition of the Laws of Louisiana, Relating to Free Public Schools* (Baton Rouge: printed at the Office of the *Delta,* 1847), 1; *Louisiana Senate Journal,* First Session, 1846, 12 (second quote).

6. *Proceedings and Debates of the* Proceedings of the *Convention of Louisiana,* 903–904.

7. See Judith K. Shafer, "Reform or Experiment? The Louisiana Constitution of 1845," and Wayne M. Everard, "Louisiana's 'Whig' Constitution Revisited: The Constitution of 1852," both in Glenn R. Conrad, ed., *The Louisiana Purchase Bicentennial Series in Louisiana History,* vol. 4, *Antebellum Louisiana, 1830–1860,* Part B, "Politics," ed. Carolyn E. DeLatte (Lafayette: Center for Louisiana Studies, University of Louisiana at Lafayette, 2004); Sacher, *A Perfect War of Politics,* 137–41, 163–70.

8. *Louisiana Constitution* (1845) title VII, art. 133–139, 352–353; Richard Loucks, *An Exposition of the Laws of Louisiana,* 1–13. For a discussion of the government's use of sixteenth section lands, see William C. Reavis, "Federal Aid for Education," *Annals of the American Academy of Political and Social Science* 265 (1949): 56; Walter I. Trattner, "The Federal Government and Needy Citizens in Nineteenth-Century America," *Political Science Quarterly* 103, no. 2 (1988): 350; Paul W. Gates, "An Overview of American Land Policy," *Agricultural History* 50, no. 1 (1976): 219; Charles H. Judd, "Federal Support of Public Education," *The Elementary School Journal* 36, no. 7 (1936): 498; Edgar W. Knight, *Public Education in the South* (Boston: Ginn, 1922), 187.

9. *Louisiana Senate Journal,* First Session, 1846, 12 (first quote); "Report of the State Superintendent of Public Education," *Louisiana Legislative Documents,* 1847, 12 (second quote).

10. Loucks, *Exposition of the Laws of Louisiana,* 7–9; "Report of the State Superintendent of Public Education," *Louisiana Legislative Documents,* 1847, 12.

11. Loucks, *Exposition of the Laws of Louisiana,* 9–12.

12. "Report of the State Superintendent of Education," *Louisiana Legislative Documents,* 1847, 12. For an example of hopeful parish superintendents, see the various parish reports attached to the "Report of the State Superintendent of Education," *Louisiana Legislative Documents,* 1851, 6–48.

13. "Report of the State Superintendent of Education," *Louisiana Legislative Documents,* 1848, 2–15; "Report of the State Superintendent of Education," *Louisiana Legislative Documents,* 1851, 7 (quote).

14. "Report of the State Superintendent of Education," *Louisiana Legislative Documents,* 1851, 11.

15. *Mississippi House Journal,* Regular Session, 1840–1841, 17–19.

16. *Mississippi House Journal,* Regular Session, 1844, 16–17.

17. Knight, *Public Education in the South,* 161.

18. Edward Mayes, *History of Education in Mississippi* (Washington, DC: Government Printing Office), 1899, 278 (first two quotes); Dunbar Rowland, *History of Mississippi: The Heart of the South,* 2 vols. (Jackson, MS: S. J. Clarke, 1925), 1:634, 647 (third quote); *Mississippi House Journal,* Regular Session, 1846, 23–26; James Byrne Ranck, *Albert Gallatin Brown: Radical Southern Nationalist* (New York: D. Appleton-Century, 1937), 29, 40–41; Charles William Dabney, *Universal Education in the South,* 4 vols. (Chapel Hill: University of North Carolina Press, 1936), 1:345; Knight, *Public Education in the South,* 247–48; *Mississippi House Journal,* Regular Session, 1846, 23, 41–62.

19. *Mississippi House Journal,* Regular Session, 1846, 23–25.

20. *Mississippi House Journal,* Regular Session, 1846, 23–25. See the responses to Governor Brown's request for information on the sixteenth sections and schools contained in *Mississippi House Journal,* Regular Session, 1846, 41–60.

21. *Mississippi House Journal,* Regular Session, 1846, 23–25.

22. *Mississippi House Journal,* Regular Session, 1848, 23, 33–42; Mayes, *History of Education in Mississippi,* 278–79.

23. Mayes, *History of Education in Mississippi,* 279–80 (quote); Knight, *Public Education in the South,* 248; *Mississippi Free Trader and Natchez Gazette,* February 11, 1845, February 18, 1845, February 20, 1845, February 22, 1845, February 25, 1845, February 27, 1845, March 4, 1845, April 3, 1845; George Duke Humphrey, "Public Education for Whites in Mississippi: A Historical and Interpretive Study" (DEd diss., Ohio State University, 1939), 40–41.

24. *Mississippi House Journal,* Regular Session, 1848, 23; Knight, *Public Education in the South,* 249; Mayes, *History of Education in Mississippi,* 280.

25. Rowland, *History of Mississippi,* 1:700–701; Mayes, *History of Education in Mississippi,* 281; Knight, *Public Education in the South,* 249; *Mississippi House Journal,* Regular Session, 1850, 20 (quote).

26. Dabney, *Universal Education in the South,* 1:345 (quote); Knight, *Public Education in the South,* 250; *Seventh Census,* 1850, 142; *Eighth Census,* 1860, 506.

27. *Alabama Senate Journal,* Twenty-Second Annual Session, 1840–1841, 14–15 (first quote), 138; *Alabama Senate Journal,* Called Session, 1844, 129–32; *Alabama Senate Journal,* Twenty-Sixth Annual Session, 1844–1845, 148, 207; Forrest David Mathews, "The Politics of Education in the Deep South: Georgia and Alabama, 1830–1860" (PhD diss., Columbia University, 1965), 298–99 (second quote).

28. *Alabama Senate Journal,* Twenty-Seventh Annual Session, 1845–1846, 126–27.

29. *Alabama Senate Journal,* Twenty-Second Annual Session, 1840–1841, 14; *Alabama Senate Journal,* Twenty-third Annual Session, 1841–1842, 94; *Alabama Senate Journal,* First Biennial Session, 1847–1848, 24; *Alabama Senate Journal,* Second Biennial Session, 1849–1850, 34; Mathews, "The Politics of Education in the Deep South," 322–29.

30. *Alabama Senate Journal,* Second Biennial Session, 1849–1850, 34 (first quote); Mathews, "The Politics of Education in the Deep South," 335–37 (second quote).

31. Alabama Senate Journal, Third Biennial Session, 1851–1852, 29.

32. J. Mills Thornton III, *Politics and Power in a Slave Society: Alabama, 1800–1860* (Baton Rouge: Louisiana State University Press, 1978), 300; Mathews, "The Politics of Education in the Deep South," 338–45; *Alabama Senate Journal,* Third Biennial Session, 1851–1852, 29, 385–86.

33. Alabama Secretary of State, Election Files—state and national, 1823– (ongoing), Alabama Department of Archives and History, Montgomery, Alabama; hereafter cited as ADAH; *Alabama Senate Journal,* Fourth Biennial Session, 1853–54, 34–35; Mathews, "The Politics of Education in the Deep South," 345–46; Thornton, *Politics and Power in a Slave Society,* 300.

34. Thornton, *Politics and Power in a Slave Society,* 300.

35. Ibid., 324–27; *Alabama Senate Journal,* Fourth Biennial Session, 1853–1854, 57, 306 (quote); Mathews, "The Politics of Education in the Deep South," 354–55.

36. *Alabama Senate Journal,* Fourth Biennial Session, 1853–1854, 303–12.

37. Stephen B. Weeks, *History of Public School Education in Alabama* (Washington, DC: Government Printing Office, 1915), 60–61.

38. Ibid., 61.

39. Ibid.

40. Mathews, "The Politics of Education in the Deep South," 364–74.

41. *Alabama Senate Journal,* Fifth Biennial Session, 1855–1856, 9, 14, 103, 237–39, 240, 273–75, 290 (quotes); Willis Brewster, *Alabama: Her History, Resources, War Records and Public Men, from 1540 to 1872* (Montgomery, AL: Barrett and Brown, 1872; reprint, Spartanburg, SC: Reprint Company, 1975), 581–82, 620; Mathews, "The Politics of Education in the Deep South," 375–77; *Alabama Senate Journal,* Sixth Biennial Session, 1857–1858, 19–20.

42. Brewster, *Alabama: Her History,* 343; Weeks, *History of Public School Education in Alabama,* 63; William F. Perry, "The Genesis of Public Education in Alabama," in Thomas M. Owen, ed., *Publications of the Alabama Historical Society, 1897–1898* (Tuscaloosa, AL: printed for the Society, 1898), 14–27 (quote).

43. Perry, "The Genesis of Public Education in Alabama," 23–24.

44. Ibid., 20.

45. Mathews, "The Politics of Education in the Deep South," 377; Weeks, *History of Public School Education in Alabama,* 67–68.

46. *Report of William F. Perry, Superintendent of Education of the State of Alabama, made to the Governor, for the year 1857* (Montgomery, AL: N. B. Cloud, State Printer, 1858), 5 (quote); Weeks, *History of Public School Education in Alabama,* 69, 77.

47. *Alabama Senate Journal,* Seventh Biennial Session, 1859–1860, 16–17; Weeks, *History of Public School Education in Alabama,* 78n1.

48. Thornton, *Politics and Power in a Slave Society,* 301.

49. "Report from the St. Landry Parish Superintendent," contained in "Report of the State Superintendent of Education," in *Louisiana Legislative Documents,* 1851, 38 (quote); see also "Report from the Calcasieu Parish Superintendent," Louisiana Legislative Documents, 1851, 16. For examples of the importance of learning to southerners, see Buck-Ellis Family Papers, Mss. 4820; Hunter-Taylor Family Papers, Mss. 3024; Charles M. Conrad Letter, Mss. 3377; Clinton School Papers, Mss. 925; John Faulk Papers, Mss. 877; Lucy Maria Fisher Memoirs, Mss. 2497; Palfrey Family Papers, Mss. 334; Thomas McCurdy Vincent Family Papers, Mss. 3116; Albert A. Batchelor Papers, Mss. 919, 1293; Honore P. Morancy Family Papers, Mss. 2430; Ellis-Farar Family Papers, Mss. 1000, all in Louisiana and Lower Mississippi Valley Collection, Louisiana State University Libraries, Baton Rouge, LA, hereafter cited as LLMVC; see also Ker Family Papers, #4656; Ann Eliza Brumby Letter, 1858, #2787-z; Hentz Family Papers, #332, all in the Southern Historical Collection, Louis Round Wilson Special Collections

Library, University of North Carolina at Chapel Hill, hereafter cited as SHC; see also "Report of the State Superintendent of Education," in Louisiana Legislative Documents, 1848–1861; Alabama Department of Education, Correspondence Files of the State Superintendent of Education, ADAH; "Report of the State Superintendent of Education," Alabama Legislative Journals, 1854–1861.

50. Hyde, *Pistols and Politics,* 70; Raleigh A. Suarez, "Chronicle of a Failure: Public Education in Antebellum Louisiana," *Louisiana History* 12 (1971): 117–18.

51. "Constitution of Louisiana, 1852," Title II, Article 8, in *Journal of the State Convention to Form a New Constitution for Louisiana,* 1852 [New Orleans, 1852], 91; New Orleans *Daily Picayune,* October 24, 1852; *American Patriot* (Clinton, LA), February 7, 1855; Baton Rouge *Daily Advocate,* February 3, 1854; *Louisiana House Journal,* Second Session, 1859, 3–7; St. Tammany Parish Police Jury Minutes, May 5, 1842, in WPA Collection, LLMVC; *Louisiana House Journal,* 1st Session, 1850, 89–91, 101–102, 126; "Report of the Superintendent of Livingston," *Louisiana Legislative Documents,* First Session, 1852, 27; *Louisiana Senate Journal,* First Session, 1853, 29–30, 72–74; Hyde, *Pistols and Politics,* 68–69; Samuel C. Hyde Jr., "Mechanisms of Planter Power in Eastern Louisiana's Piney Woods, 1810–1860," *Louisiana History* 39, no. 1 (Winter 1998): 40.

52. "Report of the State Superintendent of Public Education," *Louisiana Legislative Documents,* 1852, 3, 14 (quote); "Report of the State Superintendent of Public Education," *Louisiana Legislative Documents,* 1853, 3; Suarez, "Chronicle of a Failure," 118.

53. *Acts passed at the Fourth Annual Session of the General Assembly of the State of Alabama, begun and held at the town of Cahawba, on the Third Monday of November, one thousand eight hundred and twenty two* (Cahawba: Wm B. Allen and Co, State Printers, 1823), 73, 77.

54. Sarah E. Lipscomb, "A Crisis of Opportunity: The Example of New Orleans and Public Education in Antebellum Louisiana" (MA thesis, Louisiana State University, 2005), 37–38.

55. "Report of the State Superintendent of Public Education," *Louisiana Legislative Documents,* 1855, 25 (first quote); 1857, 30 (second quote).

56. "Report of the State Superintendent of Education," *Louisiana Legislative Documents,* 1853, 3 (first quote); 1857, 44 (second quote); 1855, 41 (third quote); 1851, 3 (fourth quote); 1857, 6 (fifth quote); 1854, 9 (sixth quote). For complaints concerning public school adminis-trators, see "Report of the State Superintendent of Public Education," *Louisiana Legislative Documents,* 1853, 16; 1854, 63, 68, 79, 88, 113, 115, 117, 120, 124; 1855, 20, 23, 31, 41, 47, 52; 1856, 20, 52, 54, 56, 64, 71, 83, 96, 99, 103; 1857, 33, 41, 44, 79, 89, 92, 94, 98, 101, 103, 107; 1858, 35, 38, 44, 57; 13, 62, 74, 103.

57. "Report of the State Superintendent of Education," *Louisiana Legislative Documents,* 1854, 8 (first quote); 1857, 89 (second quote); 1853, 5. See also 1855, 52; 1856, 20, 21; 1857, 102.

58. "Report of the State Superintendent of Public Education," *Louisiana Legislative Doc-uments,* 1856, 4 (first quote); 1858, 44 (second quote); 1857, 44 (third quote). See also "Report of the State Superintendent of Public Education," *Louisiana Legislative Documents,* 1853, 3–8; 1854, 8–9, 63, 68, 69, 79, 88, 101, 113, 117, 120, 130; 1855, 4–5, 31, 35, 41, 44, 47, 51–52; 1856, 3–11, 52, 54, 56, 64; 1857, 3–21; 1859, 3–6.

59. "Report of the State Superintendent of Education," *Louisiana Legislative Documents,* 1852, 5 (quote). For an example of local opinions, see the comments from parish superin-

tendents of Lafayette, Washington, and West Baton Rouge Parishes in "Report of the State Superintendent of Public Education," *Louisiana Legislative Documents,* 1851, 26, 44, 46.

60. "Report of the State Superintendent of Public Education," *Louisiana Legislative Documents,* 1851, 8 (first quote); 27 (second quote); 1858, 46 (third quote). See also 1854, 63; 1857, 53.

61. "Report of the State Superintendent of Public Education," *Louisiana Legislative Documents,* 1859, 65 (first quote); 7, 64 (second quote); 1851, 27 (final quotes). See also 1849, 10; 1851, 28, 41; 1856, 21, 62; 1857, 93; 1858, 95; 1859, 7, 64.

62. Seventh Census, 1850, 481–86; Hyde, *Pistols and Politics,* 27–28; Hyde, "Mechanisms of Planter Power in Eastern Louisiana's Piney Woods," 22–27.

63. "Report of the State Superintendent of Education," *Louisiana Legislative Documents,* 1857, 63–64.

64. "Report of the State Superintendent of Education," *Louisiana Legislative Documents,* 1851, 32; see also 6–48.

65. "Report of the State Superintendent of Education," *Louisiana Legislative Documents,* 1851, 30, 37, 41 (quotes). Figures compiled from 6–48.

66. "Report of the State Superintendent of Education," *Louisiana Legislative Documents,* 1857, 35; ibid., 1861, 14; ibid., 1858, 20.

67. "Report of the State Superintendent of Education," *Louisiana Legislative Documents,* 1857, 35 (first quote); 1861, 14 (second quote); 1858, 20 (final quotes). See also 1859, 74.

68. Roger W. Shugg, *Origins of Class Struggle in Louisiana: A Social History of White Farmers and Laborers during Slavery and After, 1840–1875* (Baton Rouge: Louisiana State University Press, 1939), 74.

69. "Report of the State Superintendent of Education," *Louisiana Legislative Documents,* 1864, 6.

70. Shugg, *Origins of Class Struggle,* 74 (first quote); "Report of the State Superintendent of Education," *Louisiana Legislative Documents,* 1864, 6, 10–11 (final quotes).

71. "Report of the State Superintendent of Public Education," *Louisiana Legislative Documents,* 1853, 8.

72. William F. Perry, *Report of the Superintendent of Education of the State of Alabama, to the Governor* (Montgomery, AL: Brittain and Blue, State Printers, 1855), 3, 11–14 (quote); William F. Perry, *Report of Wm. F. Perry, Superintendent of Education of the State of Alabama, Made to the Governor, for the Year 1857* (Montgomery, AL: N. B. Cloud, State Printer, 1858), 4.

73. *Mississippi House Journal,* Regular Session, 1848, 23, 5041850, 20–21, 148–63; *Mississippi House Journal,* Regular Session, 1852, 14, 84, 715; 1854, 12; 1857, 18; 1858, 22–23; 1859, 32–33, 102–103.

74. *Mississippi House Journal,* Regular Session, 1859, 32 (quote). See also 1848, 23, 504; 1850, 20–21, 148–63; 1852, 14, 84, 715; 1854, 12; 1857, 18; 1858, 22–23; 1859, 32–33, 102–103.

75. *Mississippi House Journal,* Regular Session, 1859, 102 (quote); Daniel Walker Howe, *The Political Culture of the American Whigs* (Chicago: University of Chicago Press, 1979), 36; Thornton, *Politics and Power in a Slave Society,* 38; William J. Cooper Jr. and Thomas E. Terrill, *The American South: A History,* 4th ed., 2 vols. (Lanham, MD: Rowman and Littlefield, 1996), 1:188; Sacher, *A Perfect War of Politics,* 125, 142.

76. *Louisiana House Journal,* Seventh Legislature, First Session, 1824, 2–8 (first quote); "Report of the Livingston Parish Superintendent of Education," in "Report of the State

Superintendent of Education," *Louisiana Legislative Documents,* 1851, 27 (second quote); *Alabama Constitution* (1819), Art. 3, Sec. 5, 7; Thornton, *Politics and Power in a Slave Society,* 12; Mathews, "The Politics of Education in the Deep South, 227–28.

77. "Report of William F. Perry, Superintendent of Education of the State of Alabama, Made to the Governor, for the year 1857."

CHAPTER SIX

1. *Eighth Census,* 1860, 503-511, "Report of the Alabama State Superintendent of Education, 1858;" "Report of the Secretary of State on Public Education," *Louisiana Legislative Documents,* 1859. State education officials often report higher figures than those in the census returns.

2. James L. Leloudis, *Schooling the New South: Pedagogy, Self, and Society in North Carolina, 1880–1920* (Chapel Hill: University of North Carolina Press, 1996), 13; Lawrence A. Cremin, *Traditions of American Education* (New York: Basic Books, 1977), 65; Julia Huston Nguyen, "Molding the Minds of the South: Education in Natchez, 1817–1861" (MA thesis, Louisiana State University, 1997), 41.

3. Joseph B. Lightsey Diary, June 21–Sept 10, 1852, Mississippi Department of Archives and History, Jackson, MS, hereafter cited as MDAH; Carl O. Osthaus, "The Work Ethic of the Plain Folk: Labor and Religion in the Old South," *Journal of Southern History* 70, no. 4 (Nov. 2004): 757.

4. Lightsey Diary, August 15 [1852], MDAH.

5. Leloudis, *Schooling the New South,* 13; Cremin, *Traditions of American Education,* 19–20, 28–29, 55–56, 65; Catherine Clinton, *The Plantation Mistress: Woman's World in the Old South* (New York: Pantheon, 1982), 49–50; Thomas C. W. Ellis Diary, Buck-Ellis Family Papers, Mss. 4820, Louisiana and Lower Mississippi Valley Collection, Louisiana State University Libraries, Baton Rouge, LA, hereafter cited as LLMVC; Céline Frémaux Garcia, *Celine: Remembering Louisiana, 1850–1871,* ed. Patrick J. Geary, with a foreword by Bertram Wyatt-Brown (Athens: University of Georgia Press, 1987); John D. Pulliam and James J. Van Patten, *History of Education in America,* 7th ed. (Upper Saddle River, NJ: Merrill, 1999), 58; Nguyen, "Molding the Minds of the South," 5.

6. Thomas C. W. Ellis to E. J. Ellis, January 13, 1856, Diary Entry of Thomas C. W. Ellis, January 4, 1856, June 4, 1856, in Buck-Ellis Family Papers, Mss. 4820, LLMVC; Garcia, *Celine,* 31; Clinton, *The Plantation Mistress,* 50; see also Nguyen, "Molding the Minds of the South," 4–5; Jean A. Friedman, *The Enclosed Garden: Women and Community in the Evangelical South, 1830–1900* (Chapel Hill: University of North Carolina Press, 1985), 99.

7. *Weekly Advocate* (Baton Rouge), March 1, 1848 (first quote); *Mobile Daily Register,* August 31, 1850. Worsted is a type of yarn.

8. Silliman Female Collegiate Institute pamphlet, 1854–1855, in Hunter-Taylor Family Papers, Mss. 3024, LLMVC; *Mobile Daily Register,* January 11, 1853 (first quote); Clinton School Papers, Mss. 925, LLMVC; *Weekly Advocate* (Baton Rouge, LA), June 5, 1847 (final quotes).

9. Loyce Braswell Miles, "Forgotten Scholars: Female Secondary Education in Three Deep South States" (PhD diss.: Mississippi State University, 2003), 185–89.

10. Ibid., 182–83.

11. "Report of the State Superintendent of Education," *Louisiana Legislative Documents,* 1851, 15–16, 19, 25, 29, 46.

12. *Fourth Annual Report of the Board of Visitors of the Natchez Institute: also, the Report of the Board of Examiners, July 4, 1849* (Natchez, MS: printed at the Courier Book and Job Office), 1849.

13. *Mississippi Free Trader and Natchez Gazette,* July 29, 1845.

14. *Daily Advertiser* (Mobile, AL), May 2, 1850.

15. Nannie Cage to "ever dear Friend," April 1864; Lizzie Connell to [Cornelia Randolph Stewart], April 16, 1864, both in Albert A. Batchelor Papers, Mss. 919, 1293, LLMVC (quote); William Jackson to "Ma," February 25, 1861, in Honore P. Morancy Family Papers, Mss. 2430, LLMVC.

16. Fisher (Lucy Maria W. F. P.) Memoirs, [typescript] Mss. 2497, LLMVC, 14–15.

17. *Daily Advertiser* (Mobile, AL), May 5, 1850 (quote); William Jackson to "Ma," February 25, 1861, in Honore P. Morancy Family Papers, Mss. 2430, LLMVC.

18. Lizzie Stewart to Albert A. Batchelor, February 18, 1861, in Albert A. Batchelor Family Papers, Mss. 919, 1293, LLMVC (first quote); Mary H. Baker to Isaac L. Baker, November 9, 1816, in Ker Family Papers, #4656, Southern Historical Collection, Louis Round Wilson Special Collections Library, University of North Carolina at Chapel Hill, hereafter cited as SHC; Mary Ker to Isaac L. Baker, November 29, 1820, in Ker Family Papers, #4656, SHC; Richard G. Ellis to "my dear sister," January 2, 1815, in Ellis-Farar Papers, Mss. 1000, LLMVC (second quote).

19. *Daily Advertiser* (Mobile, AL), October 13, 1850 (first quote); *Mobile Daily Register,* October 14, 1851 (second quote).

20. R. M. Brumby to Ann Eliza Brumby, April 3, 1858, #2787, SHC.

21. *Mississippi Free Trader and Natchez Gazette,* March 22, 1845 (first quote); May 31, 1845 (final quotes).

22. *Mississippi Free Trader and Natchez Gazette,* September 9, 1845 (first quote); "Report of the State Superintendent of Education," Louisiana Legislative Documents, 1858, 102 (second quote); 1859, 85; see also 1858, 96–102; 1859, 84–91; [*First] Annual Reports of the Council of Municipality Number Two, of the city of New Orleans, on the Condition of its Public Schools* (New Orleans: printed at the office of the *Picayune,* 1845), 9–10.

23. "Report of the State Superintendent of Education," *Louisiana Legislative Documents,* 1851, 24 (first quote); 1851, 46 (second quote). For favorable comments about teachers in rural areas, see also "Report of the State Superintendent of Education," *Louisiana Legislative Documents,* 1851, 6, 11, 14, 15, 17–222, 24–32, 34, 38–40, 42–46.

24. "Report of the State Superintendent of Public Education," *Louisiana Legislative Documents,* 1854, 68. For disappointing reports of public school teachers throughout the state, see also "Report of the State Superintendent of Public Education," *Louisiana Legislative Documents,* 1848, 6; 1849, 2, 7; 1851, 5, 16, 17, 23, 30, 37; 1854, 8–9, 56, 68, 79, 113; 1855, 20, 35, 41, 52; 1856, 11, 22, 52, 56, 90, 96, 99, 101, 103; 1857, 8–10, 33, 55, 89, 94; 1858, 6, 11, 28, 68, 89, 95; 1859, 10, 22, 37, 62, 65.

25. *Mississippi Free Trader and Natchez Gazette,* February 18, 1845.

26. "Report of the State Superintendent of Public Education," *Louisiana Legislative Documents,* 1851, 34.

27. John Palfrey to Mark Pickard, January 26, 1811, Palfrey Family Papers, Mss. 333, LLMVC.

28. John Palfrey to William Palfrey, August 4, 1832, Palfrey Family Papers, Mss. 333, LLMVC.

29. Martha Batchelor to Albert Batchelor, March 2, 1861, Albert A. Batchelor Papers, Mss. 919, LLMVC.

30. Anne Jackson to Mrs. Honore P. Morancy, May 17, 1864; Anne Jackson to Mrs. Honore P. Morancy, September 26, 1864, Honore P. Morancy Family Papers, Mss. 2430, LLMVC.

31. Charles Batchelor to Albert Batchelor, January 16, 1857 (quote); Charles Batchelor to Albert Batchelor, June 6, 1856, Albert A. Batchelor Papers, Mss. 919, LLMVC.

32. T. W. Mieure to Albert Batchelor, September 27, 1860 (quote); see also T. W. Mieure to Albert Batchelor, August 30, 1860; Charlie Batchelor to Albert Batchelor, August 6, 1860; T. W. Mieure to Albert Batchelor, October 16, 1860; Martha Batchelor to Albert Batchelor, November 16, 1860, December 11, 1860; Jessie M. Menzies to Albert A. Batchelor, March 15, 1861, all in Albert A. Batchelor Papers, Mss 919, LLMVC.

33. Mollie Batchelor to Albert Batchelor, February 18, 1861 (quote), March 18, 1862, Albert A. Batchelor Papers, Mss 919, LLMVC (first quote); Mary C. Lancaster to Mr. and Mrs. Joseph B. Lancaster, November 21, 1840, Thomas McCurdy Vincent Papers, Mss. 3116, LLMVC; Diary entry for September 1, 1856, Daniel Barlow Gorham Diary, Mss. 3096, LLMVC (second quote).

34. Isaac L. Baker to Joshua Baker Jr., May 28, 1809 (quote); Mary K. Baker to Isaac L. Baker, May 20, 1816, November 16, 1816, February 23, 1817, April 7, 1817, June 20, 1817, June 28, 1817, January 23, 1818, Mary K. Baker to Mrs. Sarah Metcalfe, July 23, 1818, all in Ker Family Papers, #4656, SHC.

35. Mary Baker to Sarah Metcalfe, July 23, 1818 (quote); Isaac L. Baker to Joshua Baker Jr., May 28, 1809 (quote); Mary K. Baker to Isaac L. Baker, May 20, 1816, November 16, 1816, February 23, 1817, April 7, 1817, June 20, 1817, June 28, 1817, January 23, 1818, all in Ker Family Papers, #4656, SHC.

36. Nannie Cage to [Cornelia Randolph Stewart], March 6, 1862 (first quote); Lizzie Connell to [Cornelia Randolph Stewart], April 16, 1864; Lizzie Connell to [Cornelia Randolph Stewart], June 30, 1864 (second quote); Nannie Cage to [Cornelia Randolph Stewart], January 31, 1864 (third quote); Lizzie Connell to [Cornelia Randolph Stewart], January 17, 1863, all in Albert A. Batchelor Papers, Mss 919, LLMVC; Ann Morancy to Mrs. Honore P. Morancy, November 19, 1841, all in Honore P. Morancy Family Papers, Mss. 2430, LLMVC (final quote).

37. Mary C. Lancaster to Mr. and Mrs. J. B. Lancaster, November 21, 1840, Thomas McCurdy Vincent Family Papers, Mss. 3116, LLMVC.

38. Mary E. Taylor to Stella Hunter, May 27, 1856, Hunter-Taylor Papers, Mss. 3024, LLMVC.

39. Sereno Taylor to Stella Hunter, November 11, 1857; Sereno Taylor to Eugene Hunter, n.d., Hunter-Taylor Papers, Mss. 3024, LLMVC .

40. School catalog of the Silliman Female Collegiate Institute, 1854–1855, ibid.

41. Sereno Taylor to Stella and Eugene Hunter, September 10, 1855; Sereno Taylor to Stella Hunter, December 31, 1859, ibid.

42. Mary Taylor to Stella Hunter, October 19, 1855, ibid.

43. Young ladies of the First Ward Girls' School to Joseph Reynes, May 20, 1853, Joseph Reynes Family Papers, Mss. 1038, LLMVC; John M. Bonner to Mrs. Eliza A. Bonner, December 8, 1850, Samuel C. Bonner and Family Papers, Mss. 1472, 1507, LLMVC.

BIBLIOGRAPHY

PRIMARY SOURCES

Manuscripts

Louisiana and Lower Mississippi Valley Collections, Louisiana State University Libraries, Baton Rouge, Louisiana

Affleck, Thomas, Papers.

Batchelor, Albert A., Papers.

Bonner, Samuel C. Family, Papers.

Buck-Ellis Family, Papers.

Clinton School, Papers.

Conrad, Charles M., Letter.

Ellis-Farar Family, Papers.

Embree, Joseph Family, Papers.

Faulk, John, Papers.

Fisher, Lucy Maria, Memoir.

Gorham, Daniel Barlow, Diary.

Hamilton, William S., Papers.

Hunter-Taylor Family, Papers.

Leidigh, Jacob M., Correspondence.

Lemon, James J., Letter.

Morancy, Honore P. Family, Papers.

Palfrey Family, Papers.

Reynes, Joseph Family, Papers.

Vincent, Thomas McCurdy Family, Papers.

Walworth, Douglas Family, Papers.

W. P. A. Collection. Louisiana Historical Records Survey Louisiana Police Jury Minutes Transcriptions, 1811–1940.

Southern Historical Collection, Louis Round Wilson Special Collections Library, University of North Carolina at Chapel Hill

Brumby, Ann Eliza, Letter.

Hentz Family, Papers.

Ker Family, Papers.

Slack Family, Papers.

Mississippi Department of Archives and History, Jackson, Mississippi

Hagaman, Abraham, Memoir.

Lightsey, (Joseph Benjamin), Diary.

Alabama Department of History and Archives, Montgomery, Alabama

Alabama Department of Education, Correspondence Files of the State Superintendent of Education.

Alabama Secretary of State, Election Files—state and national, 1823– (ongoing).

Newspapers

Alabama Journal (Montgomery, Alabama).

American Patriot (Clinton, Louisiana).

Daily Advertiser (Mobile, Alabama).

Daily Advocate (Baton Rouge, Louisiana).

Daily Picayune (New Orleans, Louisiana).

Democratic Advocate (Baton Rouge, Louisiana).

Mississippi Free Trader and Natchez Gazette (Natchez, Mississippi).

The Mobile Daily Register (Mobile, Alabama).

The Weekly Advocate (Baton Rouge, Louisiana).

Weekly Courier and Journal (Natchez, Mississippi).

Government Publications

Acts of the General Assembly of the State of Alabama, Passed at its First Session. Huntsville, AL: John Boardman, 1820; reprint, Washington, DC: T. L. Cole, 1912.

Acts passed at the Fourth Annual Session of the General Assembly of the State of Alabama, begun and held at the town of Cahawba, on the Third Monday of November, one thousand eight hundred and twenty two. Cahawba, AL: Wm. B. Allen and Co., State Printers, 1823.

Acts passed at the Seventh Annual Session of the General Assembly of the State of Alabama, begun and held in the Town of Cahawba, on the Third Monday in November, 1825. n.p., 1826.

Acts passed at the Third Annual Session of the General Assembly of the State of Alabama. Cahawba, AL: Wm. B. Allen and Co., State Printers, 1822.

Alabama Constitution (1819).

Alabama Legislative Documents, 1818–1861.

Annual Report of the Board of Directors of the Public Schools of the First District of New Orleans, for the Year ending June 30, 1856. New Orleans: printed at the office of the *Creole,* 1856.

Annual Reports of the Board of Visitors and the Board of Examiners of the Natchez Institute. Natchez, MS: printed at the *Daily Courier* office, 1857.

Annual Reports of the Board of Visitors, and the Board of Examiners, of the Natchez Institute. Natchez: printed at the *Daily Courier* office, 1860.

Annual Reports of the Council of Municipality Number Two, of the city of New Orleans, on the Condition of its Public Schools. New Orleans: printed at the office of the *Picayune,* 1845.

Eleventh Annual Report of the Board of Visitors of the Natchez Institute: made to the President and Selectmen of the City of Natchez. Natchez, MS: printed at the *Courier* office, 1856.

Fourth Annual Report of the Board of Visitors of the Natchez Institute: Also, the Report of the Board of Examiners. July 4th, 1849. Natchez, MS: printed at the Courier Book and Job office, 1849.

Journal of the House of Representatives for the State of Alabama, 1819–1861.

Journal of the House of Representatives for the State of Louisiana, 1812–1864.

Journal of the House of Representatives for the State of Mississippi, 1817–1861.

Journal of the House of Representatives for the Territory of Mississippi, 1812–1816.

Journal of the Legislative Council of the Alabama Territory, 1818.

Journal of the Legislative Council of the General Assembly of the Mississippi Territory, 1804–1815.

Journal of the Senate of the State of Alabama, 1819–1861.

Journal of the Senate of the State of Louisiana, 1812–1861.

Journal of the Senate of the State of Mississippi, 1817–1861.

Journal of the State Convention to Form a New Constitution for Louisiana. New Orleans: printed at the *Crescent* office, 1852.

Louisiana Constitution (1812).

Louisiana Constitution (1845).

Louisiana Constitution (1852).

Louisiana Legislative Documents, 1812–1864.

Mississippi Legislative Documents, 1817–1861.

Mississippi Constitution (1817).

Mississippi Constitution (1832).

Perry, William F. *Report of the Superintendent of Education of the State of Alabama, to the Governor.* Montgomery, AL: Brittain and Blue, State Printers, 1855.

Proceedings and Debates of the Proceedings of the Convention of Louisiana. Which assembled at the City of New Orleans, January 14, 1844. New Orleans: Besancon, Ferguson, 1845.

Report of William F. Perry, Superintendent of Education of the State of Alabama, Made to the Governor, for the year 1857. Montgomery, AL: N. B. Cloud, State Printer, 1858.

Report of the Board of Directors of the Public Schools of the Second Municipality. New Orleans: Die Glocke Office, 1848.

Third Annual Report of the Council of Municipality Number Two. New Orleans: printed at the office of the *Commercial Bulletin*, 1844.

United States Census Bureau, *Sixth Census, 1840.* Compendium.

———. *Seventh Census, 1850.* Compendium.

———. *Eighth Census, 1860.* Compendium.

Published Primary Sources

Bullard, Henry A., and Thomas Curry. *A New Digest of the Statute Laws of the State of Louisiana, From the Change of Government to the Year 1841, Inclusive.* New Orleans: E. Johns and Co., 1842.

Daughdrill & Walker's General Directory for the City and County of Mobile, for 1856. Mobile, AL: Book and Job Printers, 1856.

Fay, T. C. *Mobile Directory, or Stranger's Guide for 1839: Embracing Names of Firms, the Individuals Composing Them, and Citizens Generally; together with their Professions, Residence & Number, Alphabetically Arranged, with a Cross Index.* Mobile, AL: R. R. Dade, 1839.

Garcia, Céline Frémaux. *Céline: Remembering Louisiana, 1850–1871*, edited by Patrick J. Geary, with a foreword by Bertram Wyatt-Brown. Athens: University of Georgia Press, 1987.

Hooper, William. *Lecture on the Imperfections of Our Primary Schools.* Newbern, NC, 1832.

Loucks, Richard. An Exposition of the Laws of Louisiana, Relating to Free Public Schools. Baton Rouge: printed at the office of the *Delta*, 1847.

Mobile Directory and Commercial Supplement, for 1855–6, Embracing the Names of Firms, the Individuals Composing Them, Householders & Freeholders Generally, within the City Limits, Alphabetically Arranged. Mobile, AL: Strickland and Co., 1855.

Mobile Directory, Embracing the Names of the Heads of Families and Persons in Business, Alphabetically Arranged. Mobile, AL: M. McGuire and T. C. Fay, 1837.

Olmsted, Frederick Law. *A Journey in the Seaboard Slave States: With Remarks on Their Economy.* New York: Dix and Edwards, 1856.

Prentiss, George Lewis, ed. *A Memoir of S. S. Prentiss.* New York: C. Scribner's Sons, 1881.

Rowland, Dunbar, ed. *Official Letter Books of W. C. C. Claiborne, 1801–1816.* 6 vols. Jackson, MS: State Department of Archives and History, 1917.

Vale, R. P. *Mobile Directory, or Strangers' Guide, for 1842: Embracing the Names of Firms, the Individuals Composing Them, and Citizens Alphabetically Arranged; together with a Variety of Miscellaneous Information, and Advertisements.* Mobile, AL: Dade and Thompson, 1842.

Wood, E. T. *Mobile Directory, and Register, for 1844: Embracing the Names of Firms, the Individuals Composing Them, and Householders Generally Within the City Limits, Alphabetically Arranged.* Mobile, AL: Dade and Thompson, 1844.

SECONDARY SOURCES

Books

Bailyn, Bernard. *Education in the Forming of American Society: Needs and Opportunities for Study.* Chapel Hill: University of North Carolina Press, 1960; reprint, New York: Norton, 1972.

Bingham, Emily. *Mordecai: An American Family.* New York: Hill and Wang, 2003.

Brewster, Willis. *Alabama: Her History, Resources, War Records and Public Men, from 1540 to 1872.* Montgomery, AL: Barrett and Brown, 1872; reprint, Spartanburg, SC: Reprint Company, 1975.

Clark, Willis G. *History of Education in Alabama 1702–1889.* Washington, DC: Government Printing Office, 1889.

Clinton, Catherine. *The Plantation Mistress: Woman's World in the Old South.* New York: Pantheon, 1982.

Cooper, William J., and Thomas E. Terrill. *The American South: A History,* 4th ed. 2 vols. Lanham, MD: Rowman and Littlefield, 2009.

Cremin, Lawrence A. *American Education: The Colonial Experience, 1607–1783.* New York: Harper and Row, 1970.

———. *American Education: The Metropolitan Experience, 1876–1980.* New York: Harper and Row, 1988.

———. *American Education: The National Experience.* New York: Harper and Row, 1980.

———. *The Genius of American Education.* Pittsburgh: University of Pittsburgh Press, 1965.

———. *A History of Education in American Culture.* New York: Holt, 1953.

———. *Popular Education and Its Discontents.* New York: Harper and Row, 1990.

———. *Public Education.* New York: Basic Books, 1976.

——. *Traditions of American Education*. New York: Basic Books, 1977.

Dabney, Charles William. *Universal Education in the South*. 4 vols. Chapel Hill: University of North Carolina Press, 1936.

Dalehite, William Moore. *A History of the Public Schools in Jackson, Mississippi: 1832–1972*. Baton Rouge: TJM, 1974.

DeLatte, Carolyn E., ed. *Antebellum Louisiana, 1830–1860*. Part B, "Politics," in Glenn R. Conrad, ed. *The Louisiana Purchase Bicentennial Series in Louisiana History*, vol. 4. Lafayette: Center for Louisiana Studies, University of Louisiana at Lafayette, 2004.

Delfino, Susanna, and Michele Gillespie, eds. *Neither Lady nor Slave: Working Women of the Old South*. Chapel Hill: University of North Carolina Press, 2002.

Devore, Donald E., and Joseph Logsdon. *Crescent City Schools: Public Education in New Orleans, 1841–1991*. Lafayette: Center for Louisiana Studies, University of Southwestern Louisiana, 1991.

Doss, Harriet Amos. *Cotton City: Urban Development in Antebellum Mobile*. University: University of Alabama Press, 1985.

Eaton, Clement. *The Growth of Southern Civilization, 1790–1860*. New York: Harper and Row, 1961.

Ellis, Richard E. *The Union at Risk: Jacksonian Democracy, States' Rights, and the Nullification Crisis*. New York: Oxford University Press, 1987.

Farnham, Christie Anne. *The Education of the Southern Belle: Higher Education and Student Socialization in the Antebellum South*. New York: New York University Press, 1994.

Fay, Edwin Whitfield. *The History of Education in Louisiana*. Washington, DC: Government Printing Office, 1898.

Fletcher, Joel L. *Louisiana Education since Colonial Days*. Lafayette: Southwestern Louisiana Institute, 1948.

Friedman, Jean A. *The Enclosed Garden: Women and Community in the Evangelical South, 1830–1900*. Chapel Hill: University of North Carolina Press, 1985.

Green, Fletcher M. *The Role of the Yankee in the Old South*. Athens: University of Georgia Press, 1972.

Hamilton, Peter J. *Mobile of the Five Flags: The Story of the River Basin and Coast about Mobile from the Earliest Times to the Present*. Mobile, AL: Gill Printing, 1913.

Harris, T. H. *The Story of Public Education in Louisiana*. New Orleans: by the author, 1924.

History of Education in Alabama. Bicentennial Intern Project conducted by the Alabama State Department of Education in cooperation with the Southern Regional Education Board, Bulletin no. 7, 1975.

Howe, Daniel Walker. *The Political Culture of the American Whigs*. Chicago: University of Chicago Press, 1979.

Hyde, Samuel C. Jr. *Pistols and Politics: The Dilemma of Democracy in Louisiana's Florida Parishes, 1810–1899*. Baton Rouge: Louisiana State University Press, 1996.

James, D. Clayton. *Antebellum Natchez*. Baton Rouge: Louisiana State University Press, 1968.

Katz, Michael B. *The Irony of Early School Reform: Educational Innovation in Mid-Nineteenth Century Massachusetts*. Cambridge, MA: Harvard University Press, 1968.

Kelley, Mary. *Learning to Stand and Speak: Women, Education, and Public Life in America's Republic*. Chapel Hill: University of North Carolina, 2006.

Kendall, John Smith. *History of New Orleans*. Chicago: Lewis Publishing, 1922.

Knight, Edgar W. *Public Education in the South*. Boston: Ginn and Company, 1922.

Leavitt, Mel. *A Short History of New Orleans*. San Francisco: Lexikos, 1982.

Leloudis, James L. *Schooling the New South : Pedagogy, Self, and Society in North Carolina, 1880–1920*. Chapel Hill: University of North Carolina Press, 1996.

Mayes, Edward. *History of Education in Mississippi*. Washington, DC: Government Printing Office, 1899.

Messerli, Jonathan. *Horace Mann: A Biography*. New York: Knopf, 1972.

Moore, John Hebron. *The Emergence of the Cotton Kingdom in the Old Southwest: Mississippi, 1770–1860*. Baton Rouge: Louisiana State University Press, 1988.

Owen, Thomas M., ed. *Publications of the Alabama Historical Society, 1897–1898*. Tuscaloosa, AL: printed for the Society, 1898.

Owsley, Frank Lawrence. *Plain Folk of the Old South*, with an introduction by John B. Boles. Baton Rouge: Louisiana State University Press, 1949; updated edition, 2008.

Phillips, Ulrich B. *Life and Labor in the Old South*. New York: Grosset and Dunlap, 1929; reprint, Boston: Little, Brown, 1963.

Pulliam, John D., and James J. Van Patten. *History of Education in America,* 7th ed. Upper Saddle River, NJ: Merrill, 1999.

Ranck, James Byrne. *Albert Gallatin Brown: Radical Southern Nationalist*. New York: D. Appleton-Century, 1937.

Robson, John B. *Education in Louisiana*. Natchitoches, LA: Northwestern State College, 1957.

Rowland, Dunbar. *History of Mississippi: The Heart of the South*. 2 vols. Jackson, MS: S. J. Clarke Publishing, 1925.

Rucker, Brian R. *Encyclopedia of Education in Antebellum Pensacola*. Bagdad, FL: Patagonia Press, 1999.

Sacher, John M. *A Perfect War of Politics: Parties, Politicians, and Democracy in Louisiana, 1824–1861*. Baton Rouge: Louisiana State University Press, 2007.

Scarborough, William Kauffman. *Masters of the Big House: Elite Slaveholders of the Mid-Nineteenth-Century South*. Baton Rouge: Louisiana State University Press, 2003.

Shugg, Robert W. *Origins of Class Struggle in Louisiana: A Social History of White Farmers and Laborers during Slavery and After, 1840–1875*. Baton Rouge: Louisiana State University Press, 1939.

Stowe, Steven M. *Intimacy and Power in the Old South: Ritual in the Lives of the Planters*. Baltimore: Johns Hopkins University Press, 1987.

Thornton, J. Mills III. *Politics and Power in a Slave Society: Alabama, 1800–1860*. Baton Rouge: Louisiana State University Press, 1978.

Tregle, Joseph G. Jr. *Louisiana in the Age of Jackson: A Clash of Cultures and Personalities*. Baton Rouge: Louisiana State University Press, 1999.

Weathersby, William Henington. *A History of Educational Legislation in Mississippi from 1798 to 1860*. Chicago: University of Chicago Press, 1921.

Weeks, Stephen B. *History of Public School Education in Alabama*. Washington, DC: Government Printing Office, US Bureau of Education Bulletin, no. 12, 1915; reprint, Westport, CT: Negro University Press, 1971.

Articles

Best, John Hardin. "Education in the Forming of the American South." *History of Education Quarterly* 36, no. 1 (1996): 39–51.

Galloway, Charles B. "Thomas Griffin: A Boanerges of the Early Southwest." *Publications of the Mississippi Historical Society* 7 (1903): 153–70.

Gates, Paul W. "An Overview of American Land Policy." *Agricultural History* 50, no. 1 (1976): 213–29.

Hyde, Samuel C. Jr. "Mechanisms of Planter Power in Eastern Louisiana's Piney Woods, 1810–1860." *Louisiana History* 39, no. 1 (1998): 19–44.

Judd, Charles H. "Federal Support of Public Education." *Elementary School Journal* 36, no. 7 (1936): 497–512.

McCabe, W. Gordon. "Graduates of West Point Serving in the CSA Army." *Southern Historical Society Pages* 30 (1902): 34–76.

Mobley, James William. "The Academy Movement in Louisiana." Reprinted from *The Louisiana Historical Quarterly* (1947).

Osthaus Carl O. "The Work Ethic of the Plain Folk: Labor and Religion in the Old South." *The Journal of Southern History* 70, no. 4 (2004): 745–82.

Reavis, William C. "Federal Aid for Education." *Annals of the American Academy of Political and Social Science* 265 (1949): 56–60.

Reinders, Robert C. "New England Influences on the Formation of Public Schools in New Orleans." *Journal of Southern History* 30 (1964): 181–95.

Riley, Martin Luther. "The Development of Education in Louisiana prior to Statehood." *Louisiana Historical Quarterly* 19 (1936): 595–634.

Suarez, Raleigh A. "Chronicle of a Failure: Public Education in Antebellum Louisiana." *Louisiana History* 12, no. 2 (1971): 109–22.

Tolley, Kim, and Nancy Beadie. "Socioeconomic Incentives to Teach in New York and North Carolina: Toward a More Complex Model of Teacher Labor Markets, 1800–1850." *History of Education Quarterly* 46, no. 1 (March 2006): 36–72.

Trattner, Walter I. "The Federal Government and Needy Citizens in Nineteenth-Century America." *Political Science Quarterly* 103, no. 2 (1988): 347–56.

Theses and Dissertations

Adams, Earl Wayne. "The History of Public School Finance in Mississippi." DEd diss., University of Mississippi, 1980.

Barnett, Annie Beatrice. "A History of Education in the City of Montgomery, Alabama, from 1818 to 1860." MS thesis, Alabama Polytechnic Institute, 1949.

Causey, Maggie Lea. "A Study of Education in Alabama prior to Statehood." MEd thesis, University of Alabama, 1938.

Ellis, Harriet B. "Mobile Public School Beginnings and Their Background." MS thesis, Alabama Polytechnic Institute, 1930.

Humphrey, George Duke. "Public Education for Whites in Mississippi, A Historical and Interpretive Study." DEd diss., Ohio State University, 1939.

Hyatt, Oscar W. "The Development of Secondary Education in Alabama prior to 1920." DEd diss., George Peabody College for Teachers, 1933.

Lipscomb, Sarah E. "A Crisis of Opportunity: The Example of New Orleans and Public Education in Antebellum Louisiana." MA thesis, Louisiana State University, 2005.

Mathews, Forrest David. "The Politics of Education in the Deep South: Georgia and Alabama, 1830–1860." PhD diss., Columbia University, 1965.

Miles, Loyce Braswell. "Forgotten Scholars: Female Secondary Education in Three Antebellum Deep South States." PhD diss.: Mississippi State University, 2003.

Nguyen, Julia Huston. "Molding the Minds of the South: Education in Natchez, 1817–1861." Master's thesis, Louisiana State University, 1997.

Peterson, Alma H. "A Historical Survey of the Administration of Education in New Orleans, 1718–1851." PhD diss., Louisiana State University, 1962.

Welch, Thelma. "Salary Policies for Teachers in New Orleans Public Schools, 1841–1941." Master's thesis, Tulane University, 1942.

INDEX